SELF AND MOTIVATION

SELF AND MOTIVATION

EMERGING PSYCHOLOGICAL PERSPECTIVES

Edited by Abraham Tesser, Diederik A. Stapel,
and Joanne V. Wood

AMERICAN PSYCHOLOGICAL ASSOCIATION
WASHINGTON, DC

Published by
American Psychological Association
750 First Street, NE
Washington, DC 20002
www.apa.org

To order
APA Order Department
P.O. Box 92984
Washington, DC 20090-2984

Tel: (800) 374-2721; Direct: (202) 336-5510
Fax: (202) 336-5502; TDD/TTY: (202) 336-6123
Online: www.apa.org/books/
Email: order@apa.org

In the U.K., Europe, Africa, and the Middle East, copies may be ordered from
American Psychological Association
3 Henrietta Street
Covent Garden, London
WC2E 8LU England

Typeset in Goudy by EPS Group Inc., Easton, MD

Printer: Phoenix Color, Hagerstown, MD
Cover Designer: NiDesign, Baltimore, MD
Technical/Production Editor: Casey Ann Reever

The opinions and statements published are the responsibility of the authors, and such opinions and statements do not necessarily represent the policies of the American Psychological Association.

Library of Congress Cataloging-in-Publication Data
Self and motivation : emerging psychological perspectives / edited by Abraham Tesser, Diederik A. Stapel, Joanne V. Wood.—1st ed.
    p. cm.
   Includes bibliographical references and indexes.
   ISBN 1-55798-883-8 (alk. paper)
    1. Self. 2. Motivation (Psychology). I. Tesser, Abraham. II. Stapel, Diederik A.
III. Wood, Joanne V.

BF697 .S425 2002
153.8—dc21

2001055300

British Library Cataloguing-in-Publication Data
A CIP record is available from the British Library.

Printed in the United States of America
First Edition

CONTENTS

CONTRIBUTORS

Jamie Arndt, Department of Psychological Sciences, University of Missouri–Columbia

John A. Bargh, Department of Psychology, New York University

Tanya L. Chartrand, Department of Psychology, Ohio State University, Columbus

Jamie L. Goldenberg, Department of Psychology, Boise State University, Boise, ID

Jay G. Hull, Department of Psychological and Brain Sciences, Dartmouth College, Hanover, NH

Sheena S. Iyengar, Management Department, Columbia University, New York

Jolanda Jetten, Department of Psychology, University of Amsterdam/University of Exeter, The Netherlands

Mark R. Leary, Department of Psychology, Wake Forest University, Winston-Salem, NC

Mark R. Lepper, Department of Psychology, Stanford University, Palo Alto, CA

Daan Scheepers, Department of Psychology, University of Amsterdam, The Netherlands

Russell Spears, Department of Social Psychology, University of Amsterdam, The Netherlands

Diederik A. Stapel, Department of Social & Organizational Psychology, University of Groningen, The Netherlands

June Price Tangney, Department of Psychology, George Mason University, Fairfax, VA

Abraham Tesser, Institute of Behavioral Research, University of Georgia, Athens

Joanne V. Wood, Department of Psychology, University of Waterloo, Ontario, Canada

PREFACE

It is easy to get the impression that the amount of psychological research on the self has grown tremendously in the past few decades. The data in Figure A.1 validate that impression. The figure is a plot, over time, of the number of publications (relative to all publications) found by the PsycINFO search engine using the word *self*. Clearly, research interest on the self has been rising dramatically. Not only is this topic increasing in popularity, but it has been, and continues to be, important to psychologists in an absolute sense: About 1 in 20 publications in 1970 were related to the self, and fully 1 in 7 publications in 2000 were relevant to the self.

How are psychologists to keep up with this explosive growth? The International Society for Self and Identity book series is intended to collect some of the most productive and exciting current research programs on the self and identity. This book is the second volume in that series. One of our tasks as editors was to identify those programs of research. How does one sample the most productive and exciting current research? The choices are necessarily subjective. Moreover, limitations in space and our own judgment necessarily meant that some truly outstanding research in this area would not be represented. We apologize at the outset for these inevitable lapses. We independently nominated research programs we thought qualified. With some discussion, we were able to reach a consensus. We felt fortunate to recruit the authors to write the chapters we wanted. What follows is the result of this process.

We had no formal criteria or organization in mind, other than currency and potential importance, in deciding which chapters to commission. The themes and issues that emerged across the chapters are just that—emergent. They come as a welcome surprise to us, and we hope that they provide a valid commentary on developing areas of self-research as well.

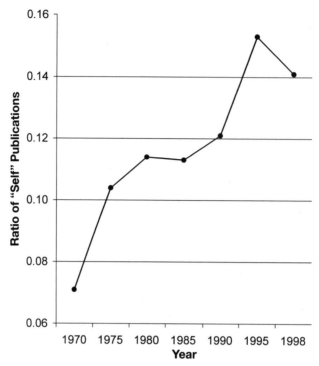

Figure A.1. Amount of psychological research on the self.
Note. The PsycINFO search engine generated these data. The number of hits to the word *self* for every 5th year, 1970–1995, was recorded. To correct for the growth in the amount of research in general, these numbers were divided by the total number of publications for each year.
From "On the Confluence of Self-Esteem Maintenance Mechanisms," by A. Tesser, 2000, *Personality and Social Psychology Review, 4,* pp. 290–299. Copyright © 2000 by Sage Publications. Reprinted with permission.

SELF AND MOTIVATION

INTRODUCTION:
AN EMPHASIS ON MOTIVATION

ABRAHAM TESSER, JOANNE V. WOOD, AND DIEDERIK A. STAPEL

Psychological thinking about the self, almost by default, invites motivational analyses. Research on the self, however, like research in many areas of psychology, has had a decidedly cognitive flavor for many years. For example, research on self schemas (Markus, 1977) is one area in which the current boom in self research had its genesis. This work documented the profound influence of chronic, cognitive self structures on perception and understanding. We also saw important work on the cognitive organization of self (Cantor & Mischel, 1979), the cognitive complexity of self (Linville, 1985), and the impact of self on memory (Rogers, Kuiper, & Kirker, 1977). The chapters in this book suggest a slight lessening of this cognitive bias. Cognitive variables remain important, to be sure, but the emergent emphasis across these chapters is clearly on motivation.

AWARENESS

The psychology of motivation raises questions about self-regulation. How do goals guide behavior? According to Tanya L. Chartrand and John

3

A. Bargh in chapter 1, many approaches to these questions assume that goals must be consciously represented to guide behavior (e.g., Rogers, 1951). In their chapter they make a different argument: that goals can be activated outside of awareness and that such goals can affect and guide behavior. Indeed, the effects of such nonconscious goals are almost indistinguishable from the effects of goals that are represented in conscious awareness.

Their auto-motive model becomes particularly interesting and productive because it is accompanied by a creative set of experiments that address the similarity between consciously and nonconsciously activated goals. In many of the experiments, some participants are provided with a conscious goal. For example, they are given trait words and asked to remember them (memory goal) or to use them to form an impression of another person (impression goal). Other participants are given a task that primes the same goals, either a memory goal or an impression goal, but does so without the participant's awareness. (Appropriate tests suggest that these participants are genuinely unaware of the primed goal.) Unaware participants appear to make the same goal-relevant response as do participants who are aware of the goal. For example, regardless of awareness, participants with an impression formation goal tend to organize information about another person more than do participants with a memory goal.

More relevant to the question of motivation, however, are behaviors that reflect persistence and affect. Again, goals activated outside of awareness produced much the same effects as consciously activated goals. For example, compared to control participants, study participants unaware of having been primed with an achievement goal tend to persist at a task longer, are more likely to resume an interrupted task, are more accurate in task performance, and feel worse as a result of poor performance. The auto-motive model's emphasis on the power of self-regulation processes outside of awareness is fascinating, and the research designed to test this approach is compelling.

SPECIFIC SELF MOTIVES AND EMOTIONS

Self-Esteem

Questions about awareness in motivated behavior tend to be generic in the sense that they are not focused on a particular motive or goal. However, a variety of motives and goals are uniquely associated with the self and identity. Perhaps the most pervasive and frequently researched motive in this context is the maintenance of self-esteem. Chapter 2 by Jamie Arndt and Jamie L. Goldenberg addresses the following two issues. First, despite the widespread acknowledgment that self-esteem is important, it is still unclear why people need self-esteem in the first place. What are the functions of self-esteem? Second, self-esteem researchers often make implicit and sometimes explicit assumptions about the relationship between self-esteem and affective reactions associated with threats to and the defense of self-esteem. However, surprisingly little attention has been paid to the empirical research that has directly tested these assumptions with physiological measures.

Arndt and Goldenberg illustrate the importance of attending to these relatively neglected aspects of self-esteem, that is, why we need it and how it is associated with arousal. Terror management theory offers an answer to why and also offers a framework through which the relationship between self-esteem and arousal can be understood. Following terror management theory, Arndt and Goldenberg argue that people need self-esteem because it provides a vital buffer against anxiety; it follows that arousal would be heavily involved in self-esteem maintenance processes.

Arndt and Goldenberg review research from a variety of domains to support this argument. This research shows that threats to self-esteem—whether in the form of negative feedback, social comparison, evaluative settings, or cognitive dissonance—have all been shown to increase physiological arousal. Moreover, in conjunction with research taking advantage of misattribution paradigms, physiologically oriented research also demonstrates that arousal influences the level at which self-esteem defenses are engaged. In sum, self processes have clear biological correlates, and those correlates are, predictably, reflected in the physiology of emotion.

Self-Determination

Motivational analyses in social psychology have long recognized the importance of self-determination. Having a choice in connection with what people do seems to increase intrinsic motivation and interest, is associated with better health outcomes, and even has been reported to lead to increased life expectancy. In short, choice seems always to be preferable to nonchoice. It turns out, according to Sheena S. Iyengar and Mark R. Lepper in chapter 3, that this may be a bias of Western culture. In a provocative chapter, Iyengar and Lepper review the research associated with self-determination or choice to document the pervasive, normative view that choice is "good." They question this view by pointing to cultural differences: Western cultures put a premium on personal independence and uniqueness; non-Western cultures value interdependence and connectedness with one's own group. Personal choice may be particularly important in a culture that values independence in that individual choice is a reflection of independence. Suppose, however, that connectedness and solidarity are particularly important. In this case, behaving in accord with the behavior and desires of other members of one's group may lead to more desirable outcomes than would exercising individual choice.

Iyengar and Lepper's argument is plausible, but is there any evidence that withholding choice results in more positive outcomes than providing choice? Most of the research in the self-determination or choice literature compares a condition in which an individual is led to believe that he or she engaged in a behavior either out of his or her own choice or because he or she was compelled to do so *by the experimenter.* Iyengar and Lepper's analysis points to a serious problem with this approach: Non-Western cultures emphasize connectedness to one's own group. Therefore, in their experiments they include a condition in which an ingroup member is the authority in "no-choice" conditions. (Because much of their research is with children, the ingroup authority is the child's mother.) Their research, reviewed in this chapter, provides strong evidence for the importance of cultural variables in understanding self-determination motivation. For example, U.S. children show greater motivation and better performance in "self-chosen" activities than they do when engaging in the same activities chosen by either the experimenter or their own mother. Asian children show a similar difference between self-chosen and experimenter-chosen conditions. However, for the Asian children, the highest level of motivation and performance is associated with a low-choice condition, that is, the condition in which their mother chooses for them.

Although we focus in this introductory discussion on the cross-cultural aspects of the research, Iyengar and Lepper's chapter also describes work on the negative consequences of too many choices for motivation. Their sophisticated theoretical analyses and intriguing empirical studies make a compelling case for the conclusion that "the appeal and the benefits of making one's own choices and the aversiveness and the costs of having one's choices dictated by others may not be as ubiquitous as has commonly been supposed."

Morality

Emotion is an integral facet of motivation. June Price Tangney argues in chapter 4 that a family of "self-conscious emotions"—shame, guilt, embarrassment, and pride—form the core of people's moral motivational system. When we commit some transgression or error, we evaluate ourselves in reference to our standards, rules, and goals. The resulting emotions serve as "an emotional moral barometer" that provides powerful feedback on our moral acceptability and that guides our subsequent behavior.

Tangney focuses in particular on the distinction between shame and guilt. Both emotions occur when one fails to meet an important standard, but they differ in the attributions one makes for that failure: Shame occurs when one attributes that failure to some fundamental defect in one's self, such as a flaw in one's character or a moral failing, whereas guilt occurs when one attributes that failure to a specific action or inaction. Although psychologists and lay people alike have tended to see shame and guilt as synonymous, Tangney persuasively argues that they are not. She reviews considerable evidence that the different emphases of the two emotions—the whole self in the case of shame and specific behavior in the case of guilt—result in distinct emotional experiences and motivations.

Specifically, guilt appears to have better consequences to the self and to society. Whereas shame motivates one to deny or hide from the shame-inducing situation, guilt leads to reparative actions, such as confessing and making amends. Shame is associated with anger and aggression; guilt is associated with empathy for other people. People who are prone to shame are also prone to depression and low self-esteem; people who are prone to guilt are less likely to use drugs or commit suicide. Shame-prone people are more likely to engage in criminal activity; guilt-prone people are more likely to engage in community service. In short, Tangney argues, guilt is the "moral emotion of choice."

In a welcome and unusual section of the chapter, Tangney goes on to draw implications of the guilt–shame distinction for the criminal justice system, for parenting, and for the classroom. Tangney's analysis is an inspiring reminder that our investigations of emotions and motivations have a purpose beyond that of educating fellow psychologists through journal articles; they also have the potential to improve society.

THE SOCIAL CONTEXT

The chapters that we have reviewed up to this point are decidedly intrapersonal in nature. However, humans are social beings, and the biases and motives that affect our self-functioning inevitably affect our interpersonal relationships as well. Moreover, the very sense of who we are as unique individuals cannot be separated from the identity of others in our own groups. These are the issues that drive the final chapters in this volume. In chapter 5, Mark R. Leary theorizes about how aspects of the self affect and are affected by interpersonal dynamics. In chapter 6, Russell Spears, Jolanda Jetten, and Daan Scheepers alert us to the complexities of constructing and maintaining a distinctive identity in a group context.

Interpersonal Dynamics

In a creative and integrative chapter, Leary focuses on five properties of the self and takes them beyond the self; he draws out their implications for interpersonal functioning. These properties include (a) the motive to differentiate the self from others; (b) egocentricity, or the tendency to fail to recognize that one's own views of the world are biased and self-centered; (c) self-esteem, which involves experiencing changes in self-evaluations and affect as a function of events; (d) egotism, or the tendency to foster and defend mental representations of oneself; and (e) self-reflection, which involves the tendency to be fundamentally absorbed in self-relevant thought. Leary illustrates how each cognitive or motivational process directs people's responses to other people.

In the section on self-esteem, Leary reviews evidence that both trait-level and situational differences in self-esteem are associated with interpersonal functioning. People with dispositionally low self-esteem, for example, have a high need for approval from other people and are highly sensitive to others' rejection. One's situational self-esteem rises and declines with changes in social acceptance and rejection, respectively. Leary describes his "sociometer model," which proposes that self-esteem functions as a barometer of one's acceptance and rejection by other people. He also describes how this model can account for many findings concerning the relation between interpersonal phenomena and self-esteem.

Another example of Leary's integrative approach concerns self–other differentiation. Here, Leary considers two models. First, Aron and Aron's model (e.g., Aron & Aron, 2000) concerns how people incorporate other individuals into their sense of self, leading them to act as if the other's characteristics and fortunes are their own. For example, when a woman makes a social faux pas at a dinner party, her husband may shrink with embarrassment. Or when she receives an award, he may be as proud as she. The second model, social identity theory, conceptualizes the self–other link differently. Rather than individuals including others in the self, individuals view the self and other as either belonging or not belonging to the same category. One's social categories, rather than specific individuals, are incorporated as part of the self. This is what motivates one to treat members of one's ingroup differently from nonmembers. Leary identifies interesting points of convergence and divergence between these two alternative conceptualizations—Aron and Aron's model versus social identity theory—in their implications for social relationships. Overall, Leary's chapter makes a novel contribution to the literature on the self and the literature on close relationships, and it charts a promising path for future research on their integration.

Distinctiveness in the Collective

Leary focuses on the need of individuals to cognitively differentiate themselves from others. Spears, Jetten, and Scheepers argue that this motive also plays an essential role in group dynamics. Their approach rests on the central assumption that people have and aspire to collective identities that distinguish them from other groups. In an original and thought-provoking chapter, Spears and colleagues propose that many examples of intergroup differentiation and discrimination may be understood more easily and relatively parsimoniously by considering the role of the need for group distinctiveness. They propose a theoretical framework, TIDE (tripartite integration of distinctiveness effects), to integrate previous explanations of group behavior.

The TIDE model proposes three distinctiveness processes. First, creative distinctiveness occurs in cases in which the status of a group is unclear, and there is a quest to define a distinctive group identity. Creative distinctiveness processes are set in motion when group identity is insufficiently defined. Interestingly, Spears and colleagues report findings that suggest that the desire for group distinctiveness is independent of the motive for self-esteem or self-enhancement. One may strive for distinctiveness to increase self-esteem, but not necessarily. Second, reactive distinctiveness refers to the situation in which group identity is already clearly defined but in which group distinctiveness is threatened by comparison with a similar, superior outgroup. Reactive distinctiveness can thus be more defensive in nature than creative distinctiveness processes. Third, reflective distinctiveness refers to processes that reflect reality. Here, distinctiveness processes are perceptual rather than motivational: They reflect existing intergroup differences. This articulation of distinctiveness processes allows the TIDE model to account for a variety of differentiation and discrimination effects that—at first sight—seem contradictory. It also helps integrate aspects of earlier theoretical approaches to differentiation such as social identity, self-categorization, and interdependence.

AN INTEGRATIVE MODEL

Research on the self has been quite popular and appears to be increasing in popularity. However, much of the research, although cumulative, seems to collect within specific, sometimes fragmented, research programs. Indeed, some of this occurs in the present volume. Authors connect research on emotions with morality, work on choice, and so forth. Few attempt to integrate such programs of research, and even fewer attempt a formal integrative model. Jay G. Hull in chapter 7 is an exception.

Hull has thoroughly reviewed the literature on the structure and functioning of the self and summarizes much of this knowledge in his model. The model is integrative and formal in that it is stated in terms of a system of equations whose implications can be objectively determined by way of computer simulation. The model is dynamic in that it exhibits interesting behavior simply as a function of time. These interesting dynamics flow, partly, from the nonlinear (e.g., threshold) relationships among some of the variables. This chapter is a nontechnical summary intended to introduce readers to some of this work (e.g., Hull, 2000).

The Hull model of self-regulation is based on a hierarchical view of self-knowledge. Behavior affects perception of one's own traits; social role performance; and, ultimately, an evaluative sense of identity—Am I a good or bad person? The model itself consists of a perceptual system to detect and remember discrepancies from standards, a system for making inferences about the self, an affective system, a motivational system, and a behavioral system. Each system is either directly or indirectly connected with all the other systems. Thus, all systems have mutual and reciprocal influence on one another.

The model behaves the way we expect it to with respect to known outcomes and, at the same time, makes new predictions. For example, there is much literature on "self-awareness." The Hull model suggests that self-awareness effects are due to heightened accessibility of self-knowledge. Indeed, increasing the accessibility of the self-knowledge parameter in the presence of a discrepancy between behavior and a comparison standard causes the model to produce many of the effects reported in the literature: greater perceived discrepancies, increased negative affect, and increased trait-related behaviors. Each of these responses is plausible and associated with interesting temporal dynamics. The model also makes predictions that have not yet been tested. For example, increased self-awareness should result in a discrepant trait becoming less relevant to global self-evaluation, decreased feelings of self-efficacy, greater flexibility in what is acceptable performance, and more compensation by performances on other aspects of self.

The model that Hull presents is simple in its detail but can appear daunting because the details have implications for one another, as they should. Here the whole is clearly greater than the sum of its parts. On a global level the model can be summarized quickly and easily: Cognition, affect, and behavior have mutual and interactive influences on one another. We applaud this integrative effort and hope that readers will spend some time with the details.

A SUMMARY

The self, like most psychological entities, consists of an organized set of beliefs, feelings, and behaviors. Psychologists' attempts to understand the self from a scientific perspective have tended, in different historical periods, to emphasize behavioral processes, cognitive processes, or affective and motivational processes. Behaviorism was followed by the cognitive revolution, and our crystal ball is beginning to detect an increasing interest in motivation. Research fashions change; different periods have had different emphases. It has always been clear, however, that a complete understanding would necessarily involve all aspects of the self. So, in spite of the increased motivational emphasis, we see it as a productive sign that each chapter in this book also shows a strong sensitivity to all three aspects of self-functioning.

The research described in the following chapters is on the cutting edge of the discipline. It includes a sophisticated approach to the role of awareness in goal striving, a comprehensive review of physiological responses in self-defense, a more nuanced and perhaps surprising understanding of the motivational significance of choice, and an analytic approach to the emotions of guilt and shame. A couple of chapters go beyond where we have been in our attempts to understand how self and identity processes function in interpersonal and intergroup contexts. Finally, we have a new, integrative formal model of much of what we know about the dynamics of self-functioning. The mixture is rich, and many of the ideas are provocative and new. We hope that readers find them useful and interesting.

REFERENCES

Aron, A., & Aron, E. (2000). Self-expansion motivation and including other in the self. In W. Ickes & S. Duck (Eds.), *The social psychology of personal relationships* (pp. 109–128). New York: John Wiley & Sons.

Cantor, N., & Mischel, W. (1979). Prototypes in person perception. In L. Berkowitz (Ed.), *Advances in experimental social psychology* (Vol. 12, pp. 3–52). New York: Academic Press.

Hull, J. G. (2000). *A dynamic theory of personality and self.* Manuscript submitted for publication.

Linville, P. W. (1985). Self-complexity and affective extremity: Don't put all of your eggs in one basket. *Social Cognition, 3,* 94–120.

Markus, H. (1977). Self-schemata and processing information about the self. *Journal of Personality and Social Psychology, 35,* 63–78.

Rogers, C. R. (1951). *Client-centered therapy: Its current practice, implications, and theory.* Boston: Houghton-Mifflin.

Rogers, T. B., Kuiper, N. A., & Kirker, W. S. (1977). Self-reference and the encoding of personal information. *Journal of Personality and Social Psychology, 35,* 677–688.

1

NONCONSCIOUS MOTIVATIONS: THEIR ACTIVATION, OPERATION, AND CONSEQUENCES

TANYA L. CHARTRAND AND JOHN A. BARGH

Self-regulation is one of the most important aspects of human existence. Deciding which goals to pursue and then engaging in goal-directed action is a fundamental process underlying many of a person's daily thoughts, feelings, and actions. The first half of the 20th century was dominated by Freudian and behavioristic models of behavior regulation, which held that behavior was determined either by biological impulses and the unconscious or by the external environment, respectively. In reaction to this, the humanistic movement, in particular Rogers's (1951) self theory, placed the conscious "self" as the most important causal agent in self-regulation. Behavior regulation was driven not by the unconscious or by the environment but rather by the self, a critical mediator between the environment and behavior.

Many current models of motivation and goal pursuit continue the tradition of maintaining continuous, conscious choice and guidance of be-

Preparation of this manuscript was supported in part by Grant R01-MH60767 from the National Institute of Mental Health to the second author.

havior—directed by the individual's chronic intents and desires—as the cornerstone and foundation of self-regulation (e.g., Bandura, 1977, 1986, 1997; Mischel, 1973). This view has intuitive appeal. We are often cognizant of deliberating among various desires and wishes and choosing which goals to actually pursue. We often consciously engage in goal-directed action and then carefully evaluate our subsequent performance. Thus, intuition tells us that the goal pursuit sequence is available to conscious awareness, and many current theories of motivation reflect and support this (Bandura, 1986; Cantor & Kihlstrom, 1987; Carver & Scheier, 1981; Deci & Ryan, 1985; Locke & Latham, 1990).

Is it possible, however, that sometimes the goal pursuit process occurs without conscious awareness? We argue that the answer to this question is a resounding "yes." There is now substantial evidence that we are in fact often not aware of our own mental processes (Nisbett & Wilson, 1977; Wilson & Brekke, 1994) or of what is guiding our daily moods, thoughts, and behavior (Bargh, 1997). For instance, the sizeable priming literature suggests that recent activation of a given category or construct can have tremendous influence on one's perceptions, judgments, moods, and behaviors (Bargh, Bond, Lombardi, & Tota, 1986; Bargh, Chen, & Burrows, 1996; Chartrand & Bargh, 2001; M. Chen & Bargh, 1999; Dijksterhuis & van Knippenberg, 1998; Dijksterhuis et al., 1999; Higgins, Rholes, & Jones, 1977). In fact, research has recently uncovered many automatic, nonconscious mental processes that affect nearly all aspects of human existence outside of the individual's awareness, intent, and control (Bargh & Chartrand, 1999). The number and range of these automatic processes is growing exponentially, and its effects seem ubiquitous. Wegner and Wheatley (1999) have gone so far as to say that the experience of free will—believing that our conscious thought causes our actions—is merely an illusion. Specifically, they argued that unconscious processes can cause one's actions and also simultaneously cause one's thoughts, creating an illusory correlation between thought and action.

Thus, researchers are building the case that people are often not aware of the true causes of their behavior. However, in discovering the various nonconscious processes that affect our daily lives, we are slowly lifting the shroud of mystery, and we can begin to explore the real origins of our actions. Because nonconscious processes have been shown to affect evaluation, mood, judgments, and behavior, it should not seem surprising that they also affect motivation and self-regulation. Nonconscious goal pursuit provides another way by which our behavior can be determined by something other than conscious reflection, deliberation, and choice.

The *auto-motive model* of self-regulation proposes that the entire goal pursuit sequence can occur outside of conscious awareness (Bargh, 1990). There is now substantial evidence that individuals frequently pursue goals that they are not aware of having. Situations can automatically activate goals frequently associated with them in the past, and these goals can then operate to guide information processing and behavior without conscious intervention at any point in the sequence. Furthermore, this nonconscious goal pursuit has consequences for mood and future behavior. It is to this model that we now turn.

THE AUTO-MOTIVE MODEL OF NONCONSCIOUS GOAL PURSUIT

The auto-motive model proposes that self-regulation can be triggered automatically by the environment (Bargh, 1990). The model holds that although many of the goals an individual pursues are the result of conscious deliberation and choice, conscious choice is not necessary for goal activation and operation. In addition to the deliberate mode of activation, goals and intentions also can be started in motion by environmental stimuli. First, the model assumes that intentions and goals are represented in memory in the same way that social attitudes, constructs, stereotypes, and schemas are represented. Second, because constructs and stereotypes are capable of being automatically activated by relevant environmental stimuli, goal representations should have this capability as well. With repeated and consistent choice (i.e., activation) of a particular goal in a certain social situation over time, the representation of that goal may become directly and automatically linked in memory to the representation of that situation. The goal will eventually come to be nonconsciously activated within that situation, independently of the individual's conscious purposes at that time.

Thus, situational features in the environment can automatically trigger goals chronically associated with those features. Moreover, once activated, the goals operate to guide subsequent cognition and behavior in the same way that consciously held goals do, all without the individual's awareness of the goals' guiding role. Thus, how a goal representation becomes activated—whether consciously or nonconsciously—has no effect on whether it operates and produces its effects.

Take the case of our friend Joe, for example. When he was growing up, he competed with his siblings for his parents' good graces. Joe came up with a strategy that worked pretty well: He tried to stir up trouble between his brothers and sisters so that they would get in trouble and he would look innocent and well-behaved by comparison. Joe would instigate fights, tattle on them, tell one the bad things the other one said about him or her, and so forth. Eventually Joe no longer had to consciously choose to compete for his parents' liking—the home environment and presence of his family automatically activated that goal in him because the representation of the goal was linked in memory to the representation of the home environment. On automatic activation of the goal, Joe engaged in the same negative behaviors he used to strategically choose to reach the goal—instigating fights, tattling, and so on—all without his awareness of why he was doing these things. Now as an adult, whenever Joe goes home to visit, the goal is still activated in him, and he finds himself stirring up trouble with his family members after all these years. Once the goal is activated, it guides his behavior just as it used to, even though he's not aware of having the goal at all.

AUTOMATIC ACTIVATION AND OPERATION OF GOALS

Information-Processing Goals

Recent research suggests that regardless of whether a goal is chosen through deliberate and conscious means or whether it is activated outside of awareness, intent, and control by the environment, an individual will pursue the goal in the same way. In one series of studies, Chartrand and Bargh (1996) demonstrated that information-processing goals can be activated nonconsciously and guide subsequent cognition. A first experiment was based on the findings of a classic social–cognitive study in the person memory literature by Hamilton, Katz, and Leirer (1980). In the original study, participants read a series of 16 behaviors with instructions either (a) to form an impression of the actor who had engaged in the various behaviors or (b) to memorize the behavioral information presented. The behaviors represented four trait categories: social/interpersonal (e.g., "had a party for some friends last week"), athletic (e.g., "went skiing in Colorado for the weekend"), intelligent ("caught the error in the mechanic's calculations"), and religious ("read the Bible in his hotel room"). Participants were given a surprise free-recall test at the end of the stimulus presentation. Participants who had been given an explicit impression formation goal recalled more behaviors and had more organization of the material in memory according to trait category (e.g., sociable, intelligent) than those told to memorize the information.

We replicated this study (Chartrand & Bargh, 1996; Experiment 1) but instead of giving participants explicit goal instructions, we activated the same information-processing goals through a supraliminal priming technique. In this "scrambled sentence task," words related either to an impression formation goal (e.g., evaluate, personality, impression, opinion) or to a memorization goal (e.g., remember, memory, retain, absorb) were embedded in the scrambled sentences. This "primed" participants with one of the two goals, without their knowledge that any goal had been activated (see also Bargh & Chartrand, 2000; Srull & Wyer, 1979). The results closely replicated those of Hamilton and colleagues (1980), suggesting that consciously choosing a goal at some point is not necessary for that goal to become active and guide subsequent cognition.

Importantly, participants were asked at the end of the experiment what they were thinking about when they read the behavioral predicates. Specifically, did they have any goal in mind, or were they trying to do anything in particular when reading the predicates? None of the participants mentioned that they were trying to memorize the information or to form an impression of the target. Because there was no subject assigned to the predicates in the sentences, it was not clear who—if anyone—engaged in these behaviors. Most indicated that they were simply paying attention (as they were instructed to do) and trying to understand the predicates.

The second study (Chartrand & Bargh, 1996; Experiment 2) was a replication of Hastie and Kumar (1979), in which participants were given an explicit goal to form an impression of a target person. In the replication, however, an impression goal was subliminally primed for half of the participants (the other half receiving neutral priming stimuli) through the parafoveal and masked brief presentations of goal-related words (e.g., impression, opinion, personality). As in the original study, those whose impression formation goal had been activated (subliminally in the replication, via explicit instructions in the original) showed evidence of online impression formation of a target person. Those without the impression goal activated presumably did not form an impression until they were asked for it by the experimenter and therefore did not show evidence of online impression formation. Again, participants did not mention having a goal to form an impression (or any similar goal) when asked at the end of the study. They pursued the goal without realizing they had it. Thus, the results of these experiments support the idea that individuals do not have to be aware or cognizant of having a goal for it to affect their information processing.

Intrinsic and Extrinsic Motivation

The goals to memorize or form an impression are concrete, specific goals. However, recent evidence by Séguin and Pelletier (2001) suggests that relatively abstract motivational orientations can operate automatically as well. The abstract motivations they focused on were intrinsic and extrinsic motivations. Previous research by Deci and Ryan (1985, 1990) has demonstrated that when activities are engaged in to satisfy intrinsic or "self-determined" motives, these activities are enjoyed for their own sake, and the individual is absorbed in the task and feels a sense of "flow." In contrast, when activities are engaged in to satisfy extrinsic or "instrumental" motives, they are not done for their own sake but rather for external reasons, including the expectation of reward or punishment. As a result, they are not enjoyed as much.

Séguin and Pelletier (2001) first primed participants (using a scrambled sentence task) with words related to either intrinsic motivation (e.g., challenge, mastering); extrinsic motivation (e.g., forced, expected); or neither (control condition). Participants next worked on several crossword puzzles in what was ostensibly a second, unrelated experiment. Results revealed that, relative to the control condition, participants who worked on the crossword puzzles with a nonconsciously operating intrinsic motivation enjoyed the task more, reported that they worked on it through their own free will, and found significantly more words on the puzzle. Those primed with an extrinsic motivation, however, enjoyed the task less, found it less interesting, found fewer words, and reported to a lesser extent that they worked on the task because of their own free will. Thus, the nonconscious intrinsic and extrinsic motives produced the same outcomes that conscious intrinsic and extrinsic motives produced.

Behavioral Goals

Can behavioral goals also become automatically activated to guide subsequent behavior? The automatic activation of goals should not be limited to information-processing motives but should include goals related to desired behavioral outcomes as well. For instance, one individual might have a self-presentational goal automatically activated whenever he is at a party, or a young girl might have an achievement goal automatically activated by the school environment. A series of studies by Bargh, Gollwitzer, Lee-Chai, Barndollar, and Trötschel (in press) have examined the nonconscious pursuit of behavioral goals. In a first study, these researchers administered a word search task in which achievement-related words were embedded for half the participants. This was intended to prime an achievement goal in the prime-condition participants. Next, participants were given five similar word search puzzles and instructed to find as many words as possible. Participants previously primed with achievement-related stimuli found significantly more words on the word search puzzles than did nonprimed participants.

In sum, then, the effects of nonconsciously operating information-processing and behavioral goals mirror those of consciously operating goals. Whether a goal becomes active via an act of will (i.e., conscious and deliberate choice), explicit instructions from an experimenter, or automatic activation through priming, the same outcomes are obtained. These results support two tenets of the auto-motive model: first, that goal structures can be automatically and nonconsciously activated, and second, that nonconscious goals, once activated, produce the same effects as conscious goals.

EVIDENCE THAT PRIMING MANIPULATIONS ACTIVATE MOTIVATIONAL STATES

Although the exposure to goal-related words in the Chartrand and Bargh (1996), Séguin and Pelletier (2001), and Bargh et al. (in press; Experiment 1) studies was intended to activate a goal state, it is possible that this simply induced goal-primed participants to construe the experimental situation that followed differently from the control participants. For instance, participants in the Bargh et al. study may have been more likely to construe it as an achievement situation if they were primed with achievement-related words, which in turn may have led them to form a conscious goal and strategy to achieve. To eliminate these alternative explanations, Bargh et al. (in press) set out to demonstrate that the "priming activates" motivational states, not just tendencies to perceive situations in a certain way. Theories of self-regulation posit that motivational states of goal pursuit have unique properties (e.g., Atkinson & Birch, 1970; Bandura, 1986; Gollwitzer, 1990; Lewin, 1951). Motivational states increase in strength over time, and individuals persist at goals in the face of obstacles and resume goal-directed action following an interruption. In a series of studies, Bargh et al. (in press) demonstrated the presence of each of these three qualities in the primed goal states.

Increase in Goal Strength Over Time

One signature of a motivational state is that activated goals increase in strength over time (until the goal is attained; Atkinson & Birch, 1970). On the other hand, perceptual priming effects (i.e., the effects of priming on subsequent judgments made of a target person) decay or decrease in strength over time (e.g., Higgins, Bargh, & Lombardi, 1985). This motivational quality is particularly useful in demonstrating a dissociation between motivation and perceptual priming effects. Because time (i.e., post-priming delay) would have different effects on goal and perceptual priming (increasing and decreasing the effects, respectively), one can conduct a clear test of dissociation between the two processes (Dunn & Kirsner, 1988).

Bargh et al. (in press; Experiment 2) conducted such a test. In an initial word search task, half the participants were primed with achievement-related words and half were not. Next, participants were given an achievement goal behavioral task or a perceptual-judgment task, either immediately or after a 5-minute delay. Thus, the study used a 2 (achievement prime words vs. neutral words) × 2 (goal-related vs. judgmental task) × 2 (delay vs. no delay) design. Participants in the goal-related behavioral task condition were given Scrabble letter tiles and asked to find as many words as they could (using only the letters they were given). Those in the

no-delay condition did the Scrabble task immediately following the priming procedure, and those in the delay condition were given a filler task
(for which they drew their own family tree) for 5 minutes before being
given the Scrabble task. Participants in the perceptual judgment task conditions read about a person who behaved in an ambiguously achieving way
(e.g., studying hard right before a test) and were asked to give their rating
of how achievement-oriented the target person was. As in the behavior
conditions, this task was given either immediately after the priming procedure or after a 5-minute delay. It was expected that for those given the
perceptual task, the achievement-related words would have a stronger impact on subsequent judgments of a target in the no-delay condition than
in the delay condition (because perceptual priming effects decay rather
than increase over time). For those given the behavioral Scrabble task,
however, the achievement goal primes were expected to have a stronger
effect on achievement behavior when there was a delay than when there
was no delay (because of the increase in motivational tendencies over
time).

Results revealed that the priming manipulations yielded a dissociation
over time between the behavioral and perceptual tasks. For the perceptual
task, when there was no delay, a significant priming effect was observed
such that achievement-primed participants rated the target as being more
achieving than did nonprimed participants. But with a 5-minute delay, this
effect disappeared. The behavioral task yielded quite different results. With
no delay, there was a significant priming effect such that achievement-
primed participants outperformed the control participants on the Scrabble
word construction task. Moreover, this effect was magnified, not dimin-
ished, after the 5-minute delay. This suggests that a motivational state was
indeed induced by the priming, independently of any perceptual priming
effect. Participants were again questioned during a postexperimental funneled debriefing and did not report consciously taking on any goal.

Persistence in the Face of Obstacles

Another study further examined the motivational qualities of the
achievement-primed state (Bargh et al., in press; Experiment 3) by testing
whether those primed with an achievement goal would persist on a task
in the face of obstacles (Gollwitzer & Moskowitz, 1996; Lewin, 1926;
Ovsiankina, 1928). An achievement goal was primed in half the participants via the same word search task used in Experiments 1 and 2. In the
next, supposedly unrelated task, participants were given 3 minutes to find
as many words in a set of Scrabble letter tiles as they could. The experimenter left the room after delivering these instructions and went next door
where a monitor was hooked up to a hidden video camera in the experimental room. This allowed the experimenter to monitor the participants'

behavior unbeknown to them. Three minutes later, the experimenter told the participants through an intercom to stop working on the Scrabble task. She was able to then record who in fact stopped working on the task and who "cheated" and continued to work after the instructions to stop. Significantly more participants in the achievement priming conditions continued to work after the stop signal than those in the control condition. Importantly, participants did not report having a conscious goal to achieve during the study. This suggests that for achievement-primed participants, an achievement goal was nonconsciously activated, which led them to persist at the achievement task in spite of an obstacle (instruction to stop).

Resumption of Goal-Directed Action After Interruption

Bargh et al. (in press; Experiment 4) also tested whether achievement-primed participants would be more likely to resume an interrupted task so as to reach the goal of completing it. Participants were again primed with an achievement goal or not in a first, "unrelated" task. They were then told that for the next experiment, they would work on two tasks: (a) finding words from a series of Scrabble tiles and (b) rating a series of cartoons on how funny they were. While participants were working on the first task, there was a staged power failure. When electric power was restored, the experimenter announced that because time had been lost, there was no longer enough time to finish both tasks. The participants were then given the choice of which one to work on, and because pretesting had shown that the second task was clearly more enjoyable, it provided a good test of how motivated they were to achieve and resume the interrupted task. Almost twice as many in the achievement-primed condition than those in the control condition chose to return to the interrupted verbal task. Again, participants showed no conscious awareness of having an achievement goal.

NEUROPHYSIOLOGICAL EVIDENCE FOR THE ACTIVATION OF GOAL STATES

The studies discussed so far suggest that automatically activated goals produce the same effects as consciously chosen goals. However, one of the basic premises of the auto-motive model is that not only should conscious and nonconscious goals produce the same effects, but they should also produce these effects in the same way. Testing this premise, Gardner, Bargh, Shellman, and Bessenoff (2001) used event-related brain potentials to compare the neurophysiological correlates of conscious and nonconscious goal pursuit. Participants engaged in four tasks, each of which involved the participants responding in some way to 75 auditorily presented nouns. Two of the tasks involved evaluation: (a) an explicit evaluation task for which participants were instructed to evaluate the nouns using the keys on a response box and (b) a primed evaluation task for which participants were first primed with an evaluation goal (using a scrambled sentence task) and then simply told to listen (but not respond) to the nouns. The remaining two tasks involved imagery: (a) an explicit imagery task for which participants were told to mentally visualize the object that each word described and then to judge whether that object was large or smaller than a file cabinet and (b) a primed imagery task for which a scrambled-sentence task primed an imagery goal in participants before they listened to the nouns. The order of evaluation and imagery tasks was counterbalanced across participants, but the implicit task was always given before the explicit task in the same domain.

Previous research has shown that when people explicitly evaluate a stimulus, there is a significant increase in activation of the basal right hemisphere around 500–600 ms after stimulus presentation (see Cacioppo, Crites, & Gardner, 1996). This "right shift" or "lateralization" of activation is unique to the evaluative response and does not occur with other processing goals, including imagery goals. Thus, Gardner et al. (2001) expected to find this right shift during the evaluation tasks (both primed and explicit) but not for the imagery tasks. This is precisely what they found; participants pursuing a nonconscious evaluation goal displayed the exact same lateralization that they displayed during conscious evaluation. Thus, even on a neurophysiological level, the same process unfolds during goal pursuit, regardless of whether that goal was consciously pursued or automatically activated by the environment.

STRUCTURE OF AUTOMATIC GOALS

In most studies of nonconscious goal pursuit, a goal is activated through a priming procedure, and once the goal is operating nonconsciously, individuals pursue that goal as if they had consciously chosen to pursue it. But how exactly does this work? On activation of the goal, what process then leads the person to actually pursue the goal? This question speaks to the structure of automatic goals. It has been assumed that the goal, once activated, automatically leads the individual to engage in various goal-directed plans and behaviors, which results in the person nonconsciously pursuing the goal (Bargh et al., in press; Chartrand & Bargh, 1996). The idea that goals become automatically associated in memory with the behavioral responses used to carry out those goals was tested recently by Aarts and Dijksterhuis (2000). These researchers hypothesized that habits are not behaviors linked directly to the environment (as classic stimulus–response [S–R] psychology posits) but rather are plans of action automatically linked to their higher order goal. When the goal is activated, the strategy or habitual plan for attaining that goal will be activated automatically as well, obviating the need for conscious planning and selection of behaviors in any given situation.

In one study, participants included university students who either habitually used their bicycle as a mode of transportation or who usually relied on a different way of travel. These habitual and nonhabitual bicycle users were either primed or not primed with the goal to travel. Specifically, those in the travel priming condition were exposed to sentences related to traveling to some location (e.g., attending a lecture, going shopping). Participants were then exposed to various location words (e.g., university) on a computer screen, each followed by a mode of transport (e.g., bicycle). Their task was to indicate as quickly and accurately as they could whether the mode of transportation would constitute a realistic means of traveling to the previously presented location. The dependent variable was response latencies on the location–bicycle links. It was predicted that habitual bike users, on being primed with the travel goal, would have increased accessibility to the associated plan of action (using a bicycle). Thus, they would respond faster to the word *bicycle* than would nonhabitual bike users, but only after being activated with the goal to travel. When the goal to travel was not activated, habitual and nonhabitual bike users were not expected to differ in their response latencies. This was precisely what the researchers found, supporting the notion that, for those who have formed a habit, there are automatic links between goals and behavioral responses often used to achieve that goal. This in turn suggests that habitual behaviors are not linked to relevant environmental events per se but rather to the mental representations of the higher order goals they serve.

AUTOMATIC ASSOCIATION BETWEEN SITUATIONS AND GOALS

In the studies discussed thus far (e.g., Bargh et al., in press; Chartrand & Bargh, 1996; Séguin & Pelletier, 2001), goals become activated through the presentation of goal synonyms during a priming task. These synonyms are presumed to activate the representation of the goal in memory, which is assumed to then activate the corresponding motivation. Thus, these studies show that goals can be directly activated through external means— bypassing conscious, deliberate choice of the goal. The goal can become automatically activated and then guide subsequent cognition and behavior. However, the auto-motive model posits a two-step process: (a) Goals become linked to situations in which they were consciously chosen in the past, and (b) the features of these situations can then directly activate the goal. Priming manipulations that directly activate the goal itself serve as a proxy for what happens in naturalistic situations when the situation automatically activates the goal. Thus, studies using this priming technique bypass the important first stage of the model: the environment activating the goal. This is an important step to show, because if the situation cannot activate the goal, then priming studies are artificially creating something that would never happen in the "real world."

Automatic Activation of Goals That Lead to Implicit Stereotyping (or Lack Thereof)

Several studies provide evidence for this first link—that between situations and goals. Spencer, Fein, Wolfe, Fong, and Dunn (1998) tested whether self-image threat makes individuals more likely to activate stereotypes when perceiving members of an ethnic minority group. These researchers hypothesized that the situation of receiving negative self-feedback would threaten the self-image, which would automatically activate a goal to restore the threatened ego:

> Based on the reasoning underlying the auto-motive model, we argue that to the extent that the motivation to restore one's threatened self-image frequently and consistently leads to the use of stereotypes on exposure to members of particular stereotyped groups, the link between self-image threat and activation of available stereotypes may become automatic. (p. 1140)

Thus, once the goal to restore the self-image is automatically activated, the goal operates to completion as if it had been consciously chosen: The individual engages in ego-restoring processes. One such ego-enhancing process may be the denigration and stereotyping of others.

To test their hypotheses, Spencer et al. (1998) replicated a well-known previous study by Gilbert and Hixon (1991). In the original study, participants were exposed to the presence of either an Asian American or a European American experimenter on a videotape. They were also either given a cognitively draining task (remembering an eight-digit number) or not. The dependent measure was completions on a word fragment task ([e.g., _hy] for which completions could either be consistent with an Asian-American stereotype [e.g., "shy"] or not [e.g., "why"]). Gilbert and Hixon (1991) found that for those not under cognitive load, the presence of an Asian American experimenter on the videotape increased the subsequent number of word-stem completions consistent with the Asian American stereotype. Importantly, this implicit stereotype effect was eliminated in the cognitive load conditions: the drain on attentional resources "knocked out" the automatic activation of the stereotype.

In several experiments, Spencer et al. (1998) gave some participants a blow to their self-esteem (i.e., negative feedback on their performance on an "ability" test) and then replicated Gilbert and Hixon's (1991) study; they found that those under self-image threat demonstrated the implicit stereotyping effect, even under cognitive load (the conditions found to eliminate the effect in the original study). These studies support the automotive model: The activation of the goal to restore self-esteem automatically leads to specific behaviors that have been frequently used to satisfy the goal in the past. To the extent that stereotyping serves the function of restoring a threatened ego (e.g., Brewer & Brown, 1998; Wood, 1989), stereotyping will be one behavior that is automatically activated by ego threat, even when cognitive resources are elsewhere. Because automatic processes are often efficient and do not depend on attentional resources (Shiffrin & Schneider, 1977), it makes sense that stereotyping could occur without these resources, if the goal had been activated.

Importantly, these studies also demonstrate that a situation can directly activate a goal. Spencer et al. (1998) did not prime participants with a goal to restore self-esteem; instead, they created the environment assumed to activate that goal. This is an ecologically valid demonstration that goals can indeed be automatically activated by the environment and then guide subsequent behavior. It should be noted, however, that it is possible that some individuals may have consciously been aware of the goal in this case (wanting to restore the ego). However, it is highly doubtful that participants would have been aware of denigrating and stereotyping targets in service of this goal. Even if they knew they wanted to put others down (which seems rather unlikely), the measure of stereotyping was too implicit and subtle to use deliberately. Thus, the prejudicial behavior was clearly nonconsciously driven by the ego restoration goal.

In another test of automatic stereotyping, Moskowitz, Wasel, Gollwitzer, and Schaal (1999) demonstrated that chronic, long-term egalitarian goals (e.g., wanting to treat others fairly) are activated automatically by a situational feature: the presence of an ethnic minority group member. Participants first completed a task that assessed whether egalitarianism and fairness to others was an important aspect of each participant's value system. Next, participants took part in an ostensibly unrelated second task in which stimuli related to gender stereotypes were presented under conditions in which it would be impossible to control the stereotype activation with effortful, strategic processes (Blair & Banaji, 1996). Participants identified by the first task as having a chronic egalitarian goal showed no signs of stereotype activation in this experiment, whereas those without such a goal did. These results suggest that those with an egalitarian goal are able to prevent the automatic activation or use of the stereotype when being presented with stereotype-consistent cues. Thus, the environmental presence of minority-group-related stimuli automatically activates the associated goal to be fair in chronic egalitarians; the situation activates the goal.

The goal then guides subsequent judgments as it always does, by inhibiting the application of the stereotype to group members.

Goals Activated by Situational Power

Another demonstration that situations can automatically activate associated goals was conducted by Bargh, Raymond, Pryor, and Strack (1995). These researchers were interested in interpersonal power. If individuals tend to pursue certain goals whenever they have power in a given situation, then it follows that those goals might become automatically linked to the power situation, such that being in power will automatically activate those goals. Previous research has established that male sexual harassers associate power and sex (e.g., Lisak & Roth, 1988; Pryor & Stoller, 1994). Thus, for these men, power should activate a sex goal. This was tested in two experiments. In the first, a sequential priming task (Neely, 1977, 1991) was used to show that an automatic association existed between the concepts of power and sex for men with a high likelihood to sexually harass but not for those with a low likelihood. Participants were exposed to subliminally presented prime words, which were each followed by a target word that they were supposed to pronounce as quickly as possible. If the prime words were power related, then this should facilitate the pronunciation of sex-related target words, but only for those high in sexual harassment tendencies. This is exactly what was found.

In a second experiment, Bargh et al. (1995) examined the behavioral consequences of this automatic association between power and sex. Male participants who had earlier been identified as having a high or low tendency to sexually harass participated in the experiment with another "participant" (actually a female confederate). Half of the participants were primed with the concept of power through a word fragment completion test, and the other half were not. The participant and confederate then worked individually on a "visual illusion" task. Next, they were brought into separate rooms and told that the experiment was actually testing impression formation and the kind of impressions that are formed with minimal interaction. The participant then rated the confederate on various scales. Critical items included how attractive he found her and whether he would like to get to know her better. For those with high likelihood to sexually harass (but not for those with low likelihood), participants primed with the power-related words thought that the confederate was more attractive and had a greater desire to get to know her better, compared to participants who were not power primed.

It should be noted that because the dependent measures in these particular studies were not motivational in nature but rather behavioral, it could be argued that there is simply a strong association between power and sex for sexual harassers, such that power primes sex, without any mediation by a goal state per se. Although this alternative explanation may be viable for these studies, it would not hold for any of the other demonstrations of nonconscious goal pursuit (Bargh et al., in press; Chartrand & Bargh, 1996; Gardner et al., 2001; Séguin & Pelletier, 2001; Spencer et al., 1998). In addition, another series of studies examining the goals automatically activated by situational power used dependent measures more directly linked to goal states.

These studies examined the notion that relationship orientation can moderate the effects of social power (S. Chen, Lee-Chai, & Bargh, 2001). It was hypothesized that people with a communal relationship orientation (Clark & Mills, 1979) associate power with social-responsibility goals and have such goals activated automatically when in power. Those with an exchange relationship orientation were assumed to chronically associate self-interest goals with power situations and so were predicted to have this type of goal automatically activated by situations of power.

In one study testing this hypothesis (S. Chen et al., 2001; Experiment 3), participants were led to a professor's office (because the lab rooms were ostensibly full) and were randomly assigned to be seated in either the professor's chair or the guest chair. This served as the power priming manipulation; those seated in the professor's chair were primed with situational power, and those in the guest chair with lack of power. The experimenter left the room briefly to get the second participant and returned saying that the second participant left a message saying that "they" (remaining non-gender-specific) would be arriving a few minutes late. The experimenter went on to explain that the study involved completing a set of 10 tasks, and each participant had to do 5 of these tasks. The experimenter gave the participant a description of the various exercises and how long each one took to complete. The participant was asked to choose 5 exercises to complete, after which he or she would be free to leave, with the understanding that the other participant would have to complete the remaining 5 when he or she arrived. The main dependent measure was the number of minutes required to complete the five tasks chosen by the participant. As predicted, among those seated in the professor's chair (but not among those in the guest chair), communals chose more minutes for themselves, compared to exchangers. This suggests that those with an exchange relationship orientation have self-interest goals automatically activated when primed with power, and those with a communal orientation have social-responsibility goals automatically activated when primed with power.

In all the studies demonstrating a link between the situation and the goal, there was no direct activation of the goal, as there was in the Bargh et al. (in press) and Chartrand and Bargh (1996) studies. The situation was primed, which in turn activated the goal, which then operated as if it had been consciously chosen. Moreover, the S. Chen et al.

(2001) studies demonstrated situational activation of goals without the priming cues being directly or semantically related to the primed construct. Instead, naturally occurring cues in the environment were used to prime power, thereby simulating one way in which power is often primed in the real world. Collectively, the studies demonstrating a link between situation and goal provide strong evidence that the environment activates goals that have been frequently and consistently chosen in that same environment in the past.

CONSEQUENCES OF AUTOMATIC GOAL PURSUIT

Regardless of whether a goal is consciously or nonconsciously determined, individuals either succeed or fail to achieve it. Research on consciously held goals has demonstrated that attaining such deliberately chosen goals improves one's mood and subsequent goal-relevant performance. Failing to reach such goals worsens one's mood and subsequent performance (Bandura, 1990, 1997; Beckmann & Heckhausen, 1988; Carver & Scheier, 1981; Gollwitzer, 1987, 1990; Gollwitzer & Wicklund, 1985; Heckhausen, 1987, 1991; Litt, 1988; Locke, Frederick, Lee, & Bobko, 1984; Nuttin & Greenwald, 1968; Weary, 1980; Weinberg, Gould, & Jackson, 1979). Do success and failure at nonconscious goal pursuit yield consequences similar to those of conscious goal pursuit?

One might argue that once a goal is activated—whether by the environment or through conscious choice—the goal is pursued in the same way (Chartrand & Bargh, 1996), and therefore the same consequences should arise from succeeding or failing at it. In fact, one could argue that mood might be especially vulnerable to influence by nonconscious processes because it frequently fluctuates during the course of a day, and people often are not aware of the source of their current mood at any given moment (Keltner, Locke, & Audrain, 1993; Schwarz & Clore, 1983, 1988, 1996; Schwarz, Servay, & Kumpf, 1985). Future goal-directed performance might also be easily affected because behavior has already been shown to be susceptible to influence from a variety of nonconscious processes (for reviews, see Bargh, 1997; Bargh & Chartrand, 1999).

Consequences for Mood

Chartrand (2001) conducted three experiments to explore the consequences of nonconscious goal pursuit. In a first study examining the consequences for mood, an achievement goal was primed in half the participants via a scrambled-sentence task. Participants were then given a "fun filler task" in the form of anagram puzzles, which were either very easy or very difficult to complete in what they were told was the "average" amount of time. This manipulated whether participants "succeeded" or "failed," without the experimenter giving participants explicit positive and negative feedback. Finally, participants were asked to report their current mood. Results revealed that for participants primed with an achievement goal, those given the easy anagram task reported being in a better mood than those given the difficult version. For participants in the no-goal condition, however, there was no reliable difference in mood between those given the easy anagram version and those given the difficult version. Importantly, postexperimental questionnaires revealed that participants did not have a conscious achievement goal during the study. The anagram task had been purposefully downplayed, and most participants thought it was a fun task included to fill up time.

A second experiment (Chartrand, 2001; Experiment 2) extended this by attempting to replicate the effects using a different priming technique (subliminal) and different type of goal (impression formation). Specifically, participants performed a parafoveal vigilance task in which words related to an impression formation goal (or neutral words) were presented to them subliminally. Next, the experimenter played an audiotape for participants, which was a recording of a male voice describing a target person. This put participants in a situation in which they could potentially form an impression of the target person if they had the goal to do so (as only the impression goal-primed participants were predicted to have). The success–failure manipulation consisted of the target person description. He was described as either performing various clumsy acts or as engaging in some clumsy acts and some agile, graceful acts. Thus, the target was either consistent or inconsistent in his behaviors, making it either easy or difficult for the participants to form a coherent impression of the target.

In addition, Experiment 2 pitted nonconscious and conscious goal pursuit against each other by including an additional control condition in which participants were given the explicit instructions to form an impression of the target person. This allowed an assessment of the relative strength or magnitude of the consequences of nonconscious goal activation, compared to those of conscious goal operation. Results revealed that among participants either explicitly given an impression formation goal or primed with such a goal, those given the consistent target description (who succeeded) were in a better mood than those given the inconsistent description (who failed). However, the consistent versus inconsistent target manipulation did not have an effect on the mood of participants who did not have a goal (conscious or nonconscious) to form an impression. Funneled debriefing questionnaires revealed that participants in the explicit-goal condition had a conscious goal to form an impression of the target, but no participants in the primed-goal or no-goal conditions reported having any similar conscious goal.

Consequences for Self-Enhancement and Stereotyping

Tesser, Martin, and Cornell (1996) argued that the common denominator among various self-enhancement mechanisms—the trigger that sets them into motion—is mood of unknown origin. Specifically, if a person is in a bad mood and does not know why, he or she will be more likely to engage in self-enhancement (using whichever mechanism is most readily available). Thus, greater self-enhancement should ensue when individuals fail at nonconscious goals (negative mystery mood) than when they succeed at nonconscious goals (positive mystery mood) or process any outcome of a conscious goal (understood moods).

A series of studies to test the self-enhancement hypotheses have been conducted (Chartrand, Cheng, & Tesser, 2001). In a first experiment, participants were supraliminally primed with an achievement goal via a scrambled sentence task (nonconscious-goal condition), explicitly told to achieve by the experimenter (conscious-goal condition), or given no goal. They were then given a series of anagrams that were presented as a fun, filler task. The anagrams were very difficult to complete in what the participants were casually told was the average amount of completion time. To assess the extent to which participants then self-enhanced, they were given a questionnaire that measured self-serving definitions of success (Dunning, 1999; Dunning, Leuenberger, & Sherman, 1995). The questionnaire began with a description of a person who had been in a successful marriage for 25 years. Various attributes were provided about this person. Participants rated the contribution of each attribute to the positive outcome (successful marriage). Participants then completed a demographic survey that asked whether they themselves had various attributes, including the ones from the earlier task. To the extent that they create self-serving definitions of success (Dunning et al., 1995), individuals are more likely to rate the qualities that they share with the target person as being greater contributors to the successful marriage than qualities that they do not share. Results indicated that those who failed at a nonconscious goal created the most self-serving definitions of success (i.e., importance ratings for qualities they share minus the importance ratings for qualities they do not share), those who had no goal created the least self-serving definitions of success, and those who failed at a conscious goal fell in between.

It should be noted that all participants in this particular study failed at the goal, which left open the possibility that any mysterious mood—positive or negative—would trigger self-enhancement equally. However, a conceptual replication was conducted during which some individuals succeeded at a nonconscious achievement goal and some failed. Results indicated that only those who failed (and not those who succeeded) exhibited self-enhancement on the self-serving bias measure.

An additional study by Chartrand et al. (2001) examined a different type of self-enhancement: stereotyping others. Fein, Spencer, and their colleagues (Fein & Spencer, 1997; Spencer et al., 1998) have demonstrated that stereotyping serves the same function that other self-enhancement mechanisms do: It boosts the ego and restores self-esteem during times of self-threat. Thus, it was predicted that those who fail at a nonconscious goal would stereotype more than those who fail at a conscious goal or no goal. Participants were primed (via a scrambled sentence task) with an achievement goal (nonconscious-goal condition), explicitly given an achievement goal by the experimenter (conscious-goal condition), or given no goal. Participants were all then given the difficult anagrams as a fun, filler task.

An additional variable was manipulated in this study as well; it was reasoned that if a negative mystery mood were driving the greater self-enhancement, then reducing the mysteriousness of the mood should attenuate the self-enhancement. Thus, half the participants were given a mood scale that provided an attribution for their mood: the previous anagram task. Specifically, the directions on the top of the mood scale stated "How did that anagram task make you feel? Please report your current mood state." The other half did not receive this form. Participants were then given the dependent variable: a measure of implicit stereotyping developed by von Hippel, Sekaquaptewa, and Vargas (1997). This Stereotypic Explanatory Bias (SEB) scale assumes that to the extent an individual is relying on his or her stereotypes, he or she will feel the need to "explain away" stereotype-inconsistent behaviors in an effort to understand what was unexpected. Higher SEB scores indicate greater implicit stereotyping. Results revealed that participants who failed at a nonconscious achievement goal and were not given an attribution for their mood state (i.e., it remained a negative mystery mood) engaged in more implicit stereotyping. As expected, however, when they were given an attribution for their mood state, the stereotyping effect was attenuated. They no longer needed to stereotype others, providing further evidence that it is being unaware of the cause of a bad mood that increases the need to self-enhance. The difference between attribution conditions was not significant for those who failed at a conscious goal or no goal.

Consequences for Subsequent Goal-Relevant Performance

Chartrand (2001; Experiment 3) also tested for possible behavioral consequences of success and failure at nonconscious goal pursuit by measuring performance on a subsequent task. Participants were either primed with an achievement goal or not. They next were administered either the easy or the difficult anagram task (manipulating success and failure, respectively). Finally, participants were given a portion of the verbal section of the Graduate Record Examination (GRE) to test their subsequent performance at a verbal task. Participants primed with an achievement goal who had succeeded on the earlier anagram task scored significantly higher on the verbal GRE than did those who had failed. There was no such difference for those not primed with an achievement goal. Again, no participant reported having a conscious goal to achieve during the study.

People may often have goals triggered by social situations and work toward them unwittingly. For instance, at a party situation a person may have a self-presentational goal activated, or in an interview an ingratiation goal, or with siblings a competition goal, without the individual's awareness or intent that the goal is operating to guide cognition and behavior. The Chartrand (2001) studies represent an attempt to better understand the consequences of such nonconscious goal pursuit. Experiments 1 and 2 provided strong evidence that success at nonconscious goal pursuit improves one's mood, whereas failure depresses one's mood. Experiment 3 demonstrated that success and failure at nonconsciously pursued goals also affect future performance; success leads to better performance, and failure leads to worse performance.

DO NONCONSCIOUS GOALS NECESSARILY MEDIATE THE STIMULUS–RESPONSE LINK?

The auto-motive model posits that goals can become automatically activated by situational features linked to those goals in memory. Bargh et al. (in press) provided evidence that individuals displayed several qualities associated with motivational states following the achievement priming manipulations in their studies. However, these tests for motivational states were not conducted in any of the other studies discussed above. Many of these studies exposed individuals to words related to a goal state in an implicit priming manipulation and found the individuals to behave in line with those goals. Results were interpreted as providing support for nonconscious motivation and goal pursuit. But does one really need the construct of goals to explain the results of these studies, or could something simpler, such as plain conditioning mechanisms, account for the effects? That is, can classic S–R behaviorism provide a more parsimonious explanation for these studies, unmediated by nonconscious motivation? When certain behaviors and reactions occur repeatedly and consistently in certain situations, eventually these situations are sufficient to trigger the relevant behaviors. Perhaps the priming manipulations in the auto-motive studies activate not goals per se but rather behavioral sequences or habitual plans.

There are several reasons this is unlikely. First, the Aarts and Dijksterhuis (2000) studies discussed above showed that habitual plans of action were automatically activated only for individuals who were first primed with the relevant goal. For those not primed, the behavioral sequences were not automatically activated by the environment. If it were just the environment activating a behavioral sequence, the priming of the goal beforehand would not be a necessary precondition of the effect, and yet it was. This suggests that strategies, plans of action, and behavioral sequences are an inextricable part of goal structure and hierarchy.

Second, in S–R behaviorism, the environment directly shapes the behavior of the individual, unmediated by any mental process. However, people who were primed with the various goals in the auto-motive studies reviewed above behaved differently than people who were not. It was the pre-activation of the goal state that caused the differences in behavior, not the situation or environment participants were in after the priming. The priming manipulations caused individual differences not explainable in terms of the stimulus environment, which precludes a radical behaviorist account of the findings.

Third, conditioning refers to single reflexive behavioral responses to single environmental stimuli, or S–R links. But in the auto-motive studies discussed above, behavior was shown to interact in a complex fashion with incoming and unpredictable environmental information over time. The goal guided the processing of the information in that different things were done with the information depending on the goal that was primed, and behavior was flexible and adaptive to that information over time (Bargh, 2001). Moreover, motivational states such as greater effort, persistence, and drive to complete the goal were shown to be present after a goal used frequently in this type of research was primed (Bargh et al., in press). None of these effects can be understood in terms of the S–R psychology model, in which each discrete response is emitted in the presence of a single controlling stimulus event. These effects are produced by internal mechanisms that operate on the information over an extended time. So, clearly, they cannot be explained by reflexive behaviors emitted in the presence of a single conditioning stimulus (Bargh, 2001).

Finally, the Chartrand (2001) studies also pose a problem for radical behaviorists. Of course, behaviorists would not be interested in the consequences of success and failure at nonconscious goal pursuit for mood, as tested in Studies 1 and 2 (Chartrand, 2001). Moreover, a behaviorist would not predict a change in future behavior based on the ease or difficulty of the anagram task. The reasons for this are twofold. First, there was no explicit success or failure feedback given and no other reward or punishment. There was no conditioning at all, so future performance in Study 3 should not have been affected. Second, even if there were some internal reward or punishment caused by the ease or difficulty, it was the same for everyone in the experiment (i.e., those primed with the goal and those not primed with the goal). A behaviorist would have predicted subsequent behavior effects for everyone in the experiment, and that did not happen.

CONCLUSION

There is substantial support for the notion that goals function the same way, regardless of whether they are instigated through conscious, deliberate means or through primed, nonconscious means. A growing body of evidence indicates that self-regulation and indeed goal-directed cognition and action are not limited to the conscious domain.

People's ability to have goals automatically activated by the environment is generally adaptive and positive. Goals become automatized to better serve our chronic desires and wishes. If goals are activated even when we are not giving them our conscious attention, then we will engage in goal-directed action even when we are not making any conscious effort to do so. This will be beneficial, because we will be more likely to achieve our immediate goals, thereby satisfying our enduring motives. The recent evidence that our capacity for conscious self-regulation is severely limited (Baumeister, Bratslavsky, Muraven, & Tice, 1998; Muraven & Baumeister, 2000; Muraven, Tice, & Baumeister, 1998) suggests that nonconscious self-regulation is necessary for everyday functioning. Self-regulation is a limited resource, so automatic goal pursuit helps us save these self-regulatory resources for when they are really needed.

The notion of an automatic process as adaptive and in service of the individual agrees with a host of other studies in the field that have shown automatic processes to be generally adaptive. For instance, our tendency to automatically mimic the behaviors, postures, and mannerisms of other people serves a positive function: It creates empathy, liking, and understanding among people (Chartrand & Bargh, 1999). The tendency to automatically evaluate stimuli in our environment as positive or negative (Bargh, Chaiken, Govender, & Pratto, 1992; Bargh, Chaiken, Raymond, & Hymes, 1996; Fazio, Sanbonmatsu, Powell, & Kardes, 1986) is also adaptive in that it provides a "running average" of the positive and negative people, things, and events in our environment. This in turn provides us with "intuition"—our sense of whether our current environment is safe and positive or dangerous and negative. In line with this, automatic evaluation has been shown to affect our mood (Chartrand & Bargh, 2001), our social judgments and interpretations of ambiguous stimuli (Ferguson & Bargh, 2001), and our behavioral tendency to approach or avoid (M. Chen & Bargh, 1999). This growing body of evidence suggests that automatic processes should not all be seen as negative, evil forces to be avoided, confronted, or reckoned with (Freud, 1901/1965; Langer, 1978, 1997; Langer, Blank, & Chanowitz, 1978) but rather as generally functional, beneficial, positive processes. Not only do they save much-needed cognitive resources, but they also usually serve the individual's chronic needs and desires.

However, the process of automatic motivation can surely go wrong.

People might have certain goals activated in inappropriate situations. Just because an individual used to choose a certain goal in a certain situation consistently and frequently does not mean that it is still appropriate in that situation. But the environment may still trigger the goal in this individual without his or her awareness or intent. This can become dangerous, especially if the goal is frequently not attained, because even though individuals do not realize they have the goal, failing at it will put them in a worse mood and worsen their future performance (Chartrand, 2001). One can further speculate that failing at a nonconscious goal may lead to frustration. According to the frustration–aggression hypothesis (Berkowitz, 1989; Dollard, Doob, Miller, Mowrer, & Sears, 1939), frustration elicits the motive to aggress, which further suggests that individuals who have failed at a nonconscious goal may be more likely to behave aggressively.

One could also speculate that nonconscious goal pursuit might contribute to certain emotional disorders. Individuals who have a maladaptive goal chronically activated by a certain situation and who always fail at it are consistently feeling bad without knowing why. This could lead to depression or perhaps to a sense of generalized, "free-floating" anxiety because they do not know why they feel that way and cannot control it. Perhaps these emotional disorders can be better understood by examining what goals the individual might be pursuing nonconsciously.

In sum, recent work on nonconscious goal pursuit suggests that self-regulation can bypass conscious mediation altogether. Individuals can have goals automatically activated by environments in which those goals were frequently and consistently chosen in the past. Such goals then operate and interact with the environment to guide subsequent cognition and behavior, in the same way that consciously held and pursued goals do. Nonconscious goal pursuit has consequences for mood and subsequent goal-relevant performance that have only begun to be explored. This new frontier promises to increase our understanding of the way we think, feel, and behave in social situations.

REFERENCES

Aarts, H., & Dijksterhuis, A. (2000). Habits as knowledge structures: Automaticity in goal-directed behavior. *Journal of Personality and Social Psychology, 78,* 53–63.

Atkinson, J. W., & Birch, D. (1970). *A dynamic theory of action.* New York: Wiley.

Bandura, A. (1977). Self-efficacy: Toward a unifying theory of behavioral change. *Psychological Review, 84,* 191–215.

Bandura, A. (1986). *Social foundations of thought and action: A social cognitive theory.* Englewood Cliffs, NJ: Prentice-Hall.

Bandura, A. (1990). Self-regulation of motivation through anticipatory and self-reactive mechanisms. In R. A. Dienstbier (Ed.), *Nebraska Symposium on Motivation: Perspectives on motivation* (Vol. 38, pp. 69–164). Lincoln: University of Nebraska Press.

Bandura, A. (1997). *Self-efficacy*. New York: Freeman.

Bargh, J. A. (1990). Auto-motives: Preconscious determinants of social interaction. In E. T. Higgins & R. M. Sorrentino (Eds.), *Handbook of motivation and cognition* (Vol. 2, pp. 93–130). New York: Guilford.

Bargh, J. A. (1997). The automaticity of everyday life. In R. S. Wyer, Jr. (Ed.), *The automaticity of everyday life: Advances in social cognition* (Vol. 10, pp. 1–61). Mahwah, NJ: Erlbaum.

Bargh, J. A. (2001). Caution: Automatic social cognition may not be habit forming. *Polish Psychological Bulletin.* [Au: please give issue and page nos.]

Bargh, J. A., Bond, R. N., Lombardi, W. J., & Tota, M. E. (1986). The additive nature of chronic and temporary sources of construct accessibility. *Journal of Personality and Social Psychology, 50,* 869–878.

Bargh, J. A., Chaiken, S., Govender, R., & Pratto, F. (1992). The generality of the automatic attitude activation effect. *Journal of Personality and Social Psychology, 62,* 893–912.

Bargh, J. A., Chaiken, S., Raymond, P., & Hymes, C. (1996). The automatic evaluation effect: Unconditionally automatic attitude activation with a pronunciation task. *Journal of Experimental Social Psychology, 32,* 185–210.

Bargh, J. A., & Chartrand, T. L. (1999). The unbearable automaticity of being. *American Psychologist, 54,* 462–479.

Bargh, J. A., & Chartrand, T. L. (2000). The mind in the middle: A practical guide to priming and automaticity research. In H. T. Reis & C. M. Judd (Eds.), *Handbook of research methods in social and personality psychology* (pp. 253–285). New York: Cambridge University Press.

Bargh, J. A., Chen, M., & Burrows, L. (1996). Automaticity of social behavior: Direct effects of trait construct and stereotype activation on action. *Journal of Personality and Social Psychology, 71,* 230–244.

Bargh, J. A., Gollwitzer, P. M., Lee-Chai, A., Barndollar, K., & Trötschel, R. (in press). Automating the will: Automatic and controlled self-regulation. *Journal of Personality and Social Psychology.*

Bargh, J. A., Raymond, P., Pryor, J., & Strack, F. (1995). Attractiveness of the underling: An automatic power–sex association and its consequences for sexual harassment and aggression. *Journal of Personality and Social Psychology, 68,* 768–781.

Baumeister, R. F., Bratslavsky, E., Muraven, M., & Tice, D. M. (1998). Ego depletion: Is the active self a limited resource? *Journal of Personality and Social Psychology, 74,* 1252–1265.

Beckmann, J., & Heckhausen, H. (1988). Handlungsbewertung und Aufmerksamkeitsumschaltung. In *Max-Planck-Gesellschaft, Jahrbuch 1988* (pp. 759–761). Gottingen, Germany: Vandenhoeck & Ruprecht.

Berkowitz, L. (1989). Frustration–aggression hypothesis: Examination and reformulation. *Psychological Bulletin, 106,* 59–73.

Blair, I. V., & Banaji, M. R. (1996). Automatic and controlled processes in stereotype priming. *Journal of Personality and Social Psychology, 70,* 1142–1163.

Brewer, M. B., & Brown, R. J. (1998). Intergroup relations. In D. T. Gilbert, S. T. Fiske, & G. Lindzey (Eds.), *Handbook of social psychology* (4th ed., Vol. 2, pp. 554–594). New York: McGraw-Hill.

Cacioppo, J. T., Crites, S. L., Jr., & Gardner, W. L. (1996). Attitudes to the right: Evaluative processing is associated with lateralized late positive event-related brain potentials. *Personality and Social Psychology Bulletin, 22,* 1205–1219.

Cantor, N., & Kihlstrom, J. F. (1987). *Personality and social intelligence.* Englewood Cliffs, NJ: Prentice-Hall.

Carver, C. S., & Scheier, M. F. (1981). *Attention and self-regulation: A control theory approach to human behaviors.* New York: Springer.

Chartrand, T. L. (2001). *Mystery moods and perplexing performance: Consequences of succeeding or failing at a nonconscious goal.* Manuscript submitted for publication, Ohio State University.

Chartrand, T. L., & Bargh, J. A. (1996). Automatic activation of impression formation and memorization goals: Nonconscious goal priming reproduces effects of explicit task instructions. *Journal of Personality and Social Psychology, 71,* 464–478.

Chartrand, T. L., & Bargh, J. A. (1999). The chameleon effect: The perception–behavior link and social interaction. *Journal of Personality and Social Psychology, 76,* 893–910.

Chartrand, T. L., & Bargh, J. A. (2001). *Consequences of automatic evaluation for mood and stereotyping.* Manuscript in preparation, Ohio State University.

Chartrand, T. L., Cheng, C. M., & Tesser, A. (2001). *Consequences of failing at nonconscious goals for self-enhancement and stereotyping.* Manuscript submitted for publication, Ohio State University.

Chen, M., & Bargh, J. A. (1999). Nonconscious approach and avoidance behavioral consequences of the automatic evaluation effect. *Personality and Social Psychology Bulletin, 25,* 215–224.

Chen, S., Lee-Chai, A. Y., & Bargh, J. A. (2001). Relationship orientation as a moderator of the effects of social power. *Journal of Personality and Social Psychology, 80,* 173–187.

Clark, M. S., & Mills, J. (1979). Interpersonal attraction in exchange and communal relationships. *Journal of Personality and Social Psychology, 37,* 12–24.

Deci, E. L., & Ryan, R. M. (1985). *Intrinsic motivation and self-determination in human behavior.* New York: Plenum.

Deci, E. L., & Ryan, R. M. (1990). A motivational approach to self: Integration in personality. In R. Dienstbier (Ed.), *Nebraska Symposium on Motivation: Perspectives on motivation* (Vol. 38, pp. 237–288). Lincoln: University of Nebraska Press.

Dijksterhuis, A., Spears, R., Postmes, T., Stapel, D., Koomen, W., van Knippenberg, A., & Scheepers, D. (1999). Seeing one thing and doing another: Contrast effects in automatic behavior. *Journal of Personality and Social Psychology, 75,* 862–871.

Dijksterhuis, A., & van Knippenberg, A. (1998). The relation between perception and behavior or how to win a game of Trivial Pursuit. *Journal of Personality and Social Psychology, 74,* 865–877.

Dollard, J., Doob, L. W., Miller, N. E., Mowrer, O. H., & Sears, R. R. (1939). *Frustration and aggression.* New Haven, CT: Yale University Press.

Dunn, J. C., & Kirsner, K. (1988). Discovering functionally independent mental processes: The principle of reversed association. *Psychological Review, 95,* 91–101.

Dunning, D. (1999). A newer look: Motivated social cognition and the schematic representation of social concepts. *Psychological Inquiry, 10,* 1–11.

Dunning, D., Leuenberger, A., & Sherman, D. A. (1995). A new look at motivated inference: Are self-serving theories of success a product of motivational forces? *Journal of Personality and Social Psychology, 69,* 58–68.

Fazio, R. H., Sanbonmatsu, D. M., Powell, M. C., & Kardes, F. R. (1986). On the automatic activation of attitudes. *Journal of Personality and Social Psychology, 50,* 229–238.

Fein, S., & Spencer, S. J. (1997). Prejudice as self-image maintenance: Affirming the self through derogating others. *Journal of Personality and Social Psychology, 73,* 31–44.

Ferguson, M. J., & Bargh, J. A. (2001). *The impact of automatic evaluation on concept accessibility and social judgment.* Manuscript submitted for publication, New York University, New York.

Freud, S. (1965). *The psychopathology of everyday life* (J. Strachey, Ed. & Trans.). New York: Norton. (Original work published 1901)

Gardner, W. L., Bargh, J. A., Shellman, A., & Bessenoff, G. (2001). *This is your brain on primes: Lateralized brain activity is the same for nonconscious and conscious evaluative processing.* Manuscript submitted for publication, Northwestern University, Evanston, IL.

Gilbert, D. T., & Hixon, J. G. (1991). The trouble of thinking: Activation and application of stereotypic beliefs. *Journal of Personality and Social Psychology, 60,* 509–517.

Gollwitzer, P. M. (1987). The implementation of identity intentions: A motivational-volitional perspective on symbolic self-completion. In F. Halisch & J. Kuhl (Eds.), *Motivation, intention, and volition* (pp. 349–369). Berlin, Germany: Springer-Verlag.

Gollwitzer, P. M. (1990). Action phases and mind-sets. In E. T. Higgins & R. M. Sorrentino (Eds.), *Handbook of motivation and cognition* (pp. 53–92). New York: Guilford.

Gollwitzer, P. M., & Moskowitz, G. (1996). Goal effects on thought and behavior. In E. T. Higgins & A. Kruglanski (Eds.), *Social psychology: Handbook of basic principles* (pp. 361–399). New York, NY: Guilford Press.

Gollwitzer, P. M., & Wicklund, R. A. (1985). The pursuit of self-defining goals. In J. Kuhl & J. Beckmann (Eds.), *Action control: From cognition to behavior* (pp. 61–85). Heidelberg, Germany: Springer-Verlag.

Hamilton, D. L., Katz, L. B., & Leirer, V. O. (1980). Organizational processes in impression formation. In R. Hastie, T. M. Ostrom, E. B. Ebbesen, R. S. Wyer, Jr., D. L. Hamilton, & D. E. Carlston (Eds.), *Person memory: The cognitive basis of social perception* (pp. 121–153). Hillsdale, NJ: Erlbaum.

Hastie, R., & Kumar, P. A. (1979). Person memory: Personality traits as organizing principles in memory for behaviors. *Journal of Personality and Social Psychology, 37*, 25–38.

Heckhausen, H. (1987). Causal attribution patterns for achievement outcomes: Individual differences, possible types and their origins. In F. E. Weinert & R. H. Kluwe (Eds.), *Metacognition, motivation, and understanding* (pp. 143–184). Hillsdale, NJ: Erlbaum.

Heckhausen, H. (1991). *Motivation and action*. Berlin, Germany: Springer-Verlag.

Higgins, E. T., Bargh, J. A., & Lombardi, W. (1985). The nature of priming effects on categorization. *Journal of Experimental Psychology: Learning, Memory, and Cognition, 11*, 59–69.

Higgins, E. T., Rholes, W. S., & Jones, C. R. (1977). Category accessibility and impression formation. *Journal of Experimental Social Psychology, 13*, 141–154.

Keltner, D., Locke, K. D., & Audrain, P. C. (1993). The influence of attributions on the relevance of negative feelings to satisfaction. *Personality and Social Psychology Bulletin, 19*, 21–30.

Langer, E. J. (1978). Rethinking the role of thought in social interaction. In J. H. Harvey, W. Ickes, & R. F. Kidd (Eds.), *New directions in attribution research* (Vol. 2, pp. 35–58). Hillsdale, NJ: Erlbaum.

Langer, E. J. (1997). *The power of mindful learning*. Reading, MA: Addison-Wesley.

Langer, E. J., Blank, A., & Chanowitz, B. (1978). The mindlessness of ostensibly thoughtful action. *Journal of Personality and Social Psychology, 36*, 635–642.

Lewin, K. (1926). Vorsatz, wille, und bedürfnis [Intention, will, and need]. *Psychologische Forschung, 7*, 330–385.

Lewin, K. (1951). *Field theory in social science*. Chicago: University of Chicago Press.

Lisak, D., & Roth, S. (1988). Motivational factors in nonincarcerated sexually aggressive men. *Journal of Personality and Social Psychology, 55*, 795–802.

Litt, M. D. (1988). Self-efficacy and perceived control: Cognitive mediators of pain tolerance. *Journal of Personality and Social Psychology, 54*, 149–160.

Locke, E. A., Frederick, E., Lee, C., & Bobko, P. (1984). Effect of self-efficacy, goals, and task strategies on task performance. *Journal of Applied Psychology, 69*, 241–251.

Locke, E. A., & Latham, G. P. (1990). *A theory of goal setting and task performance*. Englewood Cliffs, NJ: Prentice-Hall.

Mischel, W. (1973). Toward a cognitive social learning reconceptualization of personality. *Psychological Review, 80,* 252–283.

Moskowitz, G. B., Wasel, W., Gollwitzer, P. M., & Schaal, B. (1999). Preconscious control of stereotype activation through chronic egalitarian goals. *Journal of Personality and Social Psychology, 77,* 167–184.

Muraven, M., & Baumeister, R. F. (2000). Self-regulation and depletion of limited resources: Does self-control resemble a muscle? *Psychological Bulletin, 126,* 247–259.

Muraven, M., Tice, D. M., & Baumeister, R. F. (1998). Self-control as limited resource: Regulatory depletion patterns. *Journal of Personality and Social Psychology, 74,* 774–789.

Neely, J. H. (1977). Semantic priming and retrieval from lexical memory: Roles of inhibitionless spreading activation and limited-capacity attention. *Journal of Experimental Psychology: General, 106,* 226–254.

Neely, J. H. (1991). Semantic priming effects in visual word recognition: A selective review of current findings and theories. In D. Besner & G. Humphreys (Eds.), *Basic processes in reading: Visual word recognition* (pp. 264–336). Hillsdale, NJ: Erlbaum.

Nisbett, R. E., & Wilson, T. D. (1977). Telling more than we can know: Verbal reports on mental processes. *Psychological Review, 84,* 231–259.

Nuttin, J., & Greenwald, A. G. (1968). *Reward and punishment in human learning.* New York: Academic Press.

Ovsiankina, M. (1928). Die wiederaufnahme unterbrochener handlungen [The resumption of interrupted tasks]. *Psychologische Forschung, 11,* 302–379.

Pryor, J. B., & Stoller, L. M. (1994). Sexual cognition processes in men who are high in the likelihood to sexually harass. *Personality and Social Psychology Bulletin, 20,* 163–169.

Rogers, C. R. (1951). *Client-centered therapy: Its current practice, implications, and theory.* Boston: Houghton-Mifflin.

Schwarz, N., & Clore, G. L. (1983). Mood, misattribution, and judgments of well-being: Informative and directive functions of affective states. *Journal of Personality and Social Psychology, 45,* 513–523.

Schwarz, N., & Clore, G. L. (1988). How do I feel about it? Informative functions of affective states. In K. Fiedler & J. Forgas (Eds.), *Affect, cognition, and social behavior* (pp. 44–62). Toronto, Ontario, Canada: Hogrefe International.

Schwarz, N., & Clore, G. L. (1996). Feelings and phenomenal experiences. In E. T. Higgins & A. W. Kruglanski (Eds.), *Social psychology: Handbook of basic principles* (pp. 433–465). New York: Guilford.

Schwarz, N., Servay, W., & Kumpf, M. (1985). Attribution of arousal as a mediator of the effectiveness of fear-arousing communications. *Journal of Applied Social Psychology, 15,* 74–78.

Séguin, C., & Pelletier, L. G. (2001). *Automatic activation of intrinsic and extrinsic motivation.* Manuscript submitted for publication, University of Ottawa.

Shiffrin, R. M., & Schneider, W. (1977). Controlled and automatic human information processing: II. Perceptual learning, automatic attending, and a general theory. *Psychological Review, 84,* 127–190.

Spencer, S. J., Fein, S., Wolfe, C. T., Fong, C., & Dunn, M. A. (1998). Automatic activation of stereotypes: The role of self-image threat. *Personality and Social Psychology Bulletin, 24,* 1139–1152.

Srull, T. K., & Wyer, R. S., Jr. (1979). The role of category accessibility in the interpretation of information about persons: Some determinants and implications. *Journal of Personality and Social Psychology, 37,* 1660–1672.

Tesser, A., Martin, L. L., & Cornell, D. P. (1996). On the substitutability of self-protective mechanisms. In P. M. Gollwitzer & J. A. Bargh (Eds.), *The psychology of action* (pp. 48–68). New York: Guilford.

von Hippel, W., Sekaquaptewa, D., & Vargas, P. (1997). The linguistic intergroup bias as implicit indicator of prejudice. *Journal of Experimental Social Psychology, 33,* 490–509.

Weary, G. (1980). Examination of affect and egotism as mediators of bias in causal attributions. *Journal of Personality and Social Psychology, 38,* 348–357.

Wegner, D. M., & Wheatley, T. (1999). Apparent mental causation: Sources of the experience of will. *American Psychologist, 54,* 480–492.

Weinberg, R. S., Gould, D., & Jackson, A. (1979). Expectations and performance: An empirical test of Bandura's self-efficacy theory. *Journal of Sport Psychology, 1,* 320–331.

Wilson, T. D., & Brekke, N. (1994). Mental contamination and mental correction: Unwanted influences on judgments and evaluation. *Psychological Bulletin, 116,* 117–142.

Wood, J. V. (1989). Theory and research concerning social comparisons of personal attributes. *Psychological Bulletin, 106,* 231–248.

2

FROM THREAT TO SWEAT: THE ROLE OF PHYSIOLOGICAL AROUSAL IN THE MOTIVATION TO MAINTAIN SELF-ESTEEM

JAMIE ARNDT AND JAMIE L. GOLDENBERG

A variety of theorists representing diverse theoretical backgrounds concur that people have a pervasive motive to maintain self-esteem, experience several difficulties when it is threatened, and will go to great lengths to defend it in the face of such threats (e.g., Allport, 1937; Becker, 1962; Horney, 1937; James, 1890; Rank, 1937/1959; Rosenberg, 1981; Steele, 1988; Sullivan, 1953; Tesser, 1988). In advancing these ideas, self-esteem researchers often make implicit, and sometimes explicit, assumptions about the relationship between self-esteem and affective reactions to self-esteem threats and defenses. Yet despite the widespread acknowledgment of self-esteem's importance and its presumed intimate connection with anxiety and affect, surprisingly little heed has been paid to the empirical research that has directly tested these assumptions with physiological measures. The purpose of this chapter is to consider the research that bears on these issues.

A reasonable place to begin is to consider why people may be motivated to maintain self-esteem in the first place, and how these needs fit with assumptions about the role of arousal. Here, another surprise awaits us: Relatively little attention has been given to this perhaps most basic question. There are, however, some notable exceptions, and we begin with a very brief overview of these explanations. Having considered the "why" question, we turn to three issues that stem from the widespread assumptions involving arousal in self-esteem motivation: (a) Do threats to self-esteem create physiological arousal? (b) Does physiological arousal influence self-esteem defense? and (c) Do self-esteem defenses reduce physiological arousal? In concluding the chapter, we discuss how issues associated with this research, as well as future psychophysiological efforts, can inform contemporary social psychological issues in the self-esteem literature. Before starting this progression, however, we turn to a brief overview of why an examination of physiological arousal may be informative in the context of examining self-esteem, as well as some of the measures and paradigms used to this end.

WHY PSYCHOPHYSIOLOGY?

Although one of the core themes of self-esteem motivation is that it is strongly intertwined with anxiety, arousal, and affect, following Tesser and Cornell (1991), we note that this "affect hypothesis" must be viewed as tenuous. Studies using self-report methods to examine such processes as dissonance reduction, attributions, and excuse making are consistent with this perspective (e.g., Elliot & Devine, 1994; Leary, Barnes, & Griebel, 1986; Mehlman & Snyder, 1985). However, some research examining other self-esteem processes such as projection and self-affirmation is not (e.g., Holmes & Houston, 1971; Steele, 1988; Zemore & Greenough, 1973). Moreover, self-report measures are restricted to what individuals can and will describe, and people are sometimes unable or unwilling to report how or why they feel the way they do (e.g., Nisbett & Wilson, 1977; Schachter & Singer, 1962). Affect can also be manipulated by factors outside conscious awareness (e.g., Murphy & Zajonc, 1993), and the impact of primes on judgments, including judgments of mood, is often most effective when the target is not aware of being primed (e.g., Bargh, 1992; Clore, 1992). Looked at differently, combined with the idea that self-related psychological defenses are often assumed to operate outside of conscious awareness, these reservations suggest a need for research that can tap anxiety-related processes in a way that circumvents their need for conscious articulation. In addition to methodological innovations that enable the confident inference of arousal-based processes (e.g., misattribution of arousal and excitation transfer paradigms), physiological measures are increasingly popular in social psychology as a means toward this end (see Blascovich, 2000; Guglielmi, 1999).

PHYSIOLOGICAL INDICES OF AROUSAL

In this section we offer a brief overview of some of the more common physiological measures that have been used in this domain. Full coverage of these and other measures are available from several sources (see, e.g., *Principles of Psychophysiology*, 1990). Traditionally, anxiety has been characterized by responses of the sympathetic nervous system that prepare the individual for appropriate responses to impending threats (e.g., increased blood flow). This more general historical focus among social psychophysiologists on global arousal has led to an emphasis on broad electrodermal and cardiovascular measures (Blascovich & Kelsey, 1990; Cacioppo, Berntson, & Crites, 1998).

The reasoning behind measuring electrodermal responses to assess generalized anxiety is that when an individual is aroused, the eccrine glands of the sympathetic nervous system secrete sweat into ducts. This leads to a facilitation and conductance of the electrical voltage transmission between dipolar electrodes, measured via the frequencies of nonspecific skin conductance responses (NS-SCRs), skin conductance level (SCL), or with the inverse of these in the case of skin resistance (SR; see, e.g., Dawson, Schell, & Filion, 1990; Venables & Christie, 1980). In assessing cardiovascular activity, the joint influence of the sympathetic and the parasympathetic nervous systems is targeted, although emphasis in social psychophysiology tends to be on the former (Blascovich & Kelsey, 1990). Here the most commonly used techniques again measure the electrical impulses of the system, as in heart rate (HR). The general inference with these measures is that the heart beats faster and pumps more blood throughout the body in response to increased arousal. Other cardiovascular measures widely used in social psychophysiological research assess peripheral blood flow and are often quantified on the basis of the rate of blood circulation (pulse rate, PR) or by the blood amplitude or volume (e.g., finger pulse amplitude, FPA; finger pulse volume, FPV). Recent work also attempts to provide a more comprehensive picture of the differential influence of the sympathetic (e.g., pre-ejection period; PEP) and parasympathetic (e.g., vascular resistance) nervous systems, and in some cases, a more precise picture of positive versus negative arousal (e.g., Tomaka & Blascovich, 1994). Several other physiological and neurological measures are available; as one example, electromyographic (EMG) assessment of the facial muscles relies on the idea that particular facial muscle patterns are activated during the experience of specific emotional states (e.g., Darwin, 1872) and that the amplitude of responses to evocative stimuli can be used to assess positive and negative affect (e.g., Cacioppo, Petty, Losch, & Kim, 1986; Schwartz, Fair, Salt, Mandel, & Klerman, 1976).

Misattribution to Infer Physiological Arousal

In addition to physiological measures, other research methods have been used to make confident inferences about the influence of arousal in self-esteem defense. In particular, misattribution of arousal paradigms (Schachter & Singer, 1962) have been used to examine the level of self-esteem defenses when participants are provided with an alternative explanation for the physiological arousal they may be experiencing. In the first misattribution dissonance experiment, Zanna and Cooper (1974) found that psychological defenses (e.g., attitude change) in response to threat (e.g., counterattitudinal behavior) were not engaged when participants were provided with an explanation for their tension (e.g., a pill). Relatedly, Zillmann's (1978) excitation transfer theory of emotion suggests that because excitatory activity of the sympathetic nervous system decays slowly but a person's awareness of that excitation dissipates more quickly, people have the tendency to attribute (or misattribute) the residual excitation to a cognitively available and appropriate stimulus. Therefore, lacking awareness of the original source of their arousal, residues of excitation may be transferred from a previously arousing task (e.g., physical exercise) to a subsequent situation and intensify feelings as diverse as anger or sexual excitement (e.g., Cantor, Zillmann, & Bryant, 1975).

Some Issues and Concerns

Although the number of paradigms and measures invite the possibility of distinguishing physiologically between what is construed as an affective or as an arousal response, psychophysiological investigations of self-esteem have yet to consistently accept this invitation. Rather, in the studies we review, affect and arousal have been more often treated as interchangeable concepts and measured via the broad electrodermal or cardiovascular indices. It is important to point out that contemporary thinking has raised several concerns about such broad measures. For example, the basis for inferring that such activity reflects increased anxiety, or negatively valenced arousal, is not permitted on inspection of the response alone, and in some cases anxiety may be associated with initial decreases in autonomic arousal. Yet interpretations of negative arousal can productively stem from a consideration of the experimental context (Cacioppo & Tassinary, 1990) and the hypotheses guiding the research. For example, after giving participants bogus negative feedback (to lower self-esteem), researchers often reasonably interpret subsequent increases in arousal as anxiety.

We should also emphasize that researchers strongly question the tacit assumption of a one-to-one relationship between a psychological stimulus and a physiological response, which has led to an overly narrow reliance on single physiological measures. More recently, the predominant contemporary perspective in social psychology has focused on an expanded constellation of measures in the hope of capturing stable patterns of bodily responses to psychological situations (e.g., Blascovich, 2000). This certainly adds a fair amount of interpretive complexity, given that physiological measures may often be perceived as discrepant with one another. Yet, by attending to these differences, researchers may gain greater insight into the particular systems that are critically involved in the response.

WHY DO WE NEED SELF-ESTEEM?

Developmental Analysis Linking Self-Esteem to Anxiety

We have the tools to assess physiology; the question becomes whether a clear theoretical rationale exists for doing so. The role of anxiety in the development of a need for self-esteem, although touched on by a few perspectives, has received its most explicit attention in terror management theory (e.g., Solomon, Greenberg, & Pyszczynski, 1991). From this perspective, based largely on the work of cultural anthropologist Ernest Becker (e.g., 1962, 1973), the juxtaposition of instinctive mechanisms aimed at preserving and continuing life with the knowledge of one's precarious existence in a possibly meaningless world creates the potential for paralyzing terror. To manage this anxiety, the theory suggests that humans invest in culture, which provides a shared symbolic conception of reality that imbues the world with meaning and provides prescriptions for value (self-esteem). The motivation for maintaining self-esteem is thus of critical importance for understanding human social behavior.

This critical relationship between self-esteem and anxiety emerges over the course of a child's development (see also Bowlby, 1969; Freud, 1959; Horney, 1937; Sullivan, 1953). As a vulnerable infant, the child is completely dependent on his or her parents for protection and fulfillment of basic needs, and the satiation of these needs becomes epitomized by the parents' love and affection. However, as the child begins to function in a social world with rules and norms, this sense of security becomes increasingly contingent on meeting parental standards of value. For example, the child learns that defecating in the neighbor's swimming pool leads to at least a mild rebuke and the absence of affection, whereas doing so in the sanctioned porcelain bowl meets with approval and praise. Thus, children learn that meeting parental standards of value leads to feelings of significance and security and that failure to do so leads to feelings of low value and anxiety. In this way, the stage is set for an association between self-esteem and anxiety.

With the dawning awareness of one's mortality and the realization of the limited capacity of their caregivers to protect them from their anxieties, children transfer their primary security base from their parents to the culture at large (see Becker, 1973). A broad range of teachings, including fairy tales, myths, schooling, entertainment, religion, and instruction, facilitate this transference by reinforcing the association between living up to certain values and goodness and security (cf. Lerner, 1980). The more the individual meets these standards of value, the more the individual acquires feelings of personal significance, or self-esteem. According to this analysis, self-esteem arises out of the context of childhood interactions with parents and significant others and culminates as a culturally constructed anxiety buffer that makes possible secure adult functioning.

Empirical Evidence for Self-Esteem as Anxiety Buffer

The terror management perspective on why self-esteem is so vital thus leads to a clear and basic prediction: Situationally increased or dispositionally high self-esteem should lead to less anxiety in response to threatening stimuli. As a first step toward assessing this hypothesis, Greenberg et al. (1992) gave participants bogus personality feedback that was either highly positive or neutral, exposed them to a graphic video segment depicting death-related scenes or to a neutral video, and had them complete a self-report measure of anxiety. Consistent with their hypothesis, the positive feedback (which manipulation checks indicated increased self-esteem) led to less reported anxiety in response to the threat video than did the neutral feedback.

In two additional studies, participants received success or neutral feedback on a test to manipulate state self-esteem (Greenberg et al., 1992; Study 2) or positive or neutral personality feedback (Study 3) and were threatened with painful electric shock while their tonic level of SR (later transformed to SCL scores) was recorded. The results of both studies indicated that when threatened with painful electric shock, participants who had their self-esteem raised, both with success and personality feedback, showed lower SCLs than did participants whose self-esteem had not been raised. Taken together, these results illustrate how physiological techniques can be used to provide convergent support for a particular hypothesis—in this case, the terror management hypothesis that increased self-esteem reduces anxiety in response to threat.

Additional Explanations

Our intent is not to review the breadth of terror management work here (for reviews, see Arndt, Goldenberg, Greenberg, Pyszczynski, & Solomon, 2000; Greenberg, Solomon, & Pyszczynski, 1997). It is important to note here that the theory provides the developmental analysis that links self-esteem maintenance to anxiety and affect. However, the self-esteem–anxiety connection also comes into play for several other perspectives. For example, the recent work of Leary and colleagues (e.g., Leary & Baumeister, 2000) attempts to answer the question of why people need self-esteem by positing that people do not in fact need self-esteem at all. Rather, from the perspective of their sociometer model, self-esteem reflects some combination of people's current inclusionary status and potential for social inclusion. In short, for Leary and Baumeister (2000), events that threaten inclusionary status are thought to create anxiety. For perspectives such as Swann's (e.g., Swann, Griffin, Predmore, & Gaines, 1987) self-verification theory, a motive to predict and control the environment engenders self-verification needs whereby people seek to confirm their self views through social interaction, even if those views happen to be negative. Such efforts are thought to be largely a cognitive process, whereas self-esteem concerns (i.e., the desire for positive feedback) are thought to be more an affective process. Consistently, Brown (e.g., 1993) has also suggested that self-esteem is rooted in affective rather than cognitive processes; rather than resulting from positive appraisals and judgments of oneself, high self-esteem is hypothesized to be primarily an affective state that in turn biases these cognitions in a favorable direction.

Generalized View of Self-Esteem Threat and Maintenance

Rather than focusing on explanations for why people need self-esteem, the lion's share of empirical attention has been directed toward understanding the mechanisms through which self-esteem is threatened, enhanced, or maintained. In the voluminous self-esteem literature, one of the more ubiquitous characteristics of self-esteem-related processes that emerges is their association with affect and arousal. We consider a few examples to illustrate the pervasiveness of arousal and affect in these processes.

The self-evaluation maintenance model (Tesser, 1988) posits that self-esteem is heavily affected by comparisons with others. For example, being outperformed by a psychologically close other on a personally relevant task threatens self-esteem because of the negative comparison in a meaningful social domain. Research has shown that in the face of such a threat, people will respond by reducing the relevance of the performance domain, the closeness to the other person, or the performance gap between oneself and the other (e.g., Tesser, 1988, for a review)—all strategies through which the potential negative reflection on self-esteem is attenuated. According to Tesser, Pilkington, and McIntosh (1989), the engine that drives these strategic defenses is the arousal instigated by the threat. Relatedly, research on the self-serving bias—the attribution of success to internal factors and failure to external factors (e.g., Miller & Ross, 1975; Snyder, Stephan, &

Rosenfield, 1976)—has also been identified as a bias rooted in the defense of self-esteem (e.g., Weary, 1980; Zuckerman, 1979), and one line of research that has identified it as such has examined the role of arousal. Stephan and Gollwitzer (1981) further articulated the role of affect in this process by positing that outcome feedback elicits a positive or negative affective response, and this affective response motivates attributional processes that function to maintain or enhance self-esteem.

In addition to these more traditional self-esteem defenses, a diverse array of social psychological phenomena with arousal or affect implications have been argued to serve self-esteem-related motives. For example, cognitive dissonance (Festinger, 1957), although not originally formulated as such, has come to be understood at least in part as a circumstance that implicates self-esteem concerns (e.g., Aronson, 1968; Solomon et al., 1991; Steele & Liu, 1983; Stone, 1999; Tesser, Martin, & Cornell, 1996). For example, a decade after Festinger proposed the theory, Aronson (1968) suggested that cognitive inconsistency causes dissonance because it threatens one's usually positive self-concept. In a similar vein, self-affirmation theory (Steele, 1988) views cognitive dissonance as a threat to the global integrity of one's self-concept. More than 40 years of research have demonstrated the various routes through which dissonance can be reduced, and in many cases, this research has targeted the role of arousal in such processes. As another example, consider that even the counterfactual simulation of alternative outcomes to negative life events, originally studied as a cognitive phenomenon, has recently been linked to the affective processes of self-esteem maintenance (see Roese, 1997).

We outline these mechanisms in brief to make one primary point: Both research and theory on traditional self-esteem defenses and other phenomena now recognized to be linked to self-esteem often make implicit or explicit assumptions about the role of affect and arousal. Recently Tesser and colleagues (e.g., Tesser et al., 1996) have ushered this issue to center stage in their extensive discourse on the substitutability of self-esteem defenses, suggesting that the common unit of exchange is affect. In the remaining sections of the chapter we examine whether self-esteem threats create physiological arousal, whether that arousal influences self-esteem defense, and whether such defenses reduce that arousal.

DO THREATS TO SELF-ESTEEM CREATE PHYSIOLOGICAL AROUSAL?

Given the evidence that self-esteem provides protection from anxiety, it should also be the case that threatening self-esteem increases anxiety. To be sure, researchers have used self-report methods to support this claim (e.g., Hodges, 1968; Leary et al., 1986; Mehlman & Snyder, 1985). In addition, several studies show that a variety of techniques that threaten self-esteem affect physiological arousal.

Cognitive Dissonance Research

Perhaps the most programmatic of these efforts has been the search for physiological arousal from cognitive dissonance, in which the first indirect attempts found that dissonance-arousing situations increased dominant responses (i.e., improved performance on simple tasks and impaired performance on complex tasks; for a review, see Kiesler & Pollak, 1976). Subsequent work using misattribution paradigms also converged to implicate the role of physiological arousal in dissonance processes (e.g., Zanna & Cooper, 1974). Notably, the dissonance literature also features several more direct assessments of physiological responses.

In the first reported experiment to use physiological techniques, Gerard (1967) used a "free-choice" paradigm (Brehm, 1956) in which participants experienced dissonance after making a choice between two similarly appraised options and then reduced dissonance by exaggerating the positive qualities of the chosen alternative in comparison to the unchosen alternative. The results of the Gerard study suggested that the provocation of dissonance is accompanied by physiological arousal, as measured by FPA. However, this study as well as others that followed (e.g., McMillen & Geiselman, 1974) were limited because they did not reliably find accompanying attitude change and therefore were unclear as to whether the manipulations actually created dissonance (see Fazio & Cooper, 1983).

For several subsequent physiological studies, researchers adopted the induced compliance paradigm, wherein participants are led to act contrary to a pre-existing attitude, and then their attempts (most often attitude change) to reduce that inconsistency are measured (e.g., Festinger & Carlsmith, 1959). Croyle and Cooper (1983) found such attitude change in a first study, and in a subsequent study found increased NS-SCRs following the same dissonance manipulation. Although they did not replicate the increased attitude shift in the second study, presumably as the authors speculated, the misattribution of the arousal to the physiological equipment eliminated the attitude change.[1] Elkin and Leippe (1986) followed a similar procedure but implemented greater efforts to reduce the likelihood of misattribution of arousal and also measured average level of SR. The results revealed increases in dissonance reduction strategies in conjunction with

---

[1]No differences were found on HR, which, as has been mentioned, may be because of the other processes (e.g., attention) that influence this measure. Similarly, in Tesser et al. (1989), stronger self-evaluation maintenance (SEM) patterns were associated with decreases in HR. Tesser et al. (1989) speculated the stronger SEM effect may have been observed among participants with a decelerated HR because this deceleration reflected a shift in attention toward the others (cf. Cacioppo & Sandman, 1978).

physiological arousal, providing stronger support for the hypothesis that cognitive dissonance has a physiological component.

Continuing this tradition, Losch and Cacioppo (1990) had participants commit (or not) to engage in counterattitudinal behavior under conditions of high or low choice (dissonance should occur only when the counterattitudinal behavior is perceived of as freely chosen). Losch and Cacioppo found that high-choice participants showed more attitude change and NS-SCRs than did low-choice participants, directly supporting the idea that inconsistency can lead to increased arousal. More recently, Harmon-Jones, Brehm, Greenberg, Simon, and Nelson (1996) similarly found that high-choice participants showed increased NS-SCRs after engaging in counterattitudinal behavior. Thus, in terms of dissonance-induced arousal, measures of skin conductance have been found to be reliable. Given the apparent sensitivity of such measures, it is somewhat surprising that studies involving more traditional self-esteem threats have relied on different physiological indices.

Negative Feedback as Threats to Self-Esteem

A more common way to induce self-esteem threat is to provide negative feedback to participants and, although such studies have typically used nonelectrodermal measures, they are consistent with the notion that such threats increase bodily arousal. In experiments in which female participants were given unfavorable feedback regarding personality or intelligence (Bennett & Holmes, 1975; Holmes & Houston, 1971), participants responded with heightened PR. In addition, Burish and Horn (1979, Study 2) administered the same type of manipulation used by Bennett and Holmes and found increased skin temperature (ST), PR, and FPV. Based on this research as well as on the dissonance findings, it appears that an array of measures are sensitive to the bodily effects of self-esteem threats.

Fear of Failure as Self-Esteem Threat

Researchers have also sought to manipulate threat to self-esteem by creating a situation that engenders concern with the potential for failure (Berglas & Jones, 1978). Knight and Borden (1979) found that the anticipation of public speaking increased HR, SR, and FPV. Interestingly, however, the only physiological measure that was sensitive to the personality difference of social anxiety was FPV, suggesting that it may indeed provide a differentially sensitive measure of reactions to self-relevant situations. Smith, Houston, and Zurawski (1984) further implicated FPV as a physiological response to evaluative threat by showing that when participants were told that their responses on a verbal intelligence test would be later evaluated, they showed elevated FPV as well as PR and self-reported anxiety.

Inability to Cope as Self-Esteem Threat

Research by Tomaka, Blascovich, and colleagues on cognitive appraisals of "motivated performance situations" also informs understanding of the physiological consequences of how people perceive a threat to their self-esteem. Applying their formula (Blascovich & Tomaka, 1996) to the present analysis, if coping ability relative to the stressful demand of the situation is perceived to be low, the situation may represent a potential threat to self-esteem. However, if coping ability meets or exceeds the threat, the situation might be perceived as a challenge. This difference between challenge and threat appraisal is in turn associated with distinct patterns of physiological activation. Challenge appraisal leads to increased cardiac performance juxtaposed with decreased vascular resistance, whereas threat increases cardiac performance without decreasing vascular resistance (Blascovich, 2000).

In conducting these studies, researchers have allowed for free appraisals of performance situations, manipulated the challenge or threat appraisal, or manipulated the physiological response (Blascovich, 2000). For example, Tomaka, Blascovich, Kelsey, and Leitten (1993) told participants they would be performing, in the presence of the experimenter, a serial subtraction task (i.e., consecutively subtracting 7 from a large number) and assessed the ratio of participants' perceived challenge to threat of the task. The results indicated that participants who appraised the task as a challenge experienced greater blood flow from the heart (specifically, PEP and cardiac output) but decreased resistance to that activity (total peripheral resistance). Subsequent research has shown that when the cognitive appraisal is manipulated, parallel physiological response patterns emerge, but interestingly, manipulating the physiological response (e.g., submersing participants' hand in cold water to lower vascular resistance) does not reproduce the different appraisals (Tomaka, Blascovich, Kibler, & Ernst, 1997). Tomaka and Blascovich (1994) also found that people who believed strongly in a just world appraised the arithmetic task as more challenging and showed increased cardiac activation and decreased vascular resistance compared with individuals who did not believe as strongly in a just world. To the extent that just-world beliefs are a component of a person's self-concept, this study suggests that the constitution of a person's self-concept can influence his or her reaction to tasks that could threaten self-esteem.

Considered in concert, this array of findings offers convergent support for the idea that various threats relevant to self-esteem can increase arousal. We next consider whether this arousal in turn influences the extent of self-esteem defense.

DOES PHYSIOLOGICAL AROUSAL INFLUENCE
SELF-ESTEEM DEFENSE?

When a variable (e.g., arousal) is claimed to function as a mediator, it is necessary to find evidence not only that the variable is affected by the manipulation (e.g., self-esteem threat), but also that fluctuations in this variable lead to changes in the behavior or outcome (e.g., self-esteem defense) in question (Baron & Kenny, 1986). Thus, the proximal cause of self-esteem defense from this view is the elevation of arousal. It is surprising, therefore, that more studies have not explicitly investigated the influence of arousal on self-esteem defense. There are, however, some noteworthy exceptions. Although some of this research comes from a classic self-esteem perspective, other relevant efforts stem from research less commonly associated with self-esteem processes. We begin by considering some of the work that deals with more traditional self-esteem defenses.

Self-Serving Attributions

Several studies have examined whether physiological arousal mediates self-serving attributions. Motivational explanations for the self-serving attributional bias posit that negative feedback that threatens self-esteem leads to discomforting arousal (e.g., Weary, 1980). To reduce that arousal, participants engage in the self-protective strategy of making external attributions for failure.

Initial efforts to examine this idea capitalized on misattribution of arousal paradigms to infer the operation of physiological influence. In one early study, Fries and Frey (1980) reasoned that if participants were provided with an alternative explanation for the source of the arousal created by failure, then attributional egotism should be attenuated. Under conditions in which participants received negative feedback on an intelligence test, some participants ingested a pill that would purportedly have either strong or weak arousing side effects. The results of two studies indicated that participants given no pill or told that it would have weak effects exhibited a self-serving pattern of attributions (i.e., they rated their effort as low), but that participants given the "strong arousal" placebo did not.

Similar effects have also been obtained in a series of studies by Stephan, Gollwitzer, and colleagues. For example, Stephan and Gollwitzer (1981) found that when participants were attached to a physiograph that ostensibly measured their arousal, they made fewer internal attributions for successful test performance if they believed they showed low levels of arousal in response to the feedback. Similarly, using an excitation transfer paradigm (e.g., Zillmann, 1978), Gollwitzer, Earle, and Stephan (1982) had participants ride an exercise bike and then make attributions following success or failure at one of three intervals. When participants were still aroused but were no longer aware of their arousal (5 minutes after the exercise, rather than 1 and 9 minutes after), they showed an exaggerated pattern of attributional egotism.

Although these studies suggest that physiological arousal mediates self-serving attributions, Brown and Rogers (1991) are among the few to directly assess the role of arousal with physiological indices.[2] In this study, after participants completed a test of "integrative orientation" and received either positive or negative feedback, their SCLs were recorded, and they then made attributions for their performance. Results indicated that success participants believed that ability played a greater role in their performance than did failure participants. Moreover, within the failure condition, high levels of arousal were negatively correlated with attributions to ability, suggesting that the more aroused participants were, the more they favored an external attribution.

Self-Evaluation Maintenance

Tesser et al. (1989) proposed that emotion plays a key role in self-evaluation maintenance (SEM) processes, and hypothesized that SEM effects would be stronger when arousal was high and attenuated when arousal was low. A first study showed that a typical finding in the SEM paradigm (behaving more charitably toward a friend than toward a stranger on a low- but not on a high-relevance task) was attenuated when participants were provided an opportunity to attribute their arousal elsewhere. In a second study, participants were exposed to either 85 or 64 dB of noise while they completed the judgment task. Although this manipulation did not effectively increase HR and PR as intended, for participants who did not attribute their arousal to the noise, higher PRs were associated with a more exaggerated SEM pattern, whereas for those who did attribute the arousal to the noise, PR did not covary with the SEM pattern. These results are consistent with the notion that arousal influences the adjustments that people make in social comparison processes to protect self-esteem.

Cognitive Dissonance

Similar work also comes from the cognitive dissonance tradition. Of the previously discussed studies, Elkin and Leippe (1986) and Harmon-

---

[2] Only one other study that we are aware of has examined physiological processes associated with self-serving biases in causal attributions. Drake and Seligman (1989) found some indication that induced left-hemisphere activation, presumed in their research to heighten positive affect, increased a tendency for self-serving attribution to hypothetical scenarios. However, in addition to the hypothetical nature of their procedures and thus the likely absence of ego involvement, it is unclear what instead of, or in addition to, positive affect was being manipulated with their hemispheric activation procedures (see, e.g., Reid, Duke, & Allen, 1998, for discussions of correlates of left-hemisphere activity).

Jones et al. (1996) conducted additional analyses that shed light on how arousal influences defensive reactions to inconsistency. Elkin and Leippe reported significant positive overall correlations between SR (transformed into conductance) and attitude change, suggesting either that the more aroused participants were the more they adjusted their attitudes, or that the more participants adjusted their attitudes, the more they were aroused. Further support for the influence of arousal on dissonance reduction was provided by Harmon-Jones et al. (1996), who showed the same pattern of correlation and, moreover, that the more choice participants perceived they had in whether to engage in the counterattitudinal behavior, the more they evidenced increased NS-SCRs.

Following the tradition of misattribution research (e.g., Zanna & Cooper, 1974), Losch and Cacioppo (1990) found that the influence of arousal on dissonance reduction can be short-circuited if individuals already have a negative label for that arousal. Losch and Cacioppo (1990) led participants to believe that wearing prism goggles would create either positive or negative feelings and had them engage in counterattitudinal behavior under conditions of high or low choice. As previously mentioned, the results revealed that high-choice participants showed more NS-SCRs than did low-choice participants. In addition, high-choice participants who were led to believe the goggles would have a positive effect showed the most attitude change, whereas high-choice, negative-cue participants did not differ from their low-choice counterparts. This suggests that although inconsistency without justification creates arousal, attitude change occurred in response to that arousal only when the arousal could not be attributed to the effects of the goggles. This work, unlike previous efforts, considers how arousal and affect might function differently.

Worldview Defense

According to terror management theory, another means by which people may defend their self-esteem is to uphold the cultural context that allows them to feel value and meaning. Consistently, after reminders of their mortality, people become more favorable to that which supports their worldview and more unfavorable to that which threatens it (see Greenberg et al., 1997, for a review). However, in contrast to some of the self-esteem defenses described earlier, self-reported negative affect does not appear to be involved with worldview defense induced by reminders of mortality.

Moreover, additional work examining the role of physiological arousal in these defenses has failed to find that the typical mortality salience treatment (two open-ended questions about death) increases physiological arousal. Rosenblatt, Greenberg, Solomon, Pyszczynski, and Lyon (1989) found that the mortality salience treatment did not increase SR, PR, and

FPV during the next 1-minute period and that what arousal there was did not covary with extent of worldview defense. More recently, Arndt, Greenberg, and Allen (2001) measured SCL, NS-SCRs, and PR in a procedure paralleling that described above and found similar effects. To investigate this issue further, Arndt, Allen, and Greenberg (2001) conducted a study measuring facial EMG, which research has found to be better suited for assessing subtle affective reactions (e.g., Cacioppo et al., 1986). In addition, following previous research (Arndt, Greenberg, Pyszczynski, & Solomon, 1997), mortality concerns were manipulated with subliminal death presentations. In this study, along with increased worldview defense, the subliminal death primes also provoked subtle negative affective reactions as indexed by activity of the corrugator muscle region. Yet, despite the emergence of effects on both EMG and target evaluations, correlational analyses provided no evidence that this affective reaction in the death prime condition influenced participants' reaction to the worldview-threatening target.

Although the terror management work raises some question of the ubiquitous involvement of arousal in self-esteem processes, the research presented thus far generally supports the hypotheses that threats to self-esteem create arousal and that arousal can influence the operation of self-esteem defense. However, a third hypothesis concerning a critical function of such defenses—that they operate at least in part to reduce physiological arousal—is on more tentative ground.

DO SELF-ESTEEM DEFENSES REDUCE PHYSIOLOGICAL AROUSAL?

Evidence certainly shows that self-esteem defense reduces self-report negative affect (e.g., Elliot & Devine, 1994; Leary et al., 1986; Mehlman & Snyder, 1985). However, such support has not been reliably obtained using physiological measures. Efforts to assess this possibility have been conducted primarily with regard to the effectiveness of projection and dissonance reduction strategies.

Projection

The general paradigm for projection studies has been to threaten participants by telling them they possess an unwanted trait, then to give some participants the opportunity to project this trait onto others, and then to assess whether this differential opportunity for projection has any effect on arousal (see, e.g., Holmes, 1978; Sherwood, 1981, for reviews). If projection serves to protect the individual from arousal, then arousal that is increased by the threat of possessing an unwanted trait should be reduced following the projection of the trait onto others.

To assess this hypothesis, Bennett and Holmes (1975) and Holmes and Houston (1971) found that negative feedback on personality or intelligence tests produced arousal as measured by self-report and PR and that individuals in the negative-feedback condition used projection as measured by attributions of poor performance to one's friends. However, neither study revealed evidence of reduced PR as a function of projection, although Bennett and Holmes (1975) did find evidence of decreased self-reported arousal.

Zemore and Greenough (1973) suggested that projection may in fact reduce arousal, although this study is shrouded in a bit of controversy.[3] Male participants were told they had scored low on masculinity and high on femininity (and subsequently showed higher self-report anxiety than did control participants), and some participants rated a previously unknown male on masculinity and femininity. The results indicated that participants in the threat condition rated the target higher on femininity, but there was no indication that projection effectively reduced stress as assessed with a self-report measure. However, with a possibly indirect measure of arousal, participants given the opportunity to project femininity onto the ambiguous target reported fewer intentions to squeeze a hand dynameter. Note that it is not entirely clear whether this measure actually reflects the reduction of arousal. Rather, it may be that this measure indicated increased efforts to defend self-esteem by inflating one's accomplishments in another domain (i.e., compensatory self-inflation; Baumeister & Jones, 1978; Greenberg & Pyszczynski, 1985).

Cognitive Dissonance

Of the physiological studies examining dissonance arousal, only Elkin and Leippe (1986) and Harmon-Jones et al. (1996) measured arousal after participants had the opportunity to use a dissonance reduction technique (attitude change). Elkin and Leippe (1986) measured skin conductance for 3 minutes in Study 1 and for 7 minutes in Study 2, and Harmon-Jones et al. (1996) recorded SCL for 3 minutes following the reduction opportunity, and in all cases there was no evidence of attenuated arousal. Yet, as with all the studies examining the effects of self-esteem defenses on physiological arousal, it may simply be that it takes considerable time for such defenses to reduce this arousal. It is interesting to note that Elkin and Leippe (1986) included a high-choice condition in which participants were not provided

---

[3] The controversy from this study stems from whether or not the effects were replicated in subsequent research. Holmes (1978) reported that Zemore personally communicated to him that he did not replicate these effects, but Sherwood (1981) noted that Zemore was unable to find this data and that Zemore and Greenough (1973) therefore stand undisputed.

with the opportunity to adjust their attitudes. Ironically, these participants were the only ones to show a significant decrease in arousal. Elkin and Leippe therefore speculated about a "don't remind me" effect; participants who were not given the explicit opportunity to change their attitude simply forgot the dissonance, and this forgetting may be a preferred way of dealing with dissonance because it takes less effort than actively adjusting one's cognitions. However, this idea raises additional questions because forced forgetting (i.e., suppression) has been shown to have physiological consequences (Pennebaker, 1989), particularly with regard to the cardiovascular system (Gross & Levenson, 1993).

Lack of Support for an Arousal Reduction Effect of Self-Esteem Defense

The available research, limited primarily to projection and dissonance paradigms, has for the most part (with Zemore & Greenough, 1973, as a possible exception) found no difference in arousal between those who defend self-esteem and those who do not. Because this idea is such a pervasive assumption in self-esteem theorizing, its apparent lack of support warrants some speculation. And indeed, there are several possible reasons why such effects have yet to be observed. First, one cannot be sure that participants in these studies did not engage in some other form of self-esteem defense. With the dissonance research, for example, participants who were denied the opportunity to reduce dissonance through attitude change may have trivialized the threats (Simon, Greenberg, & Brehm, 1995) or self-affirmed (Steele, 1988) in a manner that more effectively reduced arousal than did the opportunity for attitude adjustment. This possibility would suggest that, as Tesser and colleagues have proposed, a variety of defenses may be used in response to self-esteem threats. However, though there may be a "zoo" of such defenses, all the beasts may not be equal. Thus, it is not necessarily the case that the defenses with which participants have the opportunity to engage are the most effective options. As Stone, Wiegand, Cooper, and Aronson (1997) have shown, participants may indeed self-affirm in response to hypocrisy-induced dissonance, but when given the choice, they prefer to address the threat more directly. Future research may therefore benefit from considering the differential effectiveness of direct versus indirect forms of defense.

Yet another possibility is that the psychological defense itself introduces arousal that obscures the effectiveness of that defense on the original provocation. For example, as Elkin and Leippe (1986) proposed, adjusting one's attitude may effectively address arousal from the previous inconsistency, but it may also introduce another inconsistency that can itself increase arousal. The provocation of further arousal may also depend on the specific form of defense engaged. Moreover, with recent research showing that intrinsic and achievement bases of self-worth have differential effects on several self-esteem defenses (e.g., Arndt, Schimel, Greenberg, & Pyszczynski, in press; Kernis & Waschull, 1995; Schimel, Arndt, Pyszczynski, & Greenberg, 2001), it is also plausible that arousal reactions may depend on the base from which a sense of self-esteem is derived (see also Higgins, 1987). Another possibility is that certain defenses could protect one's conscious feelings about oneself but not one's unconscious feelings. This would help to explain why arousal and affect reduction has been more reliably found with self-report measures instead of physiological ones; that is, it may be a case of attenuating discomfort rather than arousal per se (Devine, Tauer, Barron, Elliot, & Vance, 1999).

A remaining possibility, of course, is that this assumption that self-esteem defenses reduce arousal is simply wrong. Although self-esteem threats may create arousal and this arousal may mediate the use of some defenses, it is entirely possible that such defenses are ineffective in arousal reduction. Goldenberg, Psyzczynski, Johnson, Greenberg, and Solomon (1999) offer a similar explanation of catharsis, the notion that expression of negative emotions provides relief by purging these feelings from one's system (e.g., Breuer & Freud, 1895/1966). Specifically, although research has generally failed to support the notion that expression of emotions such as aggression and sadness ameliorates the emotional state (e.g., Geen & Quanty, 1977; Gross, Fredrickson, & Levenson, 1994; but see Pennebaker, 1989), people often nevertheless seek out opportunities to express such emotions (e.g., Diener & DeFour, 1978). In a similar manner, individuals may defend their self-esteem despite its ineffectiveness in reducing the arousal provoked by the threat. Clearly, then, several complex issues need to be more fully investigated. Future efforts might record multiple physiological responses, measure arousal at later time points, examine whether reduced activity occurs for some bodily responses but not others, and investigate the extent to which the defense introduces additional arousal or facilitates the positive relabeling of arousal rather than its excitatory level.

DIRECTIONS FOR A PSYCHOPHYSIOLOGICAL APPROACH TO SELF-ESTEEM PROCESSES

As we tried to indicate with this chapter, previous research has provided the foundation from which questions and, one hopes, answers about self-esteem and arousal can be increasingly specified. In light of the research considered, the question need no longer be whether threats to self-esteem create arousal but should instead focus on what kind or pattern of arousal they create. Many of the potential tools to evaluate these issues are already in the workshop. Consider, for example, the work of Tomaka, Blascovich, and colleagues (1997). They have shown that the body responds to threat by increasing vascular resistance to blood flow from the heart, whereas when facing challenge, such resistance is reduced. This type of approach may inform how a threat is perceived such that it may increase self-esteem defense.

Research from the emerging field of social neuroscience also provides several provocative findings such as violations of social expectancies affecting different components of the Event-Related Potential (ERP) waveform (e.g., Bartholow, Fabiani, Gratton, & Bettencourt, 2001). The potential is there for these methods to be applied to research on self-esteem related processes. For example, such research efforts could inform debates between self-verification and self-enhancement processes. To the extent that self-verification strivings represent a cognitive response, whereas self-enhancement represents an affective response (Swann et al., 1987), administering self-relevant feedback and using more cognitively oriented physiological measures such as ERP, juxtaposed with the affective orientation of EMG measures, might prove worthwhile for distinguishing these two motives further. Clearly several complex issues may be involved (e.g., associations between EEG and positive affect or approach versus avoidance motivation), but the promise is there for informative application of these techniques.

What is needed, in addition, is improved specification of the emotional processes under scrutiny. In most of the studies reviewed in this chapter, researchers approached the questions using arousal and affect as interchangeable concepts. Yet it is clear that self-esteem defense may not always be engaged in response to generalized arousal but may be a response to the affective interpretation applied to that arousal (e.g., Losch & Cacioppo, 1990). Although the two may often overlap, a wide body of research indicates that in certain, often more subtle situations, participants can respond with an affective reaction in the absence of any overt arousal response (e.g., Cacioppo et al., 1986).

CONCLUSION

Our overarching goal of this chapter was to highlight what is known but also what is not known, about the role of physiological arousal in the threat and defense of self-esteem. To the extent that we need self-esteem because it provides a vital buffer against anxiety, it follows that arousal would be heavily involved in the motivation for self-esteem maintenance. Accordingly, threats to self-esteem—whether in the form of negative feedback, social comparison, evaluative situations, or cognitive dissonance—have all been shown to increase physiological arousal. Moreover, misattribution paradigms, as well as studies using physiological measures, demonstrate that arousal influences the level at which self-esteem defenses are engaged. Interestingly, less support has been found for the effectiveness of self-esteem in reducing physiological arousal. However, as was mentioned, future research might overcome the shortcomings of these prior efforts.

Yet the evidence that so many self-esteem threats create arousal provides converging support for Tesser and colleagues' position on the substitutability of self-esteem defenses. Tesser et al. (1996) suggested that rather than conceptualize the wide array of self-esteem maintenance strategies as independent motives, we can think of self-esteem maintenance as a single, higher order motive, and therefore, each of the aforementioned self-esteem defenses can be substituted for one another. This suggestion advocates affect as the primary unit of exchange. The relevant physiological findings support this hypothesis. Still, future research may determine whether certain self-esteem defense strategies are more effective against particular threats.

Although several different self-esteem relevant defenses appear to involve physiological arousal, this does not seem to be the case for all relevant defenses. A notable example concerns the work on mortality salience-induced worldview defense. Here, reminders of death do not consistently provoke arousal, and what arousal or affect there is does not relate to worldview defense reactions. There are, however, several reasons this may be the case. It may be that affect is not necessary for terror management to occur because of the existing buffers of the worldview and self-worth of participants. In addition, during the socialization process, people may learn to avert the potential for terror by engaging these defenses whenever a relevant threat is perceived. Thus, people may avoid the experience of arousal altogether. Indeed, one way to think about the theory is as an attempt to explain how people conduct their daily affairs without experiencing the fears that the awareness of mortality engenders. Consistent with this view, studies now show that worldview defense effects are triggered by the unconscious influence of death-related cognition (e.g., Arndt et al., 1997). In addition, as terror management theory contends, the threat of one's mortality is the ultimate threat against which several deeply rooted mechanisms are directed. It is "the worm at the core" (James, 1910/1978), if you will. Thus, responses to the threat of mortality—a deeply rooted fear against which psychological defenses are most often unconsciously directed—may operate differently than responses to conscious threats to one's sense of self-worth.

In sum, studying physiologically oriented responses may provide an informative way to examine the similarities and differences between processes associated with self-esteem motivation. By understanding the role of physiological arousal in self-esteem threat and defense, rather than simply relying on participants' reports of it or researchers' inferences about its antecedents, we may better understand self-esteem. Armed with this understanding, researchers may be better able to contribute to the efforts by schools, businesses, and therapists to help people navigate through the world and the threats they inevitably encounter.

REFERENCES

Allport, G. W. (1937). *Personality: A psychological interpretation*. New York: Holt.

Arndt, J., Allen, J. J. B., & Greenberg, J. (2001). Traces of terror: Subliminal death primes and facial electromyographic indices of affect. *Motivation and Emotion, 25*, 253–277.

Arndt, J., Goldenberg, J. L., Greenberg, J., Pyszczynski, T., & Solomon, S. (2000). Death can be hazardous to your heath: Adaptive and ironic consequences of defense against the terror of death. In P. R. Duberstein & J. M. Masling (Eds.), *Psychodynamic perspectives on sickness and health* (pp. 201–257). Washington, DC: American Psychological Association.

Arndt, J., Greenberg, J., & Allen, J. J. B. (2001). *The effect of mortality salience on skin conductance and pulse rate*. Unpublished data, University of Missouri–Columbia.

Arndt, J., Greenberg, J., Pyszczynski, T., & Solomon, S. (1997). Subliminal exposure to death-related stimuli increases defense of the cultural worldview. *Psychological Science, 8*, 379–385.

Arndt, J., Schimel, J., Greenberg, J., & Pyszczynski, T. (in press). The intrinsic self and defensiveness: Evidence that activating the intrinsic self reduces self-handicapping and conformity. *Personality and Social Psychology Bulletin*.

Aronson, E. (1968). Dissonance theory: Progress and problems. In R. P. Abelson, E. Aronson, W. J. McGuire, T. M. Newcomb, M. J. Rosenberg, & P. H. Tannenbaum (Eds.), *Theories of cognitive consistency: A sourcebook* (pp. 5–27). Chicago: Rand McNally.

Bargh, J. A. (1992). Why subliminality might not matter to social psychologists: Awareness of the stimulus versus awareness of its influence. In R. F. Bornstein & T. S. Pittman (Eds.), *Perception without awareness* (pp. 236–255). New York: Guilford.

Baron, R. M., & Kenny, D. A. (1986). The moderator–mediator variable distinction in social psychological research: Conceptual, strategic, and statistical considerations. *Journal of Personality and Social Psychology, 51*, 1173–1182.

Bartholow, B. D., Fabiani, M., Gratton, G., & Bettencourt, B. A. (2001). A psychophysiological examination of cognitive processing of and affective responses to social expectancy violations. *Psychological Science, 12*, 197–204.

Baumeister, R. F., & Jones, E. E. (1978). When self-presentation is constrained by the target's knowledge: Consistency and compensation. *Journal of Personality and Social Psychology, 36*, 608–618.

Becker, E. (1962). *The birth and death of meaning*. New York: Free Press.

Becker, E. (1973). *The denial of death*. New York: Free Press.

Bennett, D. H., & Holmes, D. S. (1975). Influence of denial (situational redefinition) and projection on anxiety associated with threat to self-esteem. *Journal of Personality and Social Psychology, 32,* 915–921.

Berglas, S., & Jones, E. E. (1978). Drug choice as a self-handicapping strategy in response to a non-contingent success. *Journal of Personality and Social Psychology, 36,* 405–417.

Blascovich, J. (2000). Using physiological indexes of psychological processes in social psychological research. In H. T. Reis & C. M. Judd (Eds.), *Handbook of research methods in social and personality psychology* (pp. 117–137). New York: Cambridge University Press.

Blascovich, J., & Kelsey, R. M. (1990). Using electrodermal and cardiovascular measures of arousal in social psychological research. In C. Hendrick & M. S. Clark (Eds.), *Review of personality and social psychology* (Vol. 2, pp. 45–73). Newbury Park, CA: Sage.

Blascovich, J., & Tomaka, J. (1996). The biopsychosocial model of arousal regulation. In M. P. Zanna (Ed.), *Advances in experimental social psychology* (Vol. 28, pp. 1–51). New York: Academic Press.

Bowlby, J. (1969). *Attachment and loss: Vol. 1. Attachment.* New York: Basic Books.

Brehm, J. W. (1956). Postdecision changes in the desirability of alternatives. *Journal of Abnormal and Social Psychology, 52,* 384–389.

Breuer, J., & Freud, S. (1966). *Studies on hysteria.* New York: Avon. (Original work published 1895)

Brown, J. D. (1993). Self-esteem and self-evaluation: Feeling is believing. In J. M. Suls (Ed.), *The self in social perspective: Vol. 4. Psychological perspectives on the self* (pp. 27–58). Hillsdale, NJ: Erlbaum.

Brown, J. D., & Rogers, R. J. (1991). Self-serving attributions: The role of physiological arousal. *Personality and Social Psychology Bulletin, 17,* 501–506.

Burish, T. G., & Horn, P. W. (1979). An evaluation of frontal EMG as an index of general arousal. *Behavior Therapy, 10,* 137–147.

Cacioppo, J. T., Berntson, G. G., & Crites, S. L. (1998). Social neuroscience: Principles of psychophysiological arousal and response. In D. T. Gilbert, S. T. Fiske, & G. Lindzey (Eds.), *Handbook of social psychology* (pp. 72–101). Boston: McGraw-Hill.

Cacioppo, J. T., Petty, R. E., Losch, M. E., & Kim, H. S. (1986). Electromyographic activity over facial muscles regions can differentiate the valence and intensity of affective reactions. *Journal of Personality and Social Psychology, 50,* 260–268.

Cacioppo, J. T., & Sandman, C.A. (1978). Physiological differentiation of sensory and cognitive tasks as a function of warning, processing demands, and reported unpleasantness. *Biological Psychology, 6,* 181–192.

Cacioppo, J. T., & Tassinary, L. G. (1990). Inferring psychological significance from physiological signals. *American Psychologist, 45,* 13–28.

Cantor, J. R., Zillmann, D., & Bryant, J. (1975). Enhancement of experienced sexual arousal in response to erotic stimuli through misattribution of unrelated residual excitation. *Journal of Personality and Social Psychology, 32,* 69–75.

Clore, G. L. (1992). Cognitive phenomenology: Feelings and construction of social judgments. In L. L. Martin & A. Tesser (Eds.), *The construction of social judgments* (pp. 133–164). Hillsdale, NJ: Erlbaum.

Croyle, R. T., & Cooper, J. (1983). Dissonance arousal: Physiological evidence. *Journal of Personality and Social Psychology, 45,* 782–791.

Darwin, C. (1872). *The expression of emotions in man and animals.* London: John Murray.

Dawson, M. E., Schell, A. M., & Filion, D. L. (1990). The electrodermal system. In J. T. Cacioppo & L. G. Tassinary (Eds.), *Principles of psychophysiology: Physical, social, and inferential elements* (pp. 295–324). New York: Cambridge University Press.

Devine, P. G., Tauer, J. M., Barron, K. E., Elliot, A. J., & Vance, K. M. (1999). Moving beyond attitude change in the study of dissonance-related processes. In E. Harmon-Jones & J. Mills (Eds.), *Cognitive dissonance: Progress on a pivotal theory in social psychology* (pp. 297–324). Washington, DC: American Psychological Association.

Diener, E., & DeFour, D. (1978). Does television violence enhance program popularity? *Journal of Personality and Social Psychology, 36,* 333–341.

Drake, R. A., & Seligman, M. E. (1989). Self-serving biases in causal attributions as a function of altered activation asymmetry. *International Journal of Neuroscience, 45,* 199–204.

Elkin, R. A., & Leippe, M. R. (1986). Physiological arousal, dissonance, and attitude change: Evidence for a dissonance-arousal link and a "don't remind me" effect. *Journal of Personality and Social Psychology, 51,* 55–65.

Elliot, A. J., & Devine, P. G. (1994). On the motivational nature of cognitive dissonance: Dissonance as psychological discomfort. *Journal of Personality and Social Psychology, 67,* 382–394.

Fazio, R. H., & Cooper, J. (1983). Arousal in the dissonance process. In J. T. Cacioppo & R. E. Petty (Eds.), *Social psychophysiology: A sourcebook* (pp. 122–152). New York: Guilford.

Festinger, L. (1957). *A theory of cognitive dissonance.* Stanford, CA: Stanford University Press.

Festinger, L., & Carlsmith, J. M. (1959). Cognitive consequences of forced compliance. *Journal of Abnormal and Social Psychology, 58,* 203–210.

Freud, S. (1959). *Inhibitions, symptoms, and anxiety* (A. Strachey, Trans.). New York: Norton.

Fries, A., & Frey, D. (1980). Misattribution of arousal and the effects of self-threatening information. *Journal of Experimental Social Psychology, 16,* 405–416.

Geen, R., & Quanty, M. (1977). The catharsis of aggression: An evaluation of an hypothesis. In L. Berkowitz (Ed.), *Advances in experimental social psychology* (Vol. 10, pp. 1–36). New York: Academic Press.

Gerard, H. B. (1967). Choice difficulty, dissonance, and the decision sequence. *Journal of Personality, 35,* 91–108.

Goldenberg, J. L., Pyszczynski, T., Johnson, K. D., Greenberg, J., & Solomon, S. (1999). The appeal of tragedy: The effects of mortality salience on emotional response. *Media Psychology, 1,* 313–329.

Gollwitzer, P. M., Earle, W. B., & Stephan, W. G. (1982). Affect as a determinant of egotism: Residual excitation and performance attributions. *Journal of Personality and Social Psychology, 43,* 702–709.

Greenberg, J., & Pyszczynski, T. (1985). Compensatory self-inflation: A response to the threat to self-regard of public failure. *Journal of Personality and Social Psychology, 49,* 273–280.

Greenberg, J., Solomon, S., & Pyszczynski, T. (1997). Terror management theory of self-esteem and cultural worldviews: Empirical assessments and conceptual refinements. *Advances in Experimental Social Psychology, 29,* 61–136.

Greenberg, J., Solomon, S., Pyszczynski, T., Rosenblatt, A., Burling, J., Lyon, D., Pinel, E., & Simon, L. (1992). Assessing the terror management analysis of self-esteem: Converging evidence of an anxiety-buffering function. *Journal of Personality and Social Psychology, 63,* 913–922.

Gross, J. J., Fredrickson, B. L., & Levenson, R. W. (1994). The psychophysiology of crying. *Psychophysiology, 31,* 460–468.

Gross, J. J., & Levenson, R. W. (1993). Emotional suppression: Physiology, self-report, and expressive behavior. *Journal of Personality and Social Psychology, 64,* 970–986.

Guglielmi, R. S. (1999). Psychophysiological assessment of prejudice: Past research, current status, and future directions. *Personality and Social Psychology Review, 3,* 123–157.

Harmon-Jones, E., Brehm, J. W., Greenberg, J., Simon, L., & Nelson, D. E. (1996). Evidence that the production of aversive consequences is not necessary to create cognitive dissonance. *Journal of Personality and Social Psychology, 70,* 1–12.

Higgins, E. T. (1987). Self-discrepancy theory: A theory relating self and affect. *Psychological Review, 94,* 319–340.

Hodges, W. F. (1968). Effects of ego threat and threat of pain on state anxiety. *Journal of Personality and Social Psychology, 8,* 364–372.

Holmes, D. S. (1978). Projection as a defense mechanism. *Psychological Bulletin, 85,* 677–688.

Holmes, D. S., & Houston, B. K. (1971). The defensive function of projection. *Journal of Personality and Social Psychology, 20,* 208–213.

Horney, K. (1937). *The neurotic personality of our time.* New York: Norton.

James, W. (1890). *The principles of psychology.* New York: Dover.

James, W. (1978). *The varieties of religious experience.* Garden City, NY: Image. (Original work published 1910)

Kernis, M. H., & Waschull, S. B. (1995). The interactive roles of stability and level of self-esteem: Research and theory. In M. R. Zanna (Ed.), *Advances in experimental social psychology* (pp. 93–141). Hillsdale, NJ: Erlbaum.

Kiesler, C. A., & Pollak, M. S. (1976). Arousal properties of dissonance manipulations. *Psychological Bulletin, 83,* 1014–1025.

Knight, M. L., & Borden, R. J. (1979). Autonomic and affective reactions of high and low socially-anxious individuals awaiting public performance. *Psychophysiology, 16,* 209–213.

Leary, M. R., Barnes, B. D., & Griebel, C. (1986). Cognitive, affective, and attributional effects of potential threats to self-esteem. *Journal of Social and Clinical Psychology, 4,* 461–474.

Leary, M. R., & Baumeister, R. F. (2000). The nature and function of self-esteem: Sociometer theory. In M. Zanna (Ed.), *Advances in experimental social psychology, Vol. 32* (pp. 1–62). San Diego, CA: Academic Press.

Lerner, M. J. (1980). *The belief in a just world: A fundamental delusion.* New York: Plenum.

Losch, M. E., & Cacioppo, J. T. (1990). Cognitive dissonance may enhance sympathetic tonus, but attitudes are changed to reduce negative affect rather than arousal. *Journal of Experimental Social Psychology, 26,* 289–304.

McMillen, D. L., & Geiselman, J. H. (1974). Effect of cognitive dissonance on alpha frequency activity: The search for dissonance. *Personality and Social Psychology Bulletin, 1,* 150–151.

Mehlman, R. C., & Snyder, C. R. (1985). Excuse theory: A test of the self-protective role of attributions. *Journal of Personality and Social Psychology, 49,* 994–1001.

Miller, D. T., & Ross, M. (1975). Self-serving biases in the attribution of causality: Fact or fiction? *Psychological Bulletin, 82,* 213–225.

Murphy, S. T., & Zajonc, R. B. (1993). Affect, cognition, and awareness: Affective priming with optimal and suboptimal stimulus exposure. *Journal of Personality and Social Psychology, 64,* 723–739.

Nisbett, R. E., & Wilson, T. D. (1977). Telling more than we can know: Verbal reports on mental processes. *Psychological Review, 84,* 231–259.

Pennebaker, J. W. (1989). Confession, inhibition, and disease. In L. Berkowitz (Ed.), *Advances in experimental social psychology* (Vol. 22, 211–244). San Diego, CA: Academic Press.

Rank, O. (1959). *The myth of the birth of the hero, and other writings.* New York: Vintage Books. (Original published 1937)

Reid, S. A., Duke, L. M., & Allen, J. J. B. (1998). Resting frontal electroencephalographic asymmetry in depression: Inconsistencies suggest the need to identify mediating factors. *Psychophysiology, 35,* 389–404.

Roese, N. J. (1997). Counterfactual thinking. *Psychological Bulletin, 121,* 133–148.

Rosenberg, M. (1981). The self-concept: Social product and social force. In M. Rosenberg & R. H. Turner (Eds.), *Social psychology: Sociological perspectives* (pp. 591–624). New York: Basic Books.

Rosenblatt, A., Greenberg, J., Solomon, S., Pyszczynski, T., & Lyon, D. (1989). Evidence for terror management theory I: The effects of mortality salience on reactions to those who violate or uphold cultural values. *Journal of Personality and Social Psychology, 57*, 681–690.

Schachter, S., & Singer, J. E. (1962). Cognitive, social, and physiological determinants of emotional states. *Psychological Review, 69*, 379–399.

Schimel, J., Arndt, J., Pyszczynski, T., & Greenberg, J. (2001). Being accepted for who were are: Evidence that social validation of the intrinsic self reduces general defensiveness. *Journal of Personality and Social Psychology, 80*, 35–52.

Schwartz, G. E., Fair, P. L., Salt, P., Mandel, M. R., & Klerman, G. L. (1976). Facial muscle patterning to affective imagery in depressed and nondepressed subjects. *Science, 192*, 489–491.

Sherwood, G. G. (1981). Self-serving biases in person perception: A reexamination of projection as a mechanism of defense. *Psychological Bulletin, 90*, 445–459.

Simon, L., Greenberg, J., & Brehm, J. W. (1995). Trivialization: The forgotten mode of dissonance reduction. *Journal of Personality and Social Psychology, 68*, 247–260.

Smith, T. W., Houston, B. K., & Zurawski, R. M. (1984). Finger pulse volume as a measure of anxiety in response to evaluative threat. *Psychophysiology, 21*, 260–264.

Snyder, M. L., Stephan, W. G., & Rosenfield, D. (1976). Egotism and attribution. *Journal of Personality and Social Psychology, 33*, 435–441.

Solomon, S., Greenberg, J., & Pyszczynski, T. (1991). A terror management theory of social behavior: The psychological functions of self-esteem and cultural worldviews. In M. P. Zanna (Ed.), *Advances in experimental social psychology* (pp. 91–159). San Diego, CA: Academic Press.

Steele, C. M. (1988). The psychology of self-affirmation: Sustaining the integrity of the self. In L. Berkowitz (Ed.), *Advances in experimental psychology* (Vol. 21, pp. 261–302). New York: Academic Press.

Steele, C. M., & Liu, T. J. (1983). Dissonance processes as self-affirmation. *Journal of Personality and Social Psychology, 45*, 5–19.

Stephan, W. G., & Gollwitzer, P. M. (1981). Affect as a mediator of attributional egotism. *Journal of Experimental Social Psychology, 17*, 443–458.

Stone, J. (1999). What exactly have I done? The role of self-attribute accessibility in dissonance. In E. Harmon-Jones & J. Mills (Eds.), *Cognitive dissonance: Progress on a pivotal theory in social psychology* (pp. 175–200). Washington, DC: American Psychological Association.

Stone, J., Wiegand, A. W., Cooper, J., & Aronson, E. (1997). When exemplification fails: Hypocrisy and the motive for self-integrity. *Journal of Personality and Social Psychology, 72*, 54–65.

Sullivan, H. S. (1953). *The interpersonal theory of psychiatry.* New York: Norton.

Swann, W. B., Griffin, J. J., Predmore, S. C., & Gaines, B. (1987). The cognitive–

affective crossfire: When self-consistency confronts self-enhancement. *Journal of Personality and Social Psychology, 52,* 881–889.

Tesser, A. (1988). Towards a self-evaluation maintenance model of social behavior. In L. Berkowitz (Ed.), *Advances in experimental social psychology* (Vol. 21, pp. 181–227). New York: Academic Press.

Tesser, A., & Cornell, D. P. (1991). On the confluence of self-processes. *Journal of Experimental Social Psychology, 27,* 501–526.

Tesser, A., Martin, L. L., & Cornell, D. P. (1996). On the substitutability of self-protective mechanisms. In P. M. Gollwitzer & J. A. Bargh (Eds.), *The psychology of action: Linking cognition and motivation to behavior* (pp. 48–68). New York: Guilford Press.

Tesser, A., Pilkington, C. J., & McIntosh, W. D. (1989). Self-evaluation maintenance and the mediational role of emotion: The perception of friends and strangers. *Journal of Personality and Social Psychology, 57,* 442–456.

Tomaka, J., & Blascovich, J. (1994). Effects of justice beliefs on cognitive appraisal of a subjective, physiological, and behavioral responses to potential stress. *Journal of Personality and Social Psychology, 67,* 732–740.

Tomaka, J., Blascovich, J., Kelsey, R. M., & Leitten, C. L. (1993). Subjective, physiological, and behavioral effects of threat and challenge appraisal. *Journal of Personality and Social Psychology, 65,* 248–260.

Tomaka, J., Blascovich, J., Kibler, J., & Ernst, J. M. (1997). Cognitive and physiological antecedents of threat and challenge appraisal. *Journal of Personality and Social Psychology, 73,* 63–72.

Venables, P. H., & Christie, M. J. (1980). Electrodermal activity. In I. Martin & P. H. Venables (Eds.), *Techniques in psychophysiology* (pp. 3–67). New York: Wiley.

Weary, G. (1980). Examination of affect and egotism as mediators of bias in causal attributions. *Journal of Personality and Social Psychology, 38,* 348–357.

Zanna, M. P., & Cooper, J. (1974). Dissonance and the pill: An attribution approach to studying the arousal properties of dissonance. *Journal of Personality and Social Psychology, 29,* 703–709.

Zemore, R., & Greenough, T. (1973). Reduction of ego threat following attributive projection. *Proceedings of the 81st Annual Convention of the American Psychological Association, 8,* 343–344.

Zillmann, D. (1978). Attribution and misattribution of excitatory reactions. In J. H. Harvey, W. J. Ickes, & R. F. Kidd (Eds.), *New directions in attribution research* (Vol. 2, pp. 335–370). Hillsdale, NJ: Erlbaum.

Zuckerman, M. (1979). Attribution of success and failure revisited, or: The motivational bias is alive and well in attribution theory. *Journal of Personality, 47,* 288–305.

3

CHOICE AND ITS CONSEQUENCES: ON THE COSTS AND BENEFITS OF SELF-DETERMINATION

SHEENA S. IYENGAR AND MARK R. LEPPER

No idea is more fundamental to Americans' sense of themselves as individuals and as a culture than choice. The United States has come to epitomize the "republic of choice" (Friedman, 1990)—liberty, after all, is subordinate only to life itself in the American Declaration of Independence. From the practice of a free-market economy, to the use of "pro-choice" as a persuasive device in current political debates, to the near "tyranny of choice" (Schwartz, 2000) permeating consumer markets—evident in the sometimes-overwhelming array of selections in supermarkets and coffee shops, not to mention the Internet—the glorification of choice in American society is ubiquitous. It should not be surprising, then, that Western psychological theory and research have also presumed choice to be beneficial. As the American psychologist Richard deCharms (1968) postulated,

> Looking at both sides of the coin, we may hypothesize that when a man perceives his behavior as stemming from his own choice he will cherish that behavior and its results; when he perceives his behavior as stemming from the dictates of external forces, that behavior and its

results, although identical in other respects to behavior of his own choosing, will be devalued. (p. 273)

Indeed, American psychologists have repeatedly contended that the provision of choice will prove beneficial, increasing an individual's sense of control and feelings of intrinsic motivation. Rarely has research considered the circumstances in which choice might prove psychologically detrimental. In this chapter, however, we seek to examine some of these circumstances.

In particular, this chapter begins by reviewing the classic evidence on which current assumptions about the benefits of choice are based but then turns to a growing body of more recent research that challenges the classic assumption that the provision of choice will necessarily be preferred or linked to increased levels of intrinsic motivation. More specifically, we first explore contexts in which people may actually prefer to have choices made for them by others—showing, for example, that members of more interdependent cultures may be more motivated when significant others make choices for them than when they choose for themselves. Then, we examine situations in which a limited choice set may prove more motivating than a more extensive choice set—showing, for example, that even members of highly independent cultures can sometimes find "too much choice" demotivating.

CHOICE AND INTRINSIC MOTIVATION

From its inception, experimental social psychology has been concerned with the issues of choice, perceived control, and human motivation (Adler, 1930). Kurt Lewin (1952), the father of experimental social psychology, drew on the insight that feelings of choice can be a powerful motivator by demonstrating that as long as people believed that they had freely chosen to serve healthful but otherwise undesirable food, the likelihood of their actually engaging in the activity would increase. Since Lewin's seminal study, the implicit assumption underlying many well-regarded theories in social psychology has been that the provision of choice or control will necessarily enhance intrinsic motivation.

According to cognitive dissonance theory, for example, when individuals perceive themselves as having chosen to engage in counterattitudinal behavior, such as writing essays contrary to their personal beliefs, subsequent changes in attitudes will be observed; but when they perceive themselves as having been "forced" into that same behavior, their attitudes will not change (e.g., Collins & Hoyt, 1972; Cooper & Fazio, 1984; Goethals & Cooper, 1972; Linder, Cooper, & Jones, 1967; Sherman, 1970). Likewise, as long as individuals believe that they have chosen to undertake unpleasant activities, such as administering electric shocks to themselves or eating grasshoppers, they will tend to perceive these behaviors as less unpleasant (Zimbardo, Weisenberg, Firestone, & Levy, 1965). Indeed, even when confronted with evidence to suggest that their past choices may have been suboptimal, choosers have frequently proven reluctant to abandon their commitment to their previously made decisions (Staw, 1976, 1997).

Similarly, psychologists have long argued that the provision of choice enhances feelings of personal control (e.g., Rotter, 1966; Taylor, 1989; Taylor & Brown, 1988). Simply having control over the order in which a task is performed has been shown to significantly reduce anxiety levels (Glass & Singer, 1972a, 1972b). In fact, one well-known study conducted by Langer and Rodin (1976) suggested that even the physical health of elderly patients in a nursing home could be significantly improved if the elderly patients were led to perceive themselves as having control over mundane matters within the institution (see also Schulz, 1976). Perhaps Lefcourt (1973) best summed up the essence of this research when he concluded that, "the sense of control, the illusion that one can exercise personal choice, has a definite and a positive role in sustaining life" (p. 424).

In fact, perceptions of choice have been demonstrated to have powerful motivating consequences for human behavior, even when they are only illusory. For example, some studies have shown that the mere illusion of choice can lead people to desire an activity more than they did when the same activity was overtly dictated (Dember, Galinsky, & Warm, 1992; Swann & Pittman, 1977). Other studies have shown that the exercise of choice in a chance situation, in which choice is objectively inconsequential, can nevertheless have powerful psychological consequences, as manifested in increased confidence and risk-taking (Langer, 1975). Indeed, many important theories in social psychology, including attribution theory (e.g., Kelley, 1967, 1973), dissonance theory (e.g., Collins & Hoyt, 1972; Cooper & Fazio, 1984), self-perception theory (Bem, 1967), and reactance theory (e.g., Brehm, 1966), all presume that even purely illusory perceptions of choice will have powerful effects.

Perhaps the clearest demonstration of the link between the provision of choice and human motivation, however, has come from theorists directly studying intrinsic motivation. By far, the most prominent current analysis of this concept, that of Deci and his colleagues (e.g., Deci, 1981; Deci & Ryan, 1985; see also deCharms, 1968), virtually equates intrinsic motivation with individual choice and personal "self-determination." According to this analysis, people are actors seeking to exercise and validate a sense of control over their external environments. As a result, they are theorized to enjoy, to prefer, and to persist at activities that provide them with the opportunity to make choices, to control their own outcomes, and to determine their own fates (Condry, 1977; Condry & Chambers, 1978; Deci, 1971, 1975, 1981; Deci, Driver, Hotchkiss, Robbins, & Wilson, 1993; Deci

& Ryan, 1985, 1991; Malone & Lepper, 1987; Nuttin, 1973; Ryan, 1982; Zuckerman, Porac, Lathin, Smith, & Deci, 1978).

According to this research, when individuals are given a choice, their self-determination and intrinsic motivation is increased (Deci, 1975, 1981; Deci & Ryan, 1985). In a typical study, the intrinsic motivation of participants is compared across two conditions, one in which participants are given some minor choice, such as which of six puzzles they would like to do, and a second in which participants are told by an experimenter which puzzle to undertake (Zuckerman et al., 1978). In these studies, the provision of choice has been shown to increase levels of intrinsic motivation and to enhance performance across a variety of tasks.

More recent findings suggest that the opportunity to make a choice need not be directly linked to the central activity at hand to be associated with increased levels of intrinsic motivation. A study conducted by Cordova and Lepper (1996), for instance, suggested that even the provision of small and instructionally irrelevant choices could nonetheless increase children's intrinsic motivation and learning in a computer-based math activity. Offering students even seemingly trivial, overt choices, like the option to select the names by which they would be addressed during a computer math game, substantially increased intrinsic motivation and their actual learning of the mathematical concepts involved in the game, as did a more indirect-choice manipulation in which elements of the game were personalized for each student by the introduction into the activity of individuating information and choices that each participant had provided earlier. These results are presented in Figure 3.1.

In fact, mere perceptions of choice can sometimes prove more important determinants of subsequent intrinsic motivation than the actual availability of choice. Detweiler, Mendoza, and Lepper (1996), for example, asked preschool children to draw a picture using a set of 8 colored markers. Actual choice was manipulated by either allowing the children to choose the subject of their drawing from a list of 8 possibilities or assigning the children subjects for their drawings. Orthogonally, perceptions of choice were manipulated by showing children in the high perceived-choice condition only 8 markers and emphasizing to them that they could use any of these markers that they wished, versus showing children in the low perceived-choice condition a larger set of 32 markers and emphasizing to them that they could use only the 8 markers the experimenter had selected for them. When these children's subsequent intrinsic interest in the drawing activity was assessed during a later free-play period, the effects of perceived choice clearly outweighed those of actual choice, with children in the high perceived-choice condition showing significantly greater later intrinsic interest in the activity than those in the low perceived-choice condition.

Thus, the results from many studies, in diverse contexts such as ed-

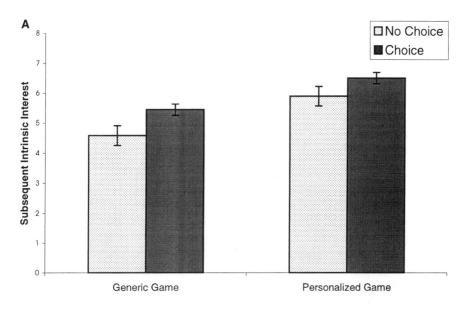

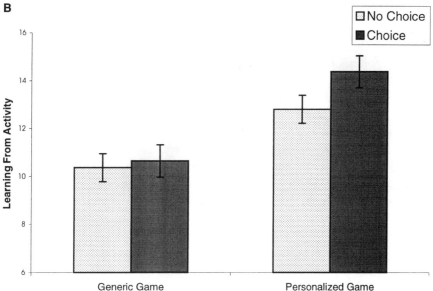

Figure 3.1. Measure of subsequent learning and intrinsic motivation in Cordova and Lepper (1996).

Note. A. Mean number of problems solved on postexperimental test, by experimental condition. Bars represent means, and lines represent standard errors. B. Mean ratings of the activity, by experimental condition, measured on 1–7 Likert scales (1–not at all interested; 7–very much interested). Bars represent means, and lines represent standard errors.

From "Intrinsic Motivation and the Process of Learning: Beneficial Effects of Contextualization, Personalization, and Choice," by D. I. Cordova and M. R. Lepper, 1996, *Journal of Educational Psychology, 88,* pp. 715–730. Copyright 1996 by American Psychological Association. Reprinted with permission.

ucation and health research, suggest that the positive consequences of choice are apparent even when choice itself is trivial, incidental, or entirely illusory. Such findings have led psychologists to assert that choice is almost invariably associated with intrinsic motivation and other beneficial effects.

Conversely, contexts in which choice is nonexistent or in which choice has been removed have been shown to produce adverse psychological effects. Seligman (1975) reported that when people encounter outcomes that they perceive as independent of their responses (i.e., over which they have no control), they lose motivation for responding, display impaired learning, and experience emotional responses that might be labeled as anxiety and depression. Even more pointedly, Brehm's work on psychological reactance (1966) showed that people whose choices had been explicitly eliminated were highly motivated to reassert their sense of personal control and individual freedom. In short, lack of choice has been hypothesized to have detrimental effects on intrinsic motivation, task performance, and health status (e.g., Brehm, 1966; Deci, Spiegel, Ryan, Koestner, & Kaufman, 1982; Schulz & Hanusa, 1978). Hence, it is not surprising that the current wisdom among psychologists is that people are invariably intrinsically motivated by contexts offering choice, whereas contexts in which choice has been removed or limited have been shown to have detrimental consequences on intrinsic motivation.

But are these blessings of choice and these costs of its absence truly as self-evident and as universal as they might first appear to be to investigators raised and living in North America? So ingrained is our assumption that people will find choice intrinsically motivating that rarely have psychologists paused to examine the more general applicability of these findings across different cultures. Despite the plethora of research findings demonstrating the benefits of choice, might there be cases, even in Western cultures, in which unlimited choices are not always preferred? In this chapter, we examine two potentially important exceptions—one cultural and one contextual—to the rule that people will always prefer the maximum level of choice possible.

CHOICE AND CULTURE

Consider, first, the question of cultural differences. Here, the seminal and highly influential cultural analysis presented by Markus and Kitayama (1991) seems to imply fairly directly that preferences for and benefits of choice might vary across different cultural contexts. In particular, Markus and Kitayama (1991) have suggested that, whereas individual agency is an essential element of the self-constructs of American individualists, it may be considerably less relevant to the self-constructs of members of more collectivistic cultures characteristic of Asia and elsewhere.

Westerners, Markus and Kitayama (1991) theorized, possess a model of the self as fundamentally independent. Such individuals strive for personal independence, desire a sense of autonomy, and seek to express their internal attributes to establish their uniqueness from others within their environments. If so, then the perception that one has chosen should be integrally linked to one's intrinsic motivation, because such contexts presumably allow for the expression of personal preferences and internal attributes, in turn allowing one to establish oneself as a volitional agent and to fulfill the goal of being independent (Nix, Ryan, Manly, & Deci, 1999).

The strength of this link, for many Americans, between the expression of choice and the desire to act volitionally can be easily illustrated with a familiar example. John goes out to dinner with friends. As he peruses the menu, he spots his favorite dish that sounds tempting—perhaps the grilled prawns. To his dismay, however, he hears the two companions sitting across from him order this same item. Suddenly, he faces a "dilemma of individuality" and must decide whether to order the same dish as originally intended, despite the fact that others have already done so. Even if he resists the temptation to change his planned order, he may still find himself obliged to offer some prefatory apology or explanation for his decision, "I hate to be such a copy-cat . . ." or "I really was planning on ordering that dish all along." In other words, what is most critical to John is that he be perceived by others and by himself as a volitional chooser.

By contrast, members of non-Western cultures are theorized to possess an interdependent model of the self (Markus & Kitayama, 1991) and to strive for the superordinate goal of a sense of interconnectedness and belongingness with their social ingroups. The mechanism through which this goal is fulfilled involves acting in accordance with one's social obligations to others, which may include the intermediate goal of maintaining harmony (De Vos, 1985; Hsu, 1985; Miller, 1988; Shweder & Bourne, 1984; Triandis, 1989, 1990, 1995). If so, the perception of having chosen may be of little intrinsic value, because choice-making contexts may be conceived of not as searches for a match to one's personal preferences but rather as searches for options that conform to the socially sanctioned standards of one's reference group, in turn allowing one to establish oneself as a dutiful agent by fulfilling one's social responsibilities.

Indeed, in some situations, the exercise of personal choice might even pose a threat to individuals whose personal preferences could prove at variance with those of their reference groups. Interdependent-selves, therefore, might actually prefer to have choices made for them, especially if the situation enables them to be relieved of the "burden" associated with identifying the socially sanctioned option and at the same time to fulfill the superordinate cultural goal of belongingness. Consequently, for members of interdependent cultures, it is not the exercise of choice that is necessary for intrinsic motivation but the perception of themselves as having fulfilled their duties and obligations toward their reference groups.

Thus, in the more interdependent cultures that comprise most of the non-Western world (Hofstede, 1991; Triandis, 1990, 1995), the apparent dilemma facing John is likely to seem ludicrous. Surely the discovery of shared preferences should be, if anything, a source of pleasure and an opportunity to display one's identification with the group. In most Eastern countries, choosing a common menu would be standard procedure when dining out, and it would be the assertion of some distinctive individual preference that might require an explanation or apology. If Yuko disliked the shellfish that was being served, her "dilemma of belongingness" would be whether just to pick politely at a dinner she could not eat or to express her distinctiveness and potentially threaten the harmony of the group around the table.

As an initial examination of the hypothesis that choice would be perceived differently by members of contrasting cultures, some preliminary ethnographic studies were conducted in which Asian and European American students' perceptions of everyday choices were examined (Iyengar & Lepper, 1999). Both American and Japanese students residing and taking classes in Kyoto, Japan, were asked to catalog the number of choices they had made within a normal work day and to provide ratings on a scale of 1 to 5 (1–not at all important; 5–very important) of how important each choice was to them. Even though the American students had typically resided in Japan for only a month—and presumably were not aware of all the choices available to them—they nevertheless perceived themselves as having nearly 50% more choices than did comparable Japanese students. Moreover, American students rated their choices as significantly more important than did Japanese students.

In subsequent studies, both Asian and European American students were asked to catalog the occasions in which they would like to have a choice and those in which they would like others to make a choice for them. Unlike the Asian students, nearly 30% of the European American students said they wished to have choices all of the time, and more than half of the European American students said that they could not imagine a specific circumstance in which they would prefer not to have a choice. Interestingly, neither of these sentiments was ever expressed by any of the Asian students. Given such differences in the way American and Japanese individuals perceive and value choice, how then might they differ in their responses to contexts offering choice, and even more importantly, to those that do not?

Two experimental studies, conducted by Iyengar and Lepper (1999), provide direct empirical support for the hypothesis that, although European American independent selves may routinely prefer to make their own choices, members of more interdependent cultures (e.g., Asian Americans) may sometimes prefer to have others make choices for them—if those making the choices are identified as important members of their reference group. In the traditional choice paradigm (Zuckerman et al., 1978), of course, it is typically a previously unknown experimenter who makes choices for the participant. Iyengar and Lepper (1999), however, compared these traditional conditions to others in which the person making choices for the participant is a member of an important reference group. Because members of interdependent cultures are theorized to view distinctions between social ingroup and outgroup members as more important, varying the identity of the chooser to reflect this distinction was predicted to significantly influence interdependent participants' responses to others' choices (Iyengar, Ross, & Lepper, 1999; Triandis, 1988, 1989, 1990; Triandis, Bontempo, Villareal, Asai, & Lucca, 1988). Any preference for relinquishing choice may be shown by interdependent selves only when the chooser is identified as a member of a relevant social ingroup.

In the first experiment, a yoked design was used in which both Asian American and European American children (ages 7–9 years) either were asked to choose an activity for themselves or were told that someone else had chosen for them. Specifically, in the personal-choice condition, participants were allowed to select which one of six activities they wished to undertake, whereas in two no-choice conditions, participants were assigned this same activity. For half of the students in these assigned-choice conditions, however, the person making the choice for them was a previously unencountered adult (i.e., the experimenter), whereas for the other students, the person making the choice was a person with whom participants shared a close, interdependent relationship (i.e., their mothers). Subsequently, these students' performance at the activity, as well as their intrinsic motivation to engage in the same activity during a later free-play period, were measured.

As earlier research would predict, the findings suggested that European Americans were most highly motivated and performed best when given a personal choice, as compared to situations in which choices were made for them, either by the experimenter or by their own mothers. Asian Americans, by contrast, were most motivated and performed best when their mothers had made the selection for them and did significantly worse when they had made the choice themselves. Like their European American counterparts, however, they did least well when the unfamiliar experimenter had made the choice for them. These findings are shown in Figure 3.2.

A second study by Iyengar and Lepper (1999) showed comparable and even more powerful cultural differences under circumstances in which the actual choices involved seemed quite trivial and in which choices were made for students by their peers rather than by their parents. This second experiment used a paradigm adapted from Cordova and Lepper (1996).

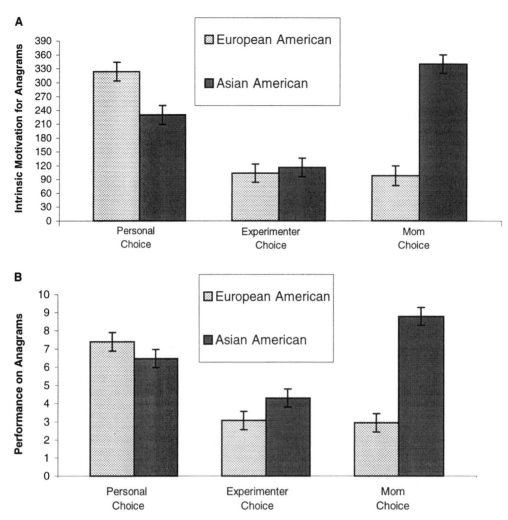

Figure 3.2. Measure of intrinsic motivation and performance in Iyengar and Lepper (1999), Experiment 1.
Note. A. Mean time spent on anagrams during a free-play period, by experimental condition. Scores are in seconds, out of a possible 360 seconds total. Bars represent means, and lines represent standard errors. B. Mean number of anagrams completed correctly, by experimental condition, out of 15 possible. Bars represent means, and lines represent standard errors.
Data from "Rethinking the Value of Choice: A Cultural Perspective on Intrinsic Motivation," by S. S. Iyengar and M. R. Lepper, 1999, *Journal of Personality and Social Psychology, 76,* pp. 349–366. Copyright 1999 by American Psychological Association. Adapted with permission.

Here, both Asian American and European American fifth-graders engaged in a computer math game under one of three conditions. In the personal-choice condition, participants were given half a dozen instructionally ir-relevant and seemingly trivial options (e.g., "Which icon would you like to have be your game piece?"). In two yoked no-choice conditions, students were told that they were being assigned these same choices on the basis of a vote taken either among their own classmates (ingroup condition) or among slightly younger children at a rival school (outgroup condition).

As in the first study, the findings were striking. European American children preferred more challenging math problems, showed more task engagement, and actually learned more when they had been allowed to make their own choices as compared to children in either of the other conditions in which choices had been made for them. Asian Americans, by contrast, were more intrinsically motivated and learned better when these choices had been made by their classmates than when they made their own choices which, in turn, produced better results than when the choices had been made for them by unfamiliar and lower status others. Figure 3.3 presents these results.

Furthermore, other studies suggest that members of interdependent cultures are less differentially influenced by self-made choices as compared to other-made choices. For instance, Heine and Lehman (1997) demonstrated that in cultures in which the value of choice is less emphasized, people appear to be less committed to their previously stated preferences. Specifically, in a study using the free-choice paradigm from cognitive dissonance research (Brehm, 1956), respondents were given a choice between two attractive CDs. Consistent with prior research, North American participants showed a considerable "spread" of preference ratings after the choice, such that liking for the chosen CD increased and liking for the unchosen CD decreased. However, no such pattern of changes in preferences was observed among Japanese participants.

Other differences are also apparent in recent comparisons of the determinants of compliance among theoretically more interdependent Polish participants and theoretically more independent European American participants (Cialdini, Wosinka, Barrett, Butner, & Gornik-Durose, 1999). Specifically, in these studies, European Americans proved more likely to engage later in those activities that they perceived themselves to have previously chosen, whereas Polish participants proved more likely to engage later in those activities that they knew their peers had previously engaged in.

Taken together, the findings from these studies are of theoretical significance in that they starkly challenge one of our most fundamental assumptions regarding human motivation. They suggest that in cultures that foster social interdependence, people seeking to fulfill their social responsibilities and obligations may prove more intrinsically motivated when choices are made for them—by someone from their social ingroup—than when they make their own choices. The findings provide, as well, a demonstration of the way in which our theories can be enriched by expanding

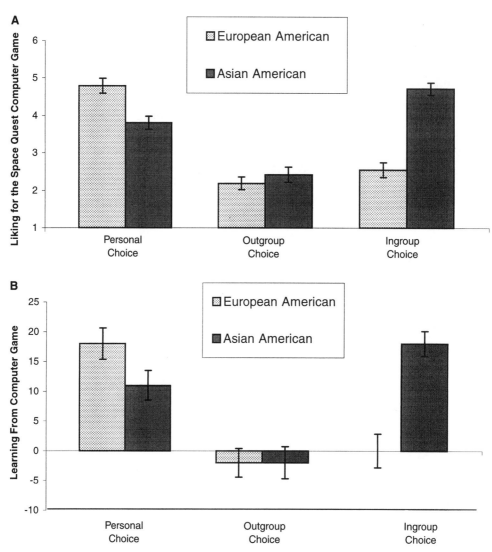

Figure 3.3. Measure of intrinsic motivation and direct learning in Iyengar and Lepper (1999), Experiment 2.
A. Mean liking for the activity, by experimental condition, measured on a 1–5 Likert scale (1–not at all interested; 5–very much interested). Bars represent means, and lines represent standard errors. B. Mean pretest to posttest change in percentage correct, by experimental condition. Bars represent means, and lines represent standard errors.
Note. Data from "Rethinking the Value of Choice: A Cultural Perspective on Intrinsic Motivation," by S. S. Iyengar and M. R. Lepper, 1999, *Journal of Personality and Social Psychology, 76,* pp. 349–366. Copyright 1999 by American Psychological Association. Adapted with permission.

our paradigms to include no-choice conditions in which the identity of the chooser is varied.

These studies of cultural differences, then, illustrate one important exception to the principle that people will always prefer contexts that offer the most freedom of choice. Might there be other contexts, even within North American culture, in which total freedom will not prove the most motivating? Might there be times when even rugged North American individualists would prefer to have their choices limited?

CHOICE AND ITS LIMITS

It is a common supposition in modern independent societies that "the more choices, the better"—that the human ability to manage choice and the human desire for choice are infinite. From classic economic theories of free enterprise to mundane marketing practices that provide customers with entire aisles devoted to potato chips or soft drinks to important life decisions in which people contemplate alternative career options or multiple investment opportunities, this belief pervades Western institutions, norms, and customs.

Although the many empirical demonstrations of the link between choice and intrinsic motivation may seem compelling, all of these studies share one seemingly trivial but potentially critical methodological characteristic—namely, that the number of choices offered is small, typically between two and six alternatives. It would appear, then, that what prior research has actually shown is that choice among relatively limited alternatives is more beneficial than no choice at all. Presumably, of course, constraints on the number of options offered in past choice studies were imposed not just for the sake of convenience, but also because what was considered theoretically counterintuitive and interesting was the demonstration that the motivational consequences of choice would extend even to contexts in which the choices were trivial, incidental, or illusory (e.g., Cordova & Lepper, 1996; Dember, Galinsky, & Warm, 1992; Langer, 1975; Langer & Rodin, 1976; Swann & Pittman, 1977).

Real-world situations, however, often provide more than a limited selection and sometimes even an overwhelming number of options. What happens when the range of alternatives becomes larger and the differences among options become relatively small? Can there be too much choice?

Certainly, there are cases when even a vast array of choices may still have beneficial effects. Imagine a group of people who arrive at a new restaurant, for example, all hoping to be able to order their personal favorite dishes. Obviously, the more items offered on the menu, the more satisfied these customers will be, on average. More generally, in "preference matching" contexts, where people enter an establishment hoping to find some specific product or service that they already know they prefer, more options will increase the likelihood that they will be successful in their searches.

On the other hand, research has shown that choosers are more likely to make suboptimal choices and to delay making choices when confronted with equally attractive or highly risky options (Mischel & Ebbesen, 1970; Shafir, Simonson, & Tversky, 1993; Shafir & Tversky, 1992; Yates & Mischel, 1979; see also Kahneman & Tversky, 1984). Higgins, Trope, and Kwon (1999), for instance, observed that children, given two equally preferred activities to choose from, subsequently demonstrated less intrinsic motivation no matter which activity they chose to engage in, as compared to children given the option of only one preferred activity.

Such responses to difficult choices may suggest that the more conflict people experience in a choice-making situation, the more their intrinsic motivation to exercise and to commit to their choice may diminish. Perhaps members of highly independent cultures will be intrinsically motivated by the actual provision of extensive choices—because such contexts allow for maximal opportunity for the achievement of personal preference matching—yet, at the same time, the act of making a choice from an excessive number of options might also result in "choice overload," in turn lessening their motivation to choose and their subsequent motivation to commit to a choice. To test this hypothesis, Iyengar and Lepper (2000) once again extended the traditional choice paradigm—this time, through the addition of extensive choices.

In particular, Iyengar and Lepper (2000) conducted a series of field and laboratory experiments in which the intrinsic motivation of participants encountering limited, versus extensive, choices was compared. One compelling field experiment took place at a neighborhood grocery store, where a tasting booth for exotic jams was arranged. As consumers passed the tasting booth, they encountered a display featuring either 6 (limited-choice condition) or 24 (extensive-choice condition) flavored jams. All those who stopped at the booth were then given a coupon for $1.00 off on the purchase of any jam by this manufacturer. The number of passersby who approached the tasting booth and the number of purchases made in these two conditions served as dependent variables.

The results suggested that, although extensive choice proved initially more enticing than limited choice, limited choice was ultimately more motivating. Thus, 60% of the passersby approached the table in the extensive-choice condition as compared to only 40% in the limited-choice condition. However, only 3% of the consumers who encountered the extensive selection actually purchased a jam, whereas 30% of those exposed to the limited selection subsequently made a purchase, as shown in Figure 3.4A. A second field study yielded similar findings (Iyengar & Lepper, 2000). In this study, students in an introductory-college-level course proved more likely to write an essay for extra credit when they had been provided a list of only 6 rather than 30 potential essay topics. Moreover, those students who chose to write essays also wrote higher quality essays if their essay topic had been picked from a smaller rather than from a more extensive choice set. These differences in quality were observed even though all participants were informed that they would receive extra credit for doing the essay regardless of the essay's quality. Consequently, there was no extrinsic incentive for writing high-caliber essays. These findings are shown in Figure 3.4B.

Laboratory experiments provide both further instantiations of this "choice overload" phenomenon and some insight concerning the potential mediators of this phenomenon. In one such study, participants were exposed to either a limited (6) or extensive (30) array of options (i.e., Godiva chocolates). In the choice conditions, participants chose and sampled a chocolate from a selection of either 6 or 30 varieties; in the no-choice conditions, participants were assigned a chocolate to sample from a selection of 6 or 30. At the time of choice, participants reported enjoying the process of choosing a chocolate more from a display of 30 than from a display of 6. Subsequently, however, participants in the extensive-choice condition proved least satisfied with and most regretful about their sampled chocolates, whereas participants in the limited-choice condition proved most satisfied with and least regretful about the chocolates they sampled. No-choice participants' responses lay in the middle. Parallel differences were also apparent on a behavioral measure of intrinsic motivation that assessed participants' subsequent preferences for receiving more chocolate rather than money as compensation for their participation in the study, as presented in Figure 3.4C.

Collectively, these findings are consistent with the hypothesis that American independent-selves indeed desire and value the provision of choices, presumably because such contexts allow for the potential fulfillment of personal preferences. At the same time, however, the exercise of choice in the face of too many alternatives may subsequently produce regret and dissatisfaction with selected choices, even among individualistic choosers. Thus, although the provision of extensive choices may initially be perceived as desirable, the actual exercise of choice in such contexts may hamper rather than enhance choosers' intrinsic motivation.

REEVALUATING CHOICE AND INTRINSIC MOTIVATION

Our analysis of the relationship between choice and intrinsic motivation suggests that the appeal and the benefits of making one's own choices and the aversiveness and the costs of having one's choices dictated by others may not be as ubiquitous as has commonly been supposed. In-

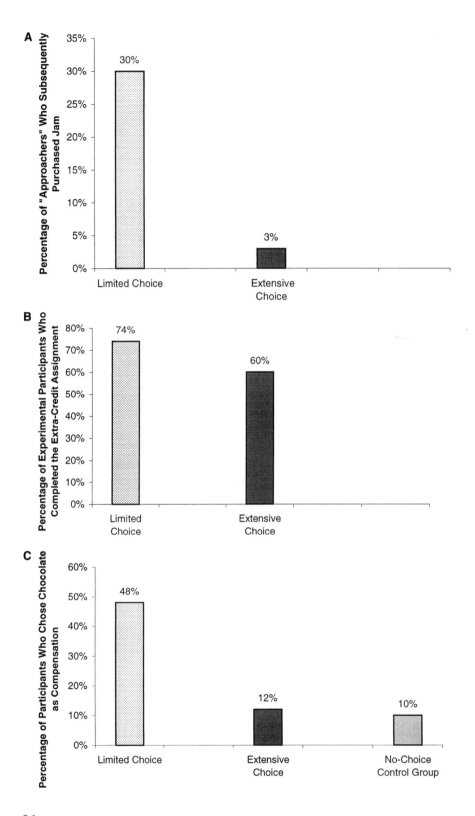

stead, the mere inclusion in traditional paradigms of experimental participants from non-Western societies and the addition of conditions in which liked or respected others make choices for the participants, or the addition of conditions in which the number of available options is significantly increased, can fundamentally change whether personal choice will be preferred and whether it will enhance or impair subsequent intrinsic motivation (Iyengar, Ross, & Lepper, 1999).

Taken together, the results from the studies described earlier show the following. First, the provision of choice may be neither as highly valued nor as intrinsically motivating among members of more interdependent non-Western cultures. Second, comparisons of intrinsic motivation across personally made and other-made choice contexts suggest the possibility that, at least for members of more collectivistic cultures, conforming to the wishes of others will not necessarily impair and may even enhance intrinsic motivation. Third, even when people from more independent cultures report and behaviorally demonstrate a desire for the provision of many choices, this desire is paradoxically not always reflected in these choosers' later intrinsic motivation toward the exercise of and commitment to their personal choices.

In considering the collective theoretical implications of these findings, we are naturally confronted by the challenge of moving beyond simple demonstrations of differences across culture and choice-making contexts to identifying the mediating mechanisms underlying the relationship between choice and intrinsic motivation (Weber & Hsee, 1999). To better understand the relationship between choice and intrinsic motivation, it is important to examine individual, cultural, and situational differences in both the perceptions and the goals of choosers across personally made and other-made choice contexts.

Recall our distinction between volitional and dutiful agency. Thus far we have argued that volitional and dutiful agents differ in the extent to which they value and prefer the provision of choice. But might these cul-

---

Figure 3.4. Consumer purchasing behavior in Iyengar and Lepper (2000), Experiment 1; student participation rates in Experiment 2; and participant reimbursement preferences in Experiment 3.
Note. A. Percentage of shoppers who subsequently purchased the product after having approached the tasting booth, by experimental condition. Bars represent percentages. B. Percentage of students in an introductory social psychology class who completed the extra-credit assignment. Bars represent percentages. C. Percentage of participants who subsequently chose chocolates as compensation for their participation. Bars represent percentages.
Data are from "When Choice Is Demotivating: Can One Desire Too Much of a Good Thing?" by S. S. Iyengar and M. R. Lepper, 2000, *Journal of Personality and Social Psychology, 76,* pp. 995–1006. Copyright 2000 by American Psychological Association. Adapted with permission.

tural differences in the preference for choice actually reflect a more fundamental difference in the way that the act of choosing itself is perceived and approached?

One potential mediator of the relationship between choice and intrinsic motivation, then, may lie in the choosers' perceptions and goals at the time of choosing. Perhaps European American volitional agents normally perceive and value choice more than do Asians and may subsequently demonstrate greater intrinsic motivation in contexts in which choice is present rather than absent because, once choice is perceived, the goal of personal preference matching appears attainable. Conversely, Asians may perceive and value choice less and subsequently exhibit greater intrinsic motivation in contexts in which they perceive themselves as acting in accordance with the wishes of known others, because for dutiful agents, the very act of choosing may be perceived as a responsibility. From this perspective, perhaps the mechanism mediating the relationship between own versus other choices and intrinsic motivation is not simply the perception that one has chosen or that one's choice has been dictated, but instead may be the perception that one has acted or chosen in accordance with important social standards—that is, considered all of one's duties towards one's relevant reference groups.

If such a hypothesis is true, we would expect volitional agents like most Americans to be more likely to perceive their day-to-day activities as matters of choice and free will, whereas dutiful agents might perceive those same daily activities as being matters of social obligation. In fact, as indicated previously, preliminary ethnographic studies conducted by Iyengar and Lepper (1999) suggested that Americans do indeed perceive their daily decisions as involving more "real" and "important" choices, as compared to their Japanese counterparts. Other related studies have also suggested that, whereas Americans perceive altruistic acts to be matters of personal choice, Hindu Indians perceive these same acts to be matters of duty and obligation (Miller, 1994; Miller & Bersoff, 1992, 1994).

If volitional agents perceive choice to be more pervasive and significant in their daily lives, then they might also be more sensitive to manipulations designed to create the illusion of choice. Indeed, classic cognitive dissonance research relies on the finding that as long as people perceive themselves as having chosen to engage in a counterattitudinal behavior—even if that perception is induced through an "illusion of choice" manipulation (e.g., "It is entirely your own choice. You don't have to, but I would really appreciate it if you would . . .")—subsequent changes in attitude and behavior will be observed (Cooper & Fazio, 1984; Linder et al., 1967).

Yet for people more concerned with and sensitive to their responsibilities to others, such an "illusion of choice" manipulation (Kelley, 1967) may not be perceived as one involving personal choice at all, and the extent to which this manipulation is intrinsically motivating may be determined by the identity of the "manipulator" rather than by the manipulation itself. In fact, recent studies suggest that, at least in the traditional "free-choice" dissonance paradigm (i.e., where participants actually make a choice and their subsequent reevaluation of the alternatives is observed), the predicted dissonance effects are not found with Japanese college students (Heine & Lehman, 1997). Thus, consistent with findings of Iyengar and Lepper (1999), dutiful agents may not only be less intrinsically motivated by contexts offering perceptions of choice but may actually have less of a perception of choice in such contexts as compared to volitional agents.

Given these contrasting choice-making goals—that of preference fulfillment versus duty fulfillment—we might expect differences in choice-seeking, choice-making heuristics and expected choice-making outcomes. Because volitional agents perceive themselves to be choosers striving to identify options that most match their personal preferences, they may be more likely to seek more options as compared to dutiful agents. In contrast, dutiful agents may seek only as many choices as enable them to identify that which fulfills their responsibilities. Consequently, volitional agents may be more attracted to extensive-choice contexts than are dutiful agents.

Similarly, as observed in the studies conducted by Cialdini and his colleagues (1999), volitional and dutiful agents may vary in the extent to which they rely on prior experience or personal judgment as compared to peer or expert judgment when making choices. Recall that in their studies, American participants proved more persuaded to engage in an activity when they believed that they had previously chosen to engage in that activity, whereas Polish participants proved more persuaded to engage in an activity that they believed peers like them had engaged in before. Thus, when making a choice, volitional agents may be more inclined to rely on the heuristic, "I know what's best for me" and as a consequence may place less emphasis and reliance on the recommendations of peers and experts. By contrast, if the primary goal of dutiful agents is to identify the appropriate choice—as defined by others—then relying on the judgments of others may be a more commonly followed heuristic.

In addition, the volitional agents' goal of identifying the options that most closely match their individual preferences may also foster greater expectations of satisfaction from a chosen option than the dutiful agents' goal of simply identifying and conforming to options determined by others. Indeed, one explanation for the observation that Asians are prone to more conformist preferences, whereas Americans are prone to more unique preferences, may be that preference-fulfillment goals create generalized expectations about the identification of individualized choice, whereas duty fulfillment goals facilitate conformist choices (Kim & Markus, 1999). Thus, volitional choosers may expect greater satisfaction from choices they have made than would dutiful choosers.

But how can we explain the paradoxical finding that independent European Americans—hypothesized to be volitional agents—exhibited a greater desire for the provision of extensive choices yet, at the same time, demonstrated less commitment to and intrinsic motivation for choosing when offered extensive choices (Iyengar & Lepper, 2000)? One explanation may be that, although volitional agents will value the provision of choices for the opportunities they potentially invite, circumstances in which the fulfillment of preference-matching goals becomes burdensome or potentially unattainable may detrimentally affect their intrinsic motivation for choosing. Although prior research has compellingly demonstrated volitional agents to be committed to choices made in contexts in which the number of choices was limited or even illusory (e.g., Cooper & Fazio, 1984; Linder et al., 1967; Zuckerman et al., 1978), perhaps the link between choice and intrinsic motivation occurs only insofar as the choice-making context preserves choosers' perceptions of preference fulfillment. Indeed, an intriguing possibility is that, as long as actual choice-making involves burdensome choosing—contexts that make the identification of personal preference matches difficult or impossible—choosers may prove more intrinsically motivated by merely "perceived" choices, that relieve them of the burden of making a potentially difficult choice, rather than by "real" choices.

As yet, the motivational consequences of extensive choices have not been studied among interdependent dutiful agents. Consider, however, the following two competing hypotheses. On the one hand, we might hypothesize that the phenomenon of choice overload would be further exacerbated among dutiful agents than among volitional agents. Because dutiful agents may rely primarily on their knowledge of what others might select, when they do face a choice, such individuals may be expected to be even more overwhelmed than volitional agents are when confronted by an overly extensive set of options. Alternatively, we may hypothesize that because dutiful agents value the provision of choices less and perceive their task to be that of duty fulfillment, exercising choice in extensive-choice contexts may prove less cognitively burdensome and, in turn, less intrinsically demotivating for them. In essence, in this latter account, although striving for personal preference fulfillment may debilitate the volitional agent's choice-making ability, the dutiful agent may be protected from the experience of choice overload because the act of choosing may promote reliance on simplifying heuristics such as, "What would others choose?"

Finally, we argue that this central distinction between volitional versus dutiful agency should extend beyond cultural differences to encompass individual and contextual differences in choice-making as well. Certainly, even those raised and living in classically independent cultures may approach choices quite differently, for instance, when they involve the selection of alternatives for others, rather than for themselves. Take, for example, the common practice within North American culture of relying on popular judgment rather than personal preference when choosing a bottle of wine for a dinner party. Hence, further studies should examine differences in choice-making perceptions and goals across contexts in which choosers are choosing for themselves as opposed to for others.

Perhaps most critically, the present analysis also suggests that manipulations that successfully shift the perceptions and goals of people making choices within a given culture from a focus on volition to a focus on duty, or vice versa, may alter people's choice-seeking behavior, use of choice-making heuristics, and expected choice-making outcomes. Thus, we would predict that situational factors that highlight, prime, or otherwise evoke a focus on goals of preference matching versus obligation fulfillment may often overcome, or even reverse, more chronic individual or cultural differences in goals and perceptions concerning choice.

In short, in the traditional Western social sciences model, personal choice is presumed to be valued and preferred because of its efficiency in promoting the net satisfaction of people in achieving their individual goals and obtaining their preferred outcomes. The present model suggests that there is much more than this to the widespread Western predilection for making choices for oneself. In addition to the likelihood of attainment of personally preferred outcomes, the exercise versus avoidance of choice also affords, at a minimum, an opportunity to assert one's individuality versus one's belongingness; an occasion to act on one's sense of autonomy versus obligation; and a chance to take, as opposed to abrogate, personal responsibility for one's actions. To understand the conditions under which choice will be preferred and will be exercised, therefore, requires attention to each of these issues.

Although some theorists may feel that this more highly nuanced and complex analysis provides "too many" theoretical alternatives, we believe that this analysis better reflects the complexity of the phenomena under study. As Whitehead (1929) warned long ago, one should "Seek simplicity, but distrust it!" (p. 22).

REFERENCES

Adler, A. (1930). Individual psychology. In C. Murchison (Ed.), *Psychologies of 1930* (pp. 395–405). Worcester, MA: Clark University Press.

Bem, D. J. (1967). Self-perception: An alternative interpretation of cognitive dissonance phenomena. *Psychological Review, 74,* 183–200.

Brehm, J. W. (May, 1956). Post-decision changes in the desirability of alternatives. *Journal of Abnormal Social Psychology,* 384–389.

Brehm, J. W. (1966). *A theory of psychological reactance.* New York: Academic Press.

Cialdini, R. B., Wosinska, W., Barrett, D. W., Butner, J., & Gornik-Durose, M.

(1999). Compliance with a request in two cultures: The differential influence of social proof and commitment/consistency on collectivists and individualists. *Personality and Social Psychology Bulletin, 25*, 1242–1253.

Collins, B. E., & Hoyt, M. G. (1972). Personal responsibility for consequences: An integration and extension of the "forced compliance" literature. *Journal of Experimental Social Psychology, 8*, 558–593.

Condry, J. (1977). Enemies of exploration: Self-initiated versus other-initiated learning. *Journal of Personality and Social Psychology, 35*, 459–477.

Condry, J. C., & Chambers, J. (1978). Intrinsic motivation and the process of learning. In M. R. Lepper & D. Greene (Eds.), *The hidden costs of reward* (pp. 61–84). Hillsdale, NJ: Erlbaum.

Cooper, J., & Fazio, R. H. (1984). A new look at dissonance theory. In L. Berkowitz (Ed.), *Advances in experimental social psychology* (Vol. 17, pp. 229–266). Orlando, FL: Academic Press.

Cordova, D. I., & Lepper, M. R. (1996). Intrinsic motivation and the process of learning: Beneficial effects of contextualization, personalization, and choice. *Journal of Educational Psychology, 88*, 715–730.

deCharms, R. (1968). *Personal causation.* New York: Academic Press.

Deci, E. L. (1971). Effects of externally mediated reward on intrinsic motivation. *Journal of Personality and Social Psychology, 18*, 105–115.

Deci, E. L. (1975). *Intrinsic motivation.* New York: Plenum Press.

Deci, E. L. (1981). *The psychology of self-determination.* Lexington, MA: Heath.

Deci, E. L., Driver, R. E., Hotchkiss, L., Robbins, R. J., & Wilson, T. D. (1993). The relation of mothers' controlling vocalization to children's intrinsic motivation. *Journal of Experimental Child Psychology, 55*, 151–162.

Deci, E. L., & Ryan, R. M. (1985). *Intrinsic motivation and self-determination in human behavior.* New York: Plenum Press.

Deci, E. L., & Ryan, R. M. (1991). A motivational approach to self: Integration in personality. In R. Dienstbier (Ed.), *Nebraska Symposium on Motivation: Perspectives on motivation* (Vol. 38, pp. 237–288). Lincoln: University of Nebraska Press.

Deci, E. L., Spiegel, N. H., Ryan, R. M., Koestner, R., & Kaufman, M. (1982). The effects of performance standards on teaching styles: The behavior of controlling teachers. *Journal of Educational Psychology, 74*, 852–859.

Dember, W. N., Galinsky, T. L., & Warm, J. S. (1992). The role of choice in vigilance performance. *Bulletin of the Psychonomic Society, 30*, 201–204.

Detweiler, J. B., Mendoza, R. J., & Lepper, M. R. (July, 1996). *Perceived versus actual choice: High perceived choice enhances children's task engagement.* Paper presented to the 8th Annual Meeting of the American Psychological Society, San Francisco, CA.

De Vos, G. A. (1985). Dimensions of the self in Japanese culture. In A. Marsella, G. De Vos, & F. L. K. Hsu (Eds.), *Culture and self* (pp. 149–184). London: Tavistock.

Friedman, L. M. (1990). *The republic of choice*. Cambridge, MA: Harvard University Press.

Glass, D. C., & Singer, J. E. (1972a). *Stress and adaptation: Experimental studies of behavioral effects of exposure to aversive events*. New York: Academic Press.

Glass, D. C., & Singer, J. E. (1972b). *Urban stress*. New York: Academic Press.

Goethals, G. R., & Cooper, J. (1972). The role of intention and postbehavioral consequences in the arousal of cognitive dissonance. *Journal of Personality and Social Psychology, 23*, 293–301.

Heine, S. J., & Lehman, D. R. (1997). Culture, dissonance, and self-affirmation. *Personality and Social Psychology Bulletin, 23*, 389–400.

Higgins, E. T., Trope, Y., & Kwon, J. (1999). Augmentation and undermining from combining activities: The role of choice in activity engagement theory. *Journal of Experimental Social Psychology, 35*, 285–307.

Hofstede, G. (1991). *Cultures and organizations: Software of the mind*. London: McGraw-Hill.

Hsu, F. L. K. (1985). The self in cross-cultural perspective. In A. J. Marsella, G. De Vos, & F. L. K. Hsu (Eds.), *Culture and self* (pp. 24–55). London: Tavistock.

Iyengar, S. S., & Lepper, M. R. (1999). Rethinking the value of choice: A cultural perspective on intrinsic motivation. *Journal of Personality and Social Psychology, 76*, 349–366.

Iyengar, S. S., & Lepper, M. R. (2000). When choice is demotivating: Can one desire too much of a good thing? *Journal of Personality and Social Psychology, 76*, 995–1006.

Iyengar, S. S., Ross, L., & Lepper, M. R. (1999). Independence from whom? Interdependence with whom? Cultural perspectives on ingroups versus outgroups. In D. A. Prentice & D. Miller (Eds.), *Cultural divides: The social psychology of cultural identity* (pp. 273–301). New York: Sage.

Kahneman, D., & Tversky, A. (1984). Choices, values, and frames. *American Psychologist, 39*, 341–350.

Kelley, H. H. (1967). Attribution theory in social psychology. In D. Levine (Ed.), *Nebraska Symposium on Motivation* (Vol. 15, pp. 192–240). Lincoln: University of Nebraska Press.

Kelley, H. H. (1973). The process of causal attribution. *American Psychologist, 28*, 107–128.

Kim, H., & Markus, H. R. (1999). Deviance or uniqueness, harmony or conformity? A cultural analysis. *Journal of Personality and Social Psychology, 77*, 785–800.

Langer, E. J. (1975). The illusion of control. *Journal of Personality and Social Psychology, 32*, 311–328.

Langer, E. J., & Rodin, J. (1976). The effects of choice and enhanced personal responsibility for the aged: A field experiment in an institutional setting. *Journal of Personality and Social Psychology, 34*, 191–198.

Lefcourt, H. M. (1973). The function of the illusions of control and freedom. *American Psychologist, 28*, 417–425.

Lewin, K. (1952). Group decision and social change. In G. E. Swanson, T. M. Newcomb, & E. L. Hartley (Eds.), *Readings in social psychology* (pp. 459–473). New York: Henry Holt.

Linder, D. E., Cooper, J., & Jones, E. E. (1967). Decision freedom as a determinant of the role of incentive magnitude in attitude change. *Journal of Personality and Social Psychology, 6*, 245–254.

Malone, T. W., & Lepper, M. R. (1987). Making learning fun: A taxonomy of intrinsic motivations for learning. In R. E. Snow & M. J. Farr (Eds.), *Aptitude, learning and instruction: Vol. 3. Conative and affective process analysis* (pp. 223–253). Hillsdale, NJ: Erlbaum.

Markus, H., & Kitayama, S. (1991). Culture and the self: Implications for cognition, emotion and motivation. *Psychological Review, 98*, 224–253.

Miller, J. G. (1988). Bridging the content–structure dichotomy: Culture and the self. In M. H. Bond (Ed.), *The cross-cultural challenge to social psychology* (pp. 266–281). Beverly Hills, CA: Sage.

Miller, J. G. (1994). Cultural diversity in the morality of caring: Individually oriented versus duty-based interpersonal moral codes. *Cross-Cultural Research, 28*, 3–39.

Miller, J. G., & Bersoff, D. M. (1992). Culture and moral judgment: How are conflicts between justice and interpersonal responsibilities resolved? *Journal of Personality and Social Psychology, 62*, 541–554.

Miller, J. G., & Bersoff, D. M. (1994). Cultural influences on the moral status of reciprocity and the discounting of endogenous motivation. *Personality and Social Psychology Bulletin, 20*, 592–602.

Mischel, W., & Ebbesen, E. B. (1970). Attention in delay of gratification. *Journal of Personality and Social Psychology, 16*, 329–337.

Nix, G. A., Ryan, R. M., Manly, J. B., & Deci, E. L. (1999). Revitalization through self-regulation: The effects of autonomous and controlled motivation on happiness and vitality. *Journal of Experimental Social Psychology, 35*, 266–284.

Nuttin, J. R. (1973). Pleasure and reward in human motivation and learning. In D. E. Berlyne & K. B. Madsen (Eds.), *Pleasure, reward, preference* (pp. 243–274). New York: Academic Press.

Rotter, J. B. (1966). Generalized expectancies for internal versus external locus of control of reinforcement. *Psychological Monographs, 80*, 1–28.

Ryan, R. M. (1982). Control and information in the interpersonal sphere: An extension of cognitive evaluation theory. *Journal of Personality and Social Psychology, 43*, 450–461.

Schulz, R. (1976). Effects of control and predictability on the physical and psychological well-being of the institutionalized aged. *Journal of Personality and Social Psychology, 33*, 563–573.

Schulz, R., & Hanusa, B. H. (1978). Long-term effects of control and predictability-enhancing interventions: Findings and ethical issues. *Journal of Personality and Social Psychology, 36,* 1194–1201.

Schwartz, B. (2000). Self-determination: The tyranny of freedom. *American Psychologist, 55,* 79–88.

Seligman, M. E. P. (1975). *Helplessness: On depression, development, and death.* San Francisco, CA: Freeman.

Shafir, E., Simonson, I., & Tversky, A. (1993). Reason-based choice. *Cognition, 49,* 11–36.

Shafir, E., & Tversky, A. (1992). Thinking through uncertainty: Non-consequential reasoning and choice. *Cognitive Psychology, 24,* 449–474.

Sherman, S. J. (1970). Attitudinal effects of unforeseen consequences. *Journal of Personality and Social Psychology, 16,* 510–520.

Shweder, R. A., & Bourne, E. J. (1984). Does the concept of the person vary cross-culturally? In R. A. Shweder & R. A. LeVine (Eds.), *Culture theory: Essays on mind, self, and emotion* (pp. 158–199). Cambridge, England: Cambridge University Press.

Staw, B. M. (1976). Knee-deep in the Big Muddy: A study of escalating commitment to a chosen course of action. *Organizational Behavior and Human Decision Processes, 16,* 27–44.

Staw, B. M. (1997). The escalation of commitment: An update and appraisal. In Z. Shapira (Ed.), *Organizational decision making: Cambridge series on judgment and decision making* (pp. 191–215). New York: Cambridge University Press.

Swann, W. B., & Pittman, T. S. (1977). Initiating play activity of children: The moderating influence of verbal cues on intrinsic motivation. *Child Development, 48,* 1128–1132.

Taylor, S. E. (1989). *Positive illusions: Creative self-deception and the healthy mind.* New York: Basic Books.

Taylor, S. E., & Brown, J. D. (1988). Illusion and well-being: A social–psychological perspective on mental health. *Psychological Bulletin, 103,* 193–210.

Triandis, H. C. (1988). Collectivism and individualism: A reconceptualization of a basic concept in cross-cultural social psychology. In G. K. Verma & C. Bagely (Eds.), *Personality, attitudes, and cognitions* (pp. 60–95). London: Macmillan.

Triandis, H. C. (1989). The self and social behavior in differing cultural contexts. *Psychological Review, 96,* 506–520.

Triandis, H. C. (1990). Cross-cultural studies of individualism and collectivism. In J. Berman (Ed.), *Nebraska Symposium on Motivation: Perspectives in motivation* (Vol. 38, pp. 41–133). Lincoln: University of Nebraska Press.

Triandis, H. C. (1995). *Individualism and collectivism.* Boulder, CO: Westview Press.

Triandis, H. C., Bontempo, R., Villareal, M. J., Asai, M., & Lucca, N. (1988). Individualism and collectivism: Cross-cultural perspectives on self and group relationships. *Journal of Personality and Social Psychology, 54,* 323–338.

Weber, E. U., & Hsee, C. K. (1999). Models and mosaics: Investigating cross-cultural differences in risk perception and risk preference. *Psychonomic Bulletin and Review, 6,* 611–617.

Whitehead, A. N. (1929). The aims of education. In *The Aims of Education and other essays* (p. 22). New York: New American Library.

Yates, B. T., & Mischel, W. (1979). Young children's preferred attentional strategies for delaying gratification. *Journal of Personality and Social Psychology, 37,* 286–300.

Zimbardo, P. G., Weisenberg, M., Firestone, I., & Levy, M. (1965). Communicator effectiveness in producing public conformity and private attitude change. *Journal of Personality, 33,* 233–255.

Zuckerman, M., Porac, J., Lathin, D., Smith, R., & Deci, E. L. (1978). On the importance of self-determination for intrinsically motivated behavior. *Personality and Social Psychology Bulletin, 4,* 443–446.

4

SELF-CONSCIOUS EMOTIONS: THE SELF AS A MORAL GUIDE

JUNE PRICE TANGNEY

Shame, guilt, embarrassment, and pride are members of a family of "self-conscious emotions" that are evoked by self-reflection and self-evaluation. This self-evaluation may be implicit or explicit, consciously experienced or transpiring beyond one's awareness. Yet in one way or another, the self is the object of these self-conscious emotions.

Somewhat ironically, these "egoistic," self-centered emotions also form the core of a person's moral motivational system. Self-conscious emotions are, at the same time, moral emotions that help motivate people to adhere to moral standards and respond appropriately (e.g., with contrition and reparation) when we do not. In the face of transgression or error, the self turns toward the self—evaluating and rendering judgment—in reference to one's standards, rules, and goals (SRGs). We feel shame when the failure to meet an important SRG is seen as a reflection of some deep-rooted and enduring defect in the self—a flaw in character, a moral failing, an inferior ability in a highly valued domain, or just plain being the wrong kind of person. We feel guilt when we focus on a specific behavior that violates an SRG, regretting the action or inaction and focusing on its consequences for the self or others. We feel embarrassment when breaching less-serious SRGs, especially violations of social roles or conventions in public settings. And we feel pride not just when any good thing happens, but specifically when our own positive attributes or actions meet or exceed our SRGs.[1] In short, shame, guilt, embarrassment, and pride function as an emotional moral barometer, providing immediate and salient feedback on one's social and moral acceptability.

Shame and guilt, in particular, are often cited as "moral emotions" because of the presumed role they play in motivating people to avoid immoral and antisocial behavior (Ausubel, 1955; Damon, 1988; Eisenberg, 1986). It is typically assumed that because these are painful emotions, they keep people "on the straight and narrow," decreasing the likelihood of transgression and impropriety. But how valid is this assumption? When it comes to actions generally considered to be moral (e.g., helping, sacrificing, telling difficult truths) or immoral (e.g., lying, cheating, stealing), how useful are shame and guilt in motivating people to "do right" and avoid "doing wrong"?

Until recently, remarkably little research has been devoted to these moral emotions. The scant literature before the 1990s yielded largely inconclusive results, in part because of difficulties in the measurement of shame and guilt and in part because of most researchers' failure to distinguish between these two closely related emotions. Over the past 10 years, however, a profusion of basic research on the nature and implications of shame and guilt has emerged. The findings have affirmed some of our assumptions and challenged many others. Most notably, a decade of research now indicates that the moral emotions are not equally "moral." In a nutshell, experiences of guilt and empathy appear to consistently motivate people in a positive direction (Eisenberg, 1986; Tangney, 1991, 1995). However, there is growing evidence that shame is a moral emotion that can easily go awry (Tangney, 1991, 1995, 1996).

In this chapter, I first summarize current theory and research in five areas that illustrate the adaptive functions of guilt, in contrast to the hidden costs of shame. Specifically, I focus on the differential relationship of shame and guilt to (a) motivation (hiding vs. amending), (b) other-oriented empathy, (c) anger and aggression, (d) deterrence of transgression and socially undesirable behavior, and (e) psychological symptomatology. The bottom line is this: When considering the welfare of the individual, his or her close relationships, or society at large, feelings of guilt (together with empathy) represent the moral emotion of choice in response to failures and transgressions.

---

[1]On some occasions we may feel pride in response to another person's behavior; that person, however, is typically someone with whom we are closely affiliated or identified (e.g., a family member, a close friend or colleague). We experience pride because that person is part of our self-definition. Similarly, the sense of group or national pride arises because of the close identification of self with the group.

In the remainder of the chapter, I examine the applied implications of this basic research on moral emotions. I focus on the relevance of research findings for the criminal justice system, parenting, and teaching.

WHAT IS THE DIFFERENCE BETWEEN SHAME AND GUILT?

People are often imprecise in their use of the terms *shame* and *guilt*. For example, in the clinical literature, it is not unusual for psychologists to refer to "feelings of shame and guilt" or to discuss the "effects of shame and guilt" without making any distinction between the two emotions. In everyday discourse, people typically avoid the term "shame" entirely, referring instead to "guilt" when they mean shame, guilt, or some combination of the two. But an extensive theoretical and empirical literature underscores striking differences in the phenomenology of these emotions (Lewis, 1971; Lindsay-Hartz, 1984; Tangney, 1989, 1993, 2001; Weiner, 1985; Wicker, Payne, & Morgan, 1983), which have important, and distinct implications for subsequent motivation and behavior.

In brief, shame and guilt are negative, self-relevant emotions that occur in response to failures or transgressions, but the focus of these emotions differs. Feelings of shame involve a negative evaluation of the global self; feelings of guilt involve a negative evaluation of a specific behavior. Although subtle, this differential emphasis on self ("*I* did that horrible thing") versus behavior ("I *did* that horrible *thing*") sets the stage for very different emotional experiences and patterns of motivations and subsequent behavior.

Shame is an acutely painful emotion that is typically accompanied by a sense of shrinking or of "being small" and by a sense of worthlessness and powerlessness. Shamed people also feel exposed. Although shame does not necessarily involve an actual observing audience to witness one's shortcomings (in fact, research has shown that, contrary to mid-century anthropological theory, shame and guilt do not differ in the degree of actual public exposure; Tangney, Marschall, Rosenberg, Barlow, & Wagner, 2001; Tangney, Miller, Flicker, & Barlow, 1996), there is often the imagery of how one's defective self would appear to others. Lewis (1971) described a split in self-functioning in which the self is both agent and object of observation and disapproval. An observing self witnesses and denigrates the focal self as unworthy and reprehensible. Not surprisingly, shame often leads to a desire to escape or to hide—to sink into the floor and disappear.

In contrast, guilt is typically a less painful and devastating experience because the primary concern is with a specific behavior and not the entire self. So guilt does not affect one's core identity. Instead, there is a sense of tension, remorse, and regret over the "bad thing done." People feeling guilt often report a nagging focus or preoccupation with the transgression, thinking of it over and over or wishing they had behaved differently or could somehow undo the harm done. Rather than motivating an avoidance response, guilt motivates reparative behavior: confession, apology, and attempts to fix the situation and undo the harm done.

SHAME AND GUILT ARE NOT EQUALLY MORAL EMOTIONS

One consistent theme emerging from empirical research is that shame and guilt are not equally moral emotions. On balance, guilt appears to be the more adaptive emotion, benefiting individuals and their relationships in a variety of ways (Baumeister, Stillwell, & Heatherton, 1994, 1995a, 1995b; Tangney, 1991, 1995). Five sets of findings help illustrate the adaptive functions of guilt in contrast to the hidden costs of shame.

Hiding vs. Amending

First, studies of shame and guilt consistently find that these emotions lead to contrasting motivations or "action tendencies" (Lewis, 1971; Lindsay-Hartz, 1984; Ferguson, Stegge, & Damhuis, 1991; Tangney, 1993; Tangney, Miller, et al., 1996; Wallbott & Scherer, 1995; Wicker et al., 1983). In the face of failure or transgression, shame typically leads to attempts to deny, hide, or escape the shame-inducing situation; guilt typically leads to reparative action—confessing, apologizing, undoing. For example, in two independent studies, we asked young adults to describe a personal shame experience and a personal guilt experience and then rate these experiences along several phenomenological dimensions (Tangney, 1993; Tangney, Miller, et al., 1996). The results across the two studies were remarkably consistent. When feeling shame as opposed to guilt, people felt more compelled to hide from others and less inclined to admit what they had done. Thus, guilt appears to motivate people in a more constructive, proactive, future-oriented direction, whereas shame motivates people toward separation, distancing, and defense.

Other-Oriented Empathy

Second, there appears to be a special link between guilt and empathy. Empathy is generally regarded as a "good" moral affective capacity or experience. There is a vast empirical literature indicating that empathy motivates altruistic, helping behavior (Eisenberg, 1986; Eisenberg & Miller, 1987; Feshbach, 1978, 1987; Feshbach & Feshbach, 1986); that it fosters warm, close interpersonal relationships; and that it inhibits antisocial behavior and interpersonal aggression (Eisenberg, 1986; Feshbach, 1984,

1987; Feshbach & Feshbach, 1969, 1982, 1986; Miller & Eisenberg, 1988). In addition, empathy has been identified as an essential component of numerous valued social processes, including positive parent–child relationships (Feshbach, 1987) and individuals' application of moral principles to real-life interpersonal situations (Hoffman, 1987).

Research has shown that guilt and empathy go hand-in-hand, whereas feelings of shame often interfere with an empathic connection (Leith & Baumeister, 1998; Tangney, 1991, 1995). This differential relationship of shame and guilt to empathy has been observed both in studies of affective styles or dispositions and in studies of emotion states.

Studies of affective dispositions focus on individual differences. When faced with a failure or transgression, to what degree is a person likely to feel shame or guilt? To assess proneness to shame and proneness to guilt, we use a scenario-based method in which respondents are presented with a range of situations often encountered in day-to-day life. Each scenario is followed by responses that capture phenomenological aspects of shame, guilt, and other theoretically relevant experiences (e.g., externalization, pride). Respondents are asked to imagine themselves in each situation and then rate their likelihood of reacting in each of the manners indicated. For example, in the adult version of our Test of Self-Conscious Affect (TOSCA; Tangney, Wagner, & Gramzow, 1989), participants are asked to imagine "You make a big mistake on an important project at work. People were depending on you, and your boss criticizes you." People then rate their likelihood of reacting with a shame response ("You would feel like you wanted to hide"), a guilt response ("You would think 'I should have recognized the problem and done a better job'"), and so forth. Across the various scenarios, the responses capture affective, cognitive, and motivational features associated with shame and guilt, respectively, as described in the theoretical, phenomenological, and empirical literature. It is important to note that these are not forced-choice measures. Respondents are asked to rate, on a 5-point scale (1, not likely–5, very likely), each of the responses. This allows for the possibility that some respondents may experience shame, guilt, both emotions, or neither emotion in connection with a given situation. See Tangney (1996) and Tangney & Dearing (in press) for a summary of research supporting the reliability and validity of the TOSCA.

Using the TOSCA, numerous independent studies have examined the relationship of shame-proneness and guilt-proneness to a dispositional capacity for interpersonal empathy (Leith & Baumeister, 1998; Tangney, 1991, 1994, 1995; Tangney & Dearing, in press; Tangney, Wagner, Fletcher, & Gramzow, 1991). The results are consistent across samples from all walks of life. Guilt-prone individuals are generally empathic individuals. In contrast, shame-proneness has been repeatedly associated with an impaired capacity for other-oriented empathy and a propensity for "self-oriented" personal-distress responses.

Similar findings are evident when we consider feelings of shame and guilt "in the moment." Individual differences aside, when people describe personal guilt experiences, they convey greater empathy for others involved than when they describe shame experiences (Leith & Baumeister, 1998; Tangney, et al., 2001). Moreover, when people are induced to feel shame, they exhibit less empathy (Marschall, 1996). Marschall experimentally manipulated feelings of shame using false negative feedback on a purported intelligence test. After participants in the shame condition publicly estimated their test scores, experimenters—exchanging shocked, surprised expressions with an assistant—told them they scored substantially below their guess. (The experiment was immediately followed with extensive "process" debriefing procedures, conducted by carefully trained and closely supervised senior research assistants.) Marschall found that people induced to feel shame subsequently reported less empathy for a student with a disability in an apparently unrelated task. The effect was most pronounced among low-shame-prone individuals. Consistent with results from our dispositional studies (Tangney, 1991, 1995), shame-prone individuals are rather unempathic across the board, regardless of whether they are shamed in the laboratory or not. However, among their less-shame-prone peers—who show a fair capacity for empathy in general—the shame induction appears to "short-circuit" participants' empathic responsiveness. In short, as a result of the shame induction, low-shame-prone people were rendered relatively unempathic—more like their shame-prone peers.

What accounts for this differential link among shame, guilt, and empathy? Developmentalists have suggested that guilt and empathy emerge along a common developmental pathway, hinging on many of the same social–cognitive achievements: increasingly complex attributions, emotion knowledge, and perspective-taking abilities (Eisenberg, 1986; Hoffman, 1982; Zahn-Waxler & Robinson, 1995). In addition, by focusing on a bad behavior (as opposed to a bad self), people who experience guilt are relatively free of the egocentric, self-involved process of shame. Instead, their focus on a specific behavior is likely to highlight the consequences of that behavior for distressed others, further facilitating an empathic response (Tangney, 1991, 1995). In contrast, the painful self-focus of shame is apt to "derail" the empathic process. As indicated by content analyses of autobiographical accounts of shame and guilt experiences, the shamed individual focuses on him or her *self*, as opposed to the harmed other (Tangney et al., 2001), and the defensive responses empirically associated with shame —denial, externalization of blame, and humiliated fury (see below)— further move the shamed individuals away from an other-oriented empathic connection.

Anger and Aggression

A third set of findings further underscores that shame and guilt are not equally moral emotions. Research has shown that there is a link between shame and anger, again observed at both the dispositional and state levels. Lewis (1971) first noted this link between shame and anger (or humiliated fury) in her clinical case studies. In years since, numerous empirical studies of children, adolescents, college students, and diverse samples of adults have indicated that shame-prone individuals are also prone to feelings of anger and hostility (Tangney, 1994, 1995; Tangney et al., 1991; Tangney, Wagner, Fletcher, & Gramzow, 1992). Not only are shame-prone individuals more prone to anger, in general, than their non-shame-prone peers, but once angered, they are also more likely to manage their anger unconstructively. In a recent cross-sectional developmental study of substantial samples of children, adolescents, college students, and adults (Tangney, Wagner, et al., 1996), proneness to shame was clearly related to maladaptive and nonconstructive responses to anger across individuals of all ages, consistent with Scheff's (1987, 1995) and Retzinger's (1987) descriptions of a "shame–rage spiral." In contrast, guilt was generally associated with constructive means of handling anger.

Similar findings have been observed at the situational level, too. For example, Wicker et al. (1983) found that college students reported a greater desire to punish others involved in personal shame versus guilt experiences. In a study of specific real-life episodes of anger among romantically involved couples, shamed partners were significantly more angry, more likely to engage in aggressive behavior, and less likely to elicit conciliatory behavior from their significant other (Tangney, 1995).

What accounts for this rather counterintuitive link between shame and anger? When feeling shame, people initially direct hostility inward ("*I am such a bad person*"). But this hostility can easily be redirected outward in a defensive attempt to protect the self, by "turning the tables" to shift the blame elsewhere—something along the lines of "Oh what a horrible person I am and, damn it, how could you make me feel that way!" (Tangney, 1995; Tangney, Wagner, Fletcher, & Gramzow, 1992). In fact, this link between proneness to shame and externalization of blame is one of the most robust findings in our research. Without exception, across some 20 independent studies of children, adolescents, college students, and noncollege adults, using various versions of our scenario-based TOSCA measure, we have found that people who are inclined to experience shame are also significantly more likely to blame the situation and other people for the very same set of failures and transgressions (Tangney, 1994; Tangney & Dearing, in press; Tangney, Wagner, Fletcher, & Gramzow, 1992).

Deterring Transgression and Socially Undesirable Behavior

Emotion researchers and practitioners in the criminal justice system widely assume that because shame is such a painful emotion, feelings of shame motivate people to avoid "doing wrong," decreasing the likelihood of transgression and impropriety (Barrett, 1995; Ferguson & Stegge, 1995; Kahan, 1997; Zahn-Waxler & Robinson, 1995). As it turns out, virtually no direct evidence supports this adaptive function of shame. To the contrary, research suggests that shame may even make things worse.

In one study (Tangney, 1994), I examined the relationship of individual differences in proneness to shame and guilt to self-reported moral behavior (assessed by the Conventional Morality Scale; Tooke & Ickes, 1988). I found that self-reported moral behaviors were substantially positively correlated with proneness to guilt but unrelated to proneness to shame. For example, compared to their less-guilt-prone peers, guilt-prone individuals were more likely to endorse such items as "I would not steal something I needed, even if I were sure I could get away with it," "I will not take advantage of other people, even when it's clear that they are trying to take advantage of me," and "Morality and ethics don't really concern me" (reverse scored). In other words, results from this study suggest that guilt but not shame motivates people to choose the "moral paths" in life.

The most direct evidence linking moral emotions with moral behavior comes from the ongoing Longitudinal Family Study of moral emotions (Tangney et al., 1991; Tangney & Dearing, in press). In this study, 380 children, their parents, and their grandparents were initially studied when children were in the fifth grade. Children were recruited from public schools in an ethnically and socioeconomically diverse suburb of Washington, DC. (Of the sample, 60% is White; 31%, Black; and 9%, "other." Most children generally came from low- to moderate-income families. The typical parents had attained a high school education.) Recently, we completed our third panel of data collection, which included an in-depth social and clinical history interview of the children at ages 18–19 years. Preliminary analyses of Panel 3 data show that moral emotional style in the fifth grade predicts critical "bottom-line" behaviors in young adulthood, including drug and alcohol use, risky sexual behavior, involvement with the criminal justice system (e.g., arrests, convictions, incarceration), suicide attempts, high school suspension, and community service involvement.

More specifically, shame-proneness assessed in the fifth grade predicted later high school suspension, drug use of various kinds (e.g., amphetamines, depressants, hallucinogens, heroin), and suicide attempts. In addition, shame-prone children were less likely to apply to college or engage in community service.

In contrast, guilt-proneness in the fifth grade was positively associated with later applying to college and doing community service. Guilt-prone fifth-graders were less likely to make suicide attempts, to use heroin, or to drive under the influence, and they began drinking at a later age. Moreover, they were less likely to be arrested, convicted, and incarcerated. In adolescence they had fewer sexual partners and were more likely to practice safe sex and use birth control.

These links between early moral emotional style and subsequent behavioral adjustment remained robust, even when controlling for family income and mothers' education. Thus, this is not simply an effect of socioeconomic status. Moreover, these findings held even when controlling for children's anger at Time 1 (fifth grade). The robustness with respect to Time 1 anger is especially impressive, given that early indices of anger and aggression are one of the most important predictors of later criminal activity and other behavioral maladjustment (Huesmann, Eron, Lefkowitz, & Walder, 1984). Our findings do not simply reflect the continuity of bad behavior (anger and aggression) often observed from childhood into adulthood.

Psychological Symptoms

Finally, proneness to shame and guilt are differentially related to psychological symptoms. The research reviewed thus far suggests that guilt is, on balance, the more moral or adaptive emotion—at least when considering social behavior and interpersonal adjustment. But one might wonder whether there is a trade-off vis-à-vis individual psychological adjustment. Does the tendency to experience guilt over one's transgressions, to feel empathy for one's victims, and to set aside one's own needs and desires in favor of the needs of others ultimately lead to increases in anxiety and depression or to decreases in self-esteem?

Apparently not. When measures are used that are sensitive to Lewis's (1971) distinction between shame about the self and guilt about a specific behavior (e.g., our scenario-based methods assessing shame-proneness and guilt-proneness with respect to specific situations), the tendency to experience shame-free guilt is essentially unrelated to psychological symptoms. Guilt-prone children, adolescents, and adults are not at increased risk for depression, anxiety, low self-esteem, and so forth. In contrast, across individuals of all ages, proneness to painful feelings of shame about the entire self has been associated with a range of psychological problems, including depression, anxiety, low self-esteem, eating disorder symptoms, and destructive responses to anger (Burggraf & Tangney, 1990; Gramzow & Tangney, 1992; Tangney, 1994; Tangney, Burggraf, & Wagner, 1995; Tangney et al., 1991; Tangney, Wagner, & Gramzow, 1992).

It is worth emphasizing that these results are clearly not caused by a generalized negative affect. In our studies of shame and guilt dispositions, we routinely conduct part correlations, where shame is factored out from guilt and vice versa. The TOSCA shame and guilt scales are substantially correlated. For example, in a large cross-sectional developmental study (Tangney, Wagner, et al., 1996), correlations between shame and guilt measures were .48 for children, .40 for adolescents, .42 for college students, and .42 for adults. This covariation between shame and guilt is likely caused by several factors. First, these emotions share several features in common—for example, both are negative emotions that involve self-relevant negative evaluations of one sort or another. Second, shame and guilt can co-occur with respect to the same situation. In isolating the unique variance of shame and guilt, respectively, we focus on individual differences in a tendency to experience shame-free guilt and guilt-free shame. Across our many studies, these part correlational results have been remarkably robust, indicating (a) that our effects are not simply due to generalized negative affect, because negative affect is essentially partialled out and (b) that there is a good portion of reliable, valid, unique variance in these shame and guilt measures. For example, even after tossing out the solid reliable variance represented by the correlation of .42 between our shame and guilt scales, shame and guilt residuals correlate meaningfully and significantly with such key variables as other-oriented empathy, constructive versus destructive responses to anger, externalization of blame, high school suspensions, drug and alcohol use, and community service. Further, these residuals are remarkably stable, showing an average stability of .52 over a 2–3-year period among adults (Tangney & Dearing, in press).

In short, shame and guilt are distinct emotions with different implications for moral motivation and behavior. In regard to the welfare of the individual, his or her close relationships, or society at large, feelings of guilt (together with empathy) represent the moral emotion of choice in response to failures and transgressions.

SOME IMPLICATIONS OF CURRENT RESEARCH ON MORAL EMOTIONS

What are the applied implications of this research showing that shame and guilt are not equally moral adaptive emotions? In the remainder of this chapter, I discuss the relevance of these findings for three important domains: (a) the criminal justice system, (b) parental discipline, and (c) the classroom context.

Criminal Justice System

Given that shame and guilt are generally seen as central to a person's moral motivational system, it is surprising that so little research has examined their links to real-world moral behavioral outcomes. In the area of criminality and recidivism, no systematic research has included a comprehensive consideration of shame and guilt. Where shame and guilt appear at all in the research literature on criminal behavior and recidivism, the consideration is brief and superficial (Blair et al., 1995; Gudjonsson & Roberts, 1983; Harry, 1992; Indermaur, 1994). Ironically, the absence of guilt or remorse is cited as one of the hallmarks of psychopathy (Hare, 1991; Rogers & Bagby, 1994; Samenow, 1984, 1989) and appears as one of the criteria for *DSM-IV* diagnosis of antisocial personality disorder (American Psychiatric Association, 1994). However, we do not know very much about moral emotions among offenders.

Without question, this is an area in which the stakes are extremely high. Crime remains one of the United States's leading problems, and most Americans agree it is a problem that we are not handling very well. Criminal activity costs America $210 billion annually—and this figure captures only the monetary dimension of cost (Anderson, 1999). Each of the 15,530 murders, 89,110 rapes, 916,380 assaults, and 2,099,700 burglaries in 1999 left indelible marks on the lives of the victims and on the network of relationships around them (Federal Bureau of Investigation, 1999). The cost of crime does not end there. Americans pay a second time, in those cases in which offenders are apprehended, convicted, and sentenced to serve time. It costs more to send someone to jail than to college. In 1996, the average cost of housing an inmate was $19,655 per year (Higgins, 1998). Moreover, on release, inmates receive not a college degree but a 2-in-3 chance of being re-incarcerated, either by committing a new offense or by violating probation or parole. Nationally, the recidivism rate was 62% in 1997 (A. J. Beck, 1997).

Two-thirds of incarcerated offenders re-offend and return to life behind bars. One-third find the path to reform, at least within the first few years after release. What distinguishes these two groups, and how can we foster a higher rate of reform? A large body of research has examined factors that predict recidivism (Andrews & Bonta, 1994; Blackburn, 1993; Gendreau, Goggin, & Little, 1996; Harris, Rice, & Quinsey, 1993; Zamble & Quinsey, 1997). Most documented predictors of recidivism represent "water under the bridge": background factors rooted in past history (e.g., unstable family life, early separation from a parent, elementary school adjustment, age of first arrest) or enduring aspects of the person (e.g., intelligence). These factors may suggest avenues of broad and difficult social change that may benefit generations far into the future. However, as Zamble and Quinsey (1997) recently pointed out, such static or "tombstone" factors do not provide points of intervention for the 1.7 million inmates currently in prison or jail.

Moral emotions represent one surprising "black hole" in the criminology literature, a factor that could potentially be "harnessed" to help inhibit recidivism and foster reform. More specifically, the knowledge gained from recent research on shame and guilt has applied implications in four areas of criminal justice.

The first area concerns intervention. Given the scant research on moral emotions among offenders in general, there is little direct evidence on how best to cultivate more adaptive patterns of moral emotions among offenders. But several innovative programs draw on a restorative justice model. *Restorative justice* is a philosophical framework that calls for active participation by the victim, the offender, and the community with the aim of repairing the fabric of community peace. For example, the Impact of Crime workshop implemented in Fairfax County, Virginia's, Adult Detention Center emphasizes principles of community, personal responsibility, and reparation. Using cognitive restructuring techniques, case workers and group facilitators challenge common distorted ways of thinking about crime, victims, and locus of responsibility. As inmates grapple with issues of responsibility, the question of blame inevitably arises. So, too, do the emotions of self-blame. On re-examining the causes of their legal difficulties and revisiting the circumstances surrounding their offense and its consequences, many inmates experience new feelings of shame or guilt, or both. Another important feature of the restorative justice approach is its guilt-inducing, shame-reducing philosophy and associated methods. Offenders are encouraged to take responsibility for their behavior, acknowledge the negative consequences to others, empathize with the distress of their victims, feel guilt for having done the wrong thing, and act on the consequent press to repair. But they are actively discouraged from feeling shame about themselves.

By their nature, interventions based on a restorative justice model tend to focus on guilt while eschewing stigmatizing shame. Such approaches could further enhance the development of an adaptive moral emotional style (high-guilt, low shame) among offenders by (a) educating offenders about the distinction between feelings of guilt about specific behaviors and feelings of shame about the self, (b) encouraging appropriate experiences of guilt and emphasizing associated constructive motivations to repair or make amends, (c) helping offenders recognize and modify maladaptive shame experiences, and (d) using inductive and educational strategies to foster a capacity for perspective-taking and other-oriented empathy.

A second critical area in which basic research on moral emotions has immediate application is judicial sentencing practices. As the costs of incarceration mount and evidence of its failure as a deterrent grows (Andrews et al., 1990; Bonta, 1996), judges understandably have begun to search for creative alternatives to traditional sentences. The recent trend toward "shaming sentences" has gained a good deal of momentum in recent years. Judges across the United States are sentencing offenders to parade around in public carrying signs broadcasting their crimes, to post signs on their front lawns warning neighbors of their vices, and to display bumper stickers detailing their offenses on their cars. Other judges have focused on sentencing alternatives based on a restorative justice model (e.g., community service and other forms of reparation), which seem to be designed, at least implicitly, to elicit feelings of guilt for the offense and its consequences rather than feelings of shame and humiliation about the self. In seeking less costly and potentially more effective alternatives, judges have been operating largely in an empirical vacuum. Regarding shaming sentences in particular, there exist no systematic data on the effectiveness or nonmonetary costs of such efforts to publicly humiliate offenders, but our findings strongly argue that this is a misguided approach to alternative sentencing. Rather than encouraging people to accept responsibility and make reparations, shame often provokes anger, aggression, denial, and externalization of blame.

A third area concerns policies and procedures in jails or prisons. Aspects of the incarceration experience itself may provoke feelings of shame and humiliation (Dunnegan, 1997; Gilligan, 1996; Smith, 1992), and it has been suggested that, particularly when punishment is perceived as unjust, such feelings of shame can lead to defiance and, paradoxically, an increase in criminal behavior (Sherman, 1993). This is especially troubling in light of Indermaur's (1994) finding that fully 90% of offenders view their sentences as unfair. Knowledge of the relative pros and cons of the different moral emotions can help inform correctional officials as they make policy decisions about specific practices (e.g., the manner in which strip searches are conducted, how inmates are addressed) or more general aspects of jail and prison environment (e.g., "direct-supervision" models of incarceration that place deputies in common living areas, as opposed to monitoring inmates down long corridors of peepholes) to minimize the potential for humiliation.

Finally, basic research on moral emotions has implications for risk assessment. Our research with nonoffender populations suggests that a consideration of offender shame and guilt may help predict recidivism, above and beyond the major variables in current models. Furthermore, given an inmate deemed "high risk," knowledge of the inmate's "moral affective profile" could help identify the most promising points for intervention for that particular individual.

Implications for Parents: Raising a Moral Child

One of the most important parts of a parent's job is to teach children to be good, moral, caring people. Parents aim to instill in their children a clear sense of right and wrong and the motivation to set things right when they do transgress. At the same time, it is important to avoid raising overly constricted, self-punitive, neurotic children who are petrified of making mistakes and far too quick to blame themselves for the woes of the world.

Parents want to help their children develop into happy, emotionally well-adjusted individuals with a solid sense of self-esteem.

How can parents best accomplish these two sometimes incompatible tasks? Parents face a fundamental conflict. On one hand, parents are the primary source of love and nurturance during a child's formative years. Parents naturally want to promote children's feelings of security, happiness, and joy while shielding them from pain and distress. On the other hand, parents must also serve as the child's primary disciplinary figures. In this role, parents take responsibility for teaching their child the difference between right and wrong and making them feel bad when they do bad things. Here is where the paradox comes in: On a regular basis, loving, responsible parents must actually induce their children to feel bad—something that can be a serious dilemma for these parents.

But concern for the welfare of a child is not at odds with discipline-induced distress, to the extent that parents keep in mind that there are good and bad ways to feel badly. Bearing in mind the adaptive functions of guilt in contrast to the costs of shame, parents can do their children a service by teaching them to feel badly about bad behaviors but not badly about themselves. In this way, parents can guide their children to be moral, responsible, happy, and well-adjusted.

What parental behaviors are likely to result in a guilt-inducing, shame-reducing style of discipline? First, when parents discipline children, they should accentuate the behavior and not the person, that is, focus on what the child has done wrong rather than on who they are. For example, adaptive feelings of guilt are more likely to result from behavior-focused here-and-now statements such as "John, you *did* a bad thing when you . . ." as opposed to "John, you're a bad (mean, clumsy, etc.) *boy*" or, "John, you're so *stupid* (careless, lazy, etc.)."

Second, parents can help children focus on the consequences of their misdeeds for others. As discussed earlier, empathy and guilt are closely linked. But compared to adults, children tend to be more self-centered and are less inclined to notice their impact on others. This is developmentally normal: the younger the child, the more self-centered he or she is. Parents can help shift the child's attention to others with statements such as, "Mary, it's not OK to hit Susie like that. Look at how that hurts Susie. She's crying." In this way, parents simultaneously focus the child's attention on the bad behavior (not a bad self) and on the consequences for others.

Third, parents can help their children develop skills to repair the harm done. Feelings of guilt typically motivate reparation. But making things right is often more easily said than done. This is especially challenging for young children, who have yet to develop the complex social and problem-solving skills necessary to formulate an effective plan for reparation. Parents can help children to identify the specific negative consequences of their actions and to devise appropriate strategies to make things right. After all, the ultimate goal of moral thought and emotion is to make things right or make positive changes for the future. In this way, parents can teach their children to effectively resolve feelings of guilt by proactively making themselves better people and the world a better place.

Fourth, parents are well advised to avoid public humiliation wherever possible. Although discipline is most effective when given immediately, there is the possibility of shaming the child, especially in settings where social approval is important (e.g., with peers). Parents can avoid unnecessarily shaming their child by adopting a respectful manner and being sensitive to the immediate social setting. Fifth, it is important to avoid teasing, derisive humor. Sarcastic humor is another potent but often unrecognized source of shame. There is a fine line between laughing *at* a child and laughing *with* him or her. Jokes meant in fun can be interpreted as a "put down," leading to a sense of being mocked, ridiculed, and shamed.

Finally, it is important to let children know they are loved, even when they have done wrong. Discipline is most effective when it is delivered in the context of a mutually respectful and loving relationship, and positive feedback is at least as important as negative feedback.

Implications for Teachers: Shame in the Classroom

Learning and failure go together, and an important part of a child's education is learning how to cope effectively with failure. Failure is unpleasant for everyone but, as highlighted by the work of educational psychologist Carol Dweck (Dweck & Leggett, 1988), there are good ways and bad ways to experience failure. Some children tackle new tasks, fail, and search for new information and strategies to get it right the second time. Their focus is on the challenge of the new task and not on themselves. Other children focus less on the task and more on the failure and its implications for their developing sense of self-worth. These children are more likely to experience shame. They are more likely to become "stuck" in shameful feelings of worthlessness and powerlessness. In fact, shame can seriously undermine children's ability to learn in a challenging environment by lessening their chance of success in future endeavors. Feeling shame, they often simply stop trying.

How can teachers provide a safe environment for children to tackle new challenges and experience inevitable failures without the destructive consequences of shame? Many of the suggestions made for parents hold for teachers as well. Students benefit when teachers accentuate the behavior and not the person. Avoiding public humiliation is equally important. Sometimes, without thinking, teachers engage in common shame-inducing practices. For example, writing the names of students on the chalkboard because of misbehavior or poor performance, punishing students by making them stand in front of the class to be chastised, and putting students "in the corner" can result in painful feelings of humiliation and shame.

Teachers can also help by discouraging children from shaming their classmates. Peers play an important role in providing feedback to children about what kinds of behaviors are socially appropriate. However, excessive amounts of teasing, criticism, and ridicule are destructive to children's developing sense of self. By monitoring and discouraging shaming interactions, teachers can help create an emotionally safe environment for classmates to learn from one another.

Finally, teachers may find it helpful to monitor the emphasis on academic competition. Enhancing students' academic motivation is an important educational goal, but students come to the classroom with differing levels of ability and family support. Teachers may inadvertently induce painful feelings of shame by adopting practices such as publicizing grades in ways that encourage social comparison, overplaying the honor roll at the expense of other students' efforts and accomplishments, and indiscriminately setting goals that amount to unrealistic expectations for some students.

I emphasize that encouraging teachers to minimize shame in the classroom is not a suggestion that experiences of failure be eliminated. Children need to develop skills to manage failure because failure is an inevitable part of life. Typically, when people try something new, attempt to learn additional skills, or otherwise aim for excellence, we initially fail. Good learners persevere in the face of failure and learn from their mistakes. In fact, children who learn this skill early on are better equipped to deal with inevitable experiences of failure throughout life. As emphasized by Dweck and Leggett (1988), children benefit from learning to view failure as an important source of information about how to master a task rather than as a reflection of their ability or worth.

CONCLUSION

Shame, guilt, embarrassment, and pride are members of a family of self-conscious emotions that are evoked by self-reflection and self-evaluation. In addition, these emotions form the core of a person's moral motivational system. Shame and guilt, in particular, are often viewed as moral emotions because of the presumed role they play in deterring immoral and antisocial behavior. But recent research suggests that shame and guilt are not equally moral or adaptive emotions. Five sets of empirical findings were discussed to illustrate the adaptive functions of guilt, in contrast to the hidden costs of shame. Together, these results underscore that feelings of guilt (together with empathy) represent the moral emotion of choice when considering the welfare of the individual, his or her close relationships, or society at large.

These findings have direct applied implications for the criminal justice system, parents, and teachers. Recognizing the distinction between shame and guilt is an important step toward making a more moral society.

REFERENCES

American Psychiatric Association. (1994). *Diagnostic and statistical manual of mental disorders* (4th ed.). Washington, DC: Author.

Anderson, David. (1999). The aggregate burden of crime. *Journal of Law and Economics, 42*(2), 611–642.

Andrews, D. A., & Bonta, J. (1994). *The psychology of criminal conduct.* Cincinnati, OH: Anderson.

Andrews, D. A., Zinger, I., Hoge, R. D., Bonta, J., Gendreau, P., & Cullen, F. T. (1990). Does correctional treatment work? A clinically relevant and psychologically informed meta-analysis. *Criminology, 3,* 369–403.

Ausubel, D. P. (1955). Relationships between shame and guilt in the socialization process. *Psychological Review, 62,* 378–390.

Barrett, K. C. (1995). A functionalist approach to shame and guilt. In J. P. Tangney & K. W. Fischer (Eds.), *Self-conscious emotions: Shame, guilt, embarrassment, and pride* (pp. 25–63). New York: Guilford.

Baumeister, R. F., Stillwell, A. M., & Heatherton, T. F. (1994). Guilt: An interpersonal approach. *Psychological Bulletin, 115,* 243–267.

Baumeister, R. F., Stillwell, A. M., & Heatherton, T. F. (1995a). Interpersonal aspects of guilt: Evidence from narrative studies. In J. P. Tangney & K. W. Fischer (Eds.), *Self-conscious emotions: Shame, guilt, embarrassment, and pride* (pp. 255–273). New York: Guilford.

Baumeister, R. F., Stillwell, A. M., & Heatherton, T. F. (1995b). Personal narratives about guilt: Role in action control and interpersonal relationships. *Basic and Applied Social Psychology, 17,* 173–198.

Beck, A. J. (1997). Recidivism of prisoners released in 1983. Bureau of Justice Statistics Special Report. http://www.ojp.usdoj.gov/bjs/pub/press/sospi91.pr

Blackburn, R. (1993). *The psychology of criminal conduct: Theory, research and practice.* Chichester, England: Wiley.

Blair, R. J. R., Sellars, C., Strickland, I., Clark, F., Williams, A. O., Smith, M., & Jones, L. (1995). Emotion attributions in the psychopath. *Personality and Individual Differences, 19,* 431–437.

Bonta, J. (1996). Risk-needs assessment and treatment. In A. T. Harland (Ed.), *Choosing correctional options that work: Defining the demand and evaluating the supply* (pp. 18–32). Thousand Oaks, CA: Sage.

Burggraf, S. A., & Tangney, J. P. (1990, June). *Shame-proneness, guilt-proneness, and attributional style related to children's depression.* Poster presented at the annual meeting of the American Psychological Society, Dallas, TX.

Damon, W. (1988). *The moral child: Nurturing children's natural moral growth.* New York: Free Press.

Dunnegan, S. W. (1997). Violence, trauma and substance abuse. *Journal of Psychoactive Drugs, 29,* 345–351.

Dweck, C. S., & Leggett, E. L. (1988). A social–cognitive approach to motivation and personality. *Psychological Review, 95,* 256–273.

Eisenberg, N. (1986). *Altruistic cognition, emotion, and behavior.* Hillsdale, NJ: Erlbaum.

Eisenberg, N., & Miller, P. A. (1987). Empathy, sympathy, and altruism: Empirical and conceptual links. In N. Eisenberg & J. Strayer (Eds.), *Empathy and its development* (pp. 292–316). New York: Cambridge University Press.

Federal Bureau of Investigation. (1999). Crime in the United States. *Uniform Crime Reports.* http://www.fbi.gov/ucr/99cius.htm

Ferguson, T. J., & Stegge, H. (1995). Emotional states and traits in children: The case of guilt and shame. In J. P. Tangney & K. W. Fischer (Eds.), *Self-conscious emotions: Shame, guilt, embarrassment, and pride* (pp. 174–197). New York: Guilford.

Ferguson, T. J., Stegge, H., & Damhuis, I. (1991). Children's understanding of guilt and shame. *Child Development, 62,* 827–839.

Feshbach, N. D. (1978). Studies of empathic behavior in children. In B. A. Maher (Ed.), *Progress in experimental personality research* (Vol. 8, pp. 1–47). New York: Academic Press.

Feshbach, N. D. (1984). Empathy, empathy training, and the regulation of aggression in elementary school children. In R. M. Kaplan, V. J. Konenci, & R. Novoco (Eds.), *Aggression in children and youth* (pp. 192–208). The Hague, Netherlands: Martinus Nijhoff.

Feshbach, N. D. (1987). Parental empathy and child adjustment/maladjustment. In N. Eisenberg & J. Strayer (Eds.), *Empathy and its development* (pp. 271–291). New York: Cambridge University Press.

Feshbach, N. D., & Feshbach, S. (1969). The relationship between empathy and aggression in two age groups. *Developmental Psychology, 1,* 102–107.

Feshbach, N. D., & Feshbach, S. (1982). Empathy training and the regulation of aggression: Potentialities and limitations. *Academic Psychology Bulletin, 4,* 399–413.

Feshbach, N. D., & Feshbach, S. (1986). Aggression and altruism: A personality perspective. In C. Zahn-Waxler, E. M. Cummings, & R. Iannotti (Eds.), *Altruism and aggression: Biological and social origins* (pp. 189–217). Cambridge, England: Cambridge University Press.

Gendreau, P., Goggin, C., & Little, T. (1996). *Predicting adult offender recidivism: What works?* (User Report 96-07). Ottawa: Department of the Solicitor General of Canada.

Gilligan, J. (1996). Exploring shame in special settings: A psychotherapeutic study. In C. Cordess & M. Cox (Eds.), *Forensic psychotherapy: Crime, psychodynamics and the offender patient: Vol. 2. Mainly practice* (pp. 475–489). London: Jessica Kingsley.

Gramzow, R., & Tangney, J. P. (1992). Proneness to shame and the narcissistic personality. *Personality and Social Psychology Bulletin, 18,* 369–376.

Gudjonsson, G. H., & Roberts, J. C. (1983). Guilt and self-concept in "secondary psychopaths." *Personality and Individual Differences, 4,* 65–70.

Hare, R. D. (1991). *The Hare Psychopathy Checklist—Revised.* Toronto, Ontario, Canada: Multi-Health Systems.

Harris, G. T., Rice, M. E., & Quinsey, V. L. (1993). Violent recidivism of mentally disordered offenders: The development of a statistical prediction instrument. *Criminal Justice and Behavior, 20,* 315–335.

Harry, B. (1992). Criminals' explanations of their criminal behavior, Part II: A possible role for psychotherapy. *Journal of Forensic Sciences, 37,* 1334–1340.

Higgins, G. (1998). *Comparison of Regional Corrections Agencies.* Correctional Standards and Oversight Committee. April, 1998. http://leg.state.mt.us/reports/reference/past_interim/cor_rpt6.htm

Hoffman, M. L. (1982). Development of prosocial motivation: Empathy and guilt. In N. Eisenberg-Berg (Ed.), *Development of prosocial behavior* (pp. 281–313). New York: Academic Press.

Hoffman, M. L. (1987). The contribution of empathy to justice and moral judgement. In N. Eisenberg & J. Strayer (Eds.), *Empathy and its development* (pp. 47–80). New York: Cambridge University Press.

Huesmann, L. R., Eron, L. D., Lefkowitz, M. M., & Walder, L. O. (1984). Stability of aggression over time and generations. *Developmental Psychology, 20,* 1120–1134.

Indermaur, D. (1994). Offenders' perceptions of sentencing. *Australian Psychologist, 29,* 140–144.

Kahan, D. M. (1997). Ignorance of law is an excuse—But only for the virtuous. *Michigan Law Review, 96,* 127–154.

Leith, K. P., & Baumeister, R. F. (1998). Empathy, shame, guilt, and narratives of interpersonal conflicts: Guilt-prone people are better at perspective taking. *Journal of Personality, 66,* 1–37.

Lewis, H. B. (1971). *Shame and guilt in neurosis.* New York: International Universities Press.

Lindsay-Hartz, J. (1984). Contrasting experiences of shame and guilt. *American Behavioral Scientist, 27,* 689–704.

Marschall, D. E. (1996). *Effects of induced shame on subsequent empathy and altruistic behavior.* Unpublished masters' thesis, George Mason University, Fairfax, VA.

Miller, P. A., & Eisenberg, N. (1988). The relation of empathy to aggressive and externalizing/antisocial behavior. *Psychological Bulletin, 103,* 324–344.

Retzinger, S. R. (1987). Resentment and laughter: Video studies of the shame-rage spiral. In H. B. Lewis (Ed.), *The role of shame in symptom formation* (pp. 151–181). Hillsdale, NJ: Erlbaum.

Rogers, R., & Bagby, M. R. (1994). Dimensions of psychopathy: A factor analytic study of the MMPI Antisocial Personality Disorder Scale. *International Journal of Offender Therapy and Comparative Criminology, 38,* 297–308.

Samenow, S. E. (1984). *Inside the criminal mind.* New York: Times Books.

Samenow, S. E. (1989). *Before it's too late: Why some kids get into trouble—And what parents can do about it.* New York: Times Books.

Scheff, T. J. (1987). The shame–rage spiral: A case study of an interminable quarrel. In H. B. Lewis (Ed.), *The role of shame in symptom formation* (pp. 109–149). Hillsdale, NJ: Erlbaum.

Scheff, T. J. (1995). Conflict in family systems: The role of shame. In J. P. Tangney & K. W. Fischer (Eds.), *Self-conscious emotions: Shame, guilt, embarrassment, and pride* (pp. 393–412). New York: Guilford.

Sherman, L. W. (1993). Defiance, deterrence, and irrelevance: A theory of the criminal sanction. *Journal of Research in Crime and Delinquency, 30,* 445–473.

Smith, J. S. (1992). Humiliation, degradation and the criminal justice system. *Journal of Primary Prevention, 12,* 209–222.

Tangney, J. P. (1989, August). *A quantitative assessment of phenomenological differences between shame and guilt.* Poster presented at the Annual Meeting of the American Psychological Association, New Orleans, LA.

Tangney, J. P. (1991). Moral affect: The good, the bad, and the ugly. *Journal of Personality and Social Psychology, 61,* 598–607.

Tangney, J. P. (1993). Shame and guilt. In C. G. Costello (Ed.), *Symptoms of depression* (pp. 161–180). New York: Wiley.

Tangney, J. P. (1994). The mixed legacy of the super-ego: Adaptive and maladaptive aspects of shame and guilt. In J. M. Masling & R. F. Bornstein (Eds.), *Empirical perspectives on object relations theory* (pp. 1–28). Washington, DC: American Psychological Association.

Tangney, J. P. (1995). Shame and guilt in interpersonal relationships. In J. P. Tangney & K. W. Fischer (Eds.), *Self-conscious emotions: Shame, guilt, embarrassment, and pride* (pp. 114–139). New York: Guilford.

Tangney, J. P. (1996). Conceptual and methodological issues in the assessment of shame and guilt. *Behaviour Research and Therapy, 34,* 741–754.

Tangney, J. P. (2001). Constructive and destructive aspects of shame and guilt. In A. C. Bohart & D. J. Stipek (Eds.), *Constructive and destructive behavior: Implications for family, school, and society* (pp. 127–145). Washington, DC: American Psychological Association.

Tangney, J. P., Burggraf, S. A., & Wagner, P. E. (1995). Shame-proneness, guilt-proneness, and psychological symptoms. In J. P. Tangney & K. W. Fischer (Eds.), *Self-conscious emotions: Shame, guilt, embarrassment, and pride* (pp. 343–367). New York: Guilford.

Tangney, J. P., & Dearing, R. (in press). *Shame and guilt.* New York: Guilford Press.

Tangney, J. P., Marschall, D. E., Rosenberg, K., Barlow, D. H., & Wagner, P. E. (2001). *Children's and adults' autobiographical accounts of shame, guilt and pride experiences: An analysis of situational determinants and interpersonal concerns.* Manuscript submitted for publication.

Tangney, J. P., Miller, R. S., Flicker, L., & Barlow, D. H. (1996). Are shame, guilt and embarrassment distinct emotions? *Journal of Personality and Social Psychology, 70,* 1256–1269.

Tangney, J. P., Wagner, P. E., Barlow, D. H., Marschall, D. E., & Gramzow, R. (1996). The relation of shame and guilt to constructive vs. destructive responses to anger across the lifespan. *Journal of Personality and Social Psychology, 70,* 797–809.

Tangney, J. P., Wagner, P. E., Fletcher, C., & Gramzow, R. (1991, April). *Intergenerational continuities and discontinuities in proneness to shame and proneness to guilt.* In J. P. Tangney (Chair), Socialization of Emotion in the Family Symposium conducted at the meeting of the Society for Research in Child Development, Seattle, WA.

Tangney, J. P., Wagner, P. E., Fletcher, C., & Gramzow, R. (1992). Shamed into anger? The relation of shame and guilt to anger and self-reported aggression. *Journal of Personality and Social Psychology, 62,* 669–675.

Tangney, J. P., Wagner, P. E., & Gramzow, R. (1989). *The Test of Self-Conscious Affect* (TOSCA). George Mason University, Fairfax, VA.

Tangney, J. P., Wagner, P. E., & Gramzow, R. (1992). Proneness to shame, proneness to guilt, and psychopathology. *Journal of Abnormal Psychology, 103,* 469–478.

Tooke, W. S., & Ickes, W. (1988). A measure of adherence to conventional morality. *Journal of Social and Clinical Psychology, 6,* 310–334.

Wallbott, H. G., & Scherer, K. R. (1995). Cultural determinants in experiencing shame and guilt. In J. P. Tangney & K. W. Fischer (Eds.), *Self-conscious emotions: Shame, guilt, embarrassment, and pride* (pp. 465–487). New York: Guilford.

Weiner, B. (1985). An attributional theory of achievement motivation and emotion. *Psychological Review, 92,* 548–573.

Wicker, F. W., Payne, G. C., & Morgan, R. D. (1983). Participant descriptions of guilt and shame. *Motivation and Emotion, 7,* 25–39.

Zahn-Waxler, C., & Robinson, J. (1995). Empathy and guilt: Early origins of feelings of responsibility. In J. P. Tangney & K. W. Fischer (Eds.), *Self-conscious emotions: Shame, guilt, embarrassment, and pride* (pp. 143–173). New York: Guilford.

Zamble, E., & Quinsey, V. L. (1997). *The criminal recidivism process.* New York: Cambridge University Press.

5

WHEN SELVES COLLIDE: THE NATURE OF THE SELF AND THE DYNAMICS OF INTERPERSONAL RELATIONSHIPS

MARK R. LEARY

The theorists who first discussed self processes from psychological perspectives viewed the self as firmly rooted in interpersonal interactions and relationships. From James's (1890) discussion of the social me to Cooley's (1902) concept of the looking glass self to Mead's (1934) analysis of self and perspective-taking, early writers saw that the capacity for self-reflexive thought was intimately involved in how people relate to one another. Although later researchers did not deny the interpersonal aspects of the self, the focus of most theory and research during the 20th century was primarily on the self as a cognitive entity that structures perceptions, motivates behaviors (e.g., in a quest for self-esteem or self-consistent information), and guides decisions and actions. Thus, concepts such as self-schema, self-efficacy, self-consistency, self-regulation, and self-enhancement dominated discussions of the self. In the past decade, however, theorists and researchers have refocused attention on the relational aspects of the self: how the self arises from social interaction and then plays an important role in influencing how people negotiate the complexities of social life.

THE NATURE OF THE SELF

Because "self" has a wide variety of meanings in both scholarly and colloquial discussions, I wish to clarify what I mean by the term. At its core, the self is the cognitive–affective apparatus that allows people to engage in abstract, symbolically mediated thought about themselves. Although certain other animals have the capacity to engage in rudimentary forms of self-awareness and perspective-taking (Gallup & Suarez, 1986), they are not able to think about themselves in the complex, abstract ways that are characteristic of human beings. This ability to take oneself as the object of one's own attention and to think consciously about oneself in complex ways is perhaps the cardinal psychological trait that distinguishes human beings from all other animals. Although we do not yet understand the neurological basis of this unique ability, human beings clearly possess some sort of cognitive–affective apparatus that most (if not all) other animals do not. This apparatus lies at the heart of what we are referring to when we use the term *self* and its variations (e.g., *self-awareness, self-evaluation, self-concept, self-regulation*).[1]

The possession of a self allows human beings to do several things that are unimaginable for most, if not all other animals. By being able to manipulate thoughts and images about oneself in one's mind—what Jaynes (1976) called the "analogue-I"—people can envision possible outcomes of likely actions, prepare for contingencies that they can anticipate happening in the future, and deliberately plan in ways that other animals cannot. Possession of a self also permits a level of self-analysis and self-evaluation that is impossible without it. People are able to form ideas of what they are like and evaluate these self-concepts. They can explicitly compare themselves to their own standards and to other people and experience self-related emotions such as pride and shame as a result. Possession of a self also allows them to think about their motives, intentions, and morals. They also treat their mental images of themselves as if they were real and respond to threats to those images in ego-defensive ways.

The ability to self-reflect has important implications for social interaction. Self-related thoughts and feelings arise in real and imagined social interactions, then feed back to influence how people behave toward other people. In many ways, interactions between individuals may be viewed as interactions between the selves of those individuals, with each person's perceptions of and responses to the other filtered through and mediated by his or her self-perceptions. To this extent, we may gain insight into rela-

---

[1] This conceptualization of the self does not preclude the possibility that self-relevant information may be processed automatically and without conscious awareness (see chapter 1, this volume), although it raises important questions regarding which of these processes are unique features of the human self and which are part of the automatic regulatory systems of all animals. Examination of these questions would take us far beyond the scope of this chapter.

tional processes by considering how they are influenced, albeit indirectly, by the operation of each individual's self.

The purpose of this chapter is to examine five properties of the human self that have implications for individuals' relationships with other people. Every adult's self appears to be characterized by these five features, suggesting that they are a natural and inherent part of the human psyche. Indeed, it is difficult to conceive of an otherwise functioning adult self that did not display each of them. Everyone who is capable of self-relevant thought (a) cognitively differentiates himself or herself from other people (self–other differentiation) while including certain other individuals as part of the self to varying degrees (self–other incorporation), (b) has difficulty recognizing that his or her views of himself or herself are biased and self-centered (egocentricity), (c) experiences changes in self-evaluations and related affect as a function of events that happen to him or her (self-esteem), (d) fosters and defends certain mental representations of himself or herself (egotism), and (e) is fundamentally absorbed in self-relevant thought (self-reflection). These are by no means the only properties of the self that have relational implications, but we confine ourselves to these five. As we show, these properties of the self channel people's responses to others in certain directions and set the stage for what happens in interpersonal life.

SELF–OTHER DIFFERENTIATION AND INCORPORATION

Every sentient organism can distinguish its own body from its environment through proprioception, but only organisms with a self can consciously distinguish themselves from other organisms and from the environment. During human development, infants come to appreciate not only that they are distinct from their caregivers but also that their perspectives and feelings are not always shared by other people (Lewis & Brooks-Gunn, 1979). At the same time, children also begin to form concepts about how they resemble and are socially connected to other individuals. This emerging sense of self allows children to view themselves as distinct entities and to contemplate how they relate to aspects of their physical and social worlds (Tesser, 1984).

Even as people differentiate themselves, however, they also incorporate aspects of their worlds into their concept of self. As James (1890) observed, a person's sense of self typically includes not only his or her own physical body and mental states but also his or her family members, friends, possessions, reputations, and so forth. These extensions of oneself are treated as part of "me," and their fortunes elicit much the same reactions as events that impinge on oneself directly. This incorporation process begins at an early age; toddlers show clear evidence that they have incorporated parents, siblings, and even toys into their sense of self (Lewis & Brooks-Gunn, 1979; Tesser, 1984). Later, in adulthood, people may react to threats to their reputations, beliefs, families, and bank accounts with as much fervor as attacks on their physical bodies.

People incorporate other people into their sense of self to varying degrees. Parents incorporate their children into their sense of self a great deal, for example, whereas siblings introject one another somewhat less. Similarly, good friends derive more of their sense of self from one another than do casual friends, who do so more than acquaintances. Romantic relationships tend to be especially characterized by including the partner as part of oneself. Along these lines, Maslow (1967) suggested that "beloved people can be incorporated into the self" (p. 103).

Presumably, the more we include another person as part of our self, the more we respond to that individual's experiences as if they were our own. For example, parents respond strongly to their children's successes and failures, and good friends often view one another's accomplishments with the same sort of pride with which they react to their own (assuming that the accomplishment does not reflect badly on them; Tesser, 1988). Conversely, the more we distinguish ourselves from another person, the less we will respond to their fortunes as if they were ours; whether we are indifferent to what happens to them or react favorably to their difficulties will depend on the degree to which our outcomes and theirs are linked. In any case, people tend to treat those who are part of their self-concept differently than those who are not.

The implication of this fact seems clear: The more that people incorporate another person into their sense of who they are, the more naturally and easily they should identify and empathize with him or her. In essence, failing to distinguish between oneself and another person should lead one to treat the other person as one treats oneself. Along these lines, Wegner (1980) suggested that certain instances of empathy may "stem in part from a basic confusion between ourselves and others" (p. 133), and Cialdini, Brown, Lewis, Luce, and Neuberg (1997) presented evidence that self–other overlap or "oneness" mediates empathic concern. Thus, empathic caring requires some degree of positive incorporation of the other individual into the self. Failures to incorporate others into the self, on the other hand, result in indifference if not animosity. Two distinct models of this process have been discussed. In one model, people incorporate another individual as part of the self, and in the other, a person's membership in one or more social groups (or relationships) is included as an aspect of the self.

Including Other People in the Self

Aron and Aron (1996, 2000) suggested that the degree to which one person includes another person in his or her self helps to determine the closeness of the relationship between the individuals. When people include another individual as part of the self, they begin to act as if some or all of the other individual's characteristics, perspectives, and resources are their own. So, for example, we may be as embarrassed by our partner's inappropriate behavior as we are by our personal misdeeds and may work as hard to further his or her well-being as we do our own.

Aron, Aron, and Smollan (1992) developed a simple, visual measure of the degree to which people include others in the self. The Inclusion of Other in the Self (IOS) scale consists of a set of seven Venn diagrams involving two circles, one labeled "self" and the other labeled "other." The Venn diagrams are arrayed on a 7-point scale ranging from no overlap between the circles to nearly complete overlap. The respondent is asked to indicate which circle best describes a particular personal relationship.

Studies have supported the idea that the IOS scale assesses the degree to which the individual includes another person as part of his or her sense of self. For example, people with higher IOS scores (i.e., presumably indicating a greater degree of inclusion of the other in one's self) take longer to rate themselves on traits on which they and their partner differ. Aron et al.'s (1992) interpretation of this finding was that the more a person has incorporated another in the self, the more confusion occurs between perceptions of oneself and perceptions of the other, resulting in slower ratings. This interpretation is consistent with Aron, Aron, Tudor, and Nelson's (1991) finding that people's reaction times were slower for traits that distinguished them from close others. In essence, once another individual is included in a person's self, the person has greater difficulty distinguishing cognitively between himself or herself and the other individual.

Evidence shows that the degree to which people include others as part of the self is related to their feelings about those relationships. Scores on the IOS scale correlate with self-reported closeness and intimacy, as well as with marital quality and ratings of love and relationship excitement (Aron et al., 1992; Aron & Fraley, 1999). Perhaps most intriguing is the fact that scores on the IOS scale correlate with whether respondents' relationships survive up to three months later. What is unclear is whether relationships in which people include their partners less as part of the self are less stable or whether, as relationships wane (for whatever reason), the degree to which people include the partner in the self diminishes, thereby predicting, but not causing, the breakup. In either case, the degree to which people incorporate other individuals into their selves has implications for feelings of closeness and for the course of relationships.

Social Identification

Social identity theory provides an alternative way of conceptualizing the link between the self and other people. Tajfel (1981) defined *social identity* as "that part of the individual's self-concept which derives from his [or her] knowledge of membership of a social group (or groups) together with the value and emotional significance attached to that membership" (p. 255). In this conceptualization, other individuals are not included in the self per se, but rather the self and others are viewed as belonging to the same socially relevant category. Through the process of self-categorization—cognitively grouping "oneself and some other class of stimuli as the same . . . in contrast to some other class of stimuli" (Turner, Hogg, Oakes, Reicher, & Wetherell, 1987, p. 44)—people come to identify with certain groups and disidentify from certain other groups.

Once self-categorization and differentiation have occurred, people react differently to members of groups with which they identify than to members of groups with which they do not identify (Brewer, 1979; Hogg & Abrams, 1988). Research shows that people readily discriminate in favor of their own groups even when the social category on which the group is based is arbitrary and they do not expect to receive any personal reward from doing so. Simply conceptualizing oneself as a member of a particular group is sufficient to produce the effect. Social identity theory suggests that the degree to which people discriminate against members of other groups in biased and prejudicial ways depends on the degree to which they identify with their ingroup—that is, the degree to which their self-categorization includes membership in the ingroup (Jarymowicz, 1998; Oakes, Haslam, & Turner, 1994).

Although social identity theory and self-categorization theory were initially proposed to account for intergroup behavior, they are applicable to interactions and relationships between individuals as well. Once one's sense of self includes membership in particular groups, one will react to individual members of other groups differently than to members of one's own. Thus, what have typically been viewed as interpersonal relationships between individuals are strongly influenced by the social (group) identities of the people involved (see Moya, 1998).

Inclusion or Categorization?

Although these two perspectives differ in important ways, they converge on the idea that people's interactions and relationships are affected by how they construe themselves in relation to other individuals and, in particular, the degree to which they differentiate themselves from others versus incorporate aspects of other people into their sense of self. According to Aron et al. (1991), other individuals are incorporated into one's sense of self, leading one to treat those individuals and their fortunes similarly to one's self and one's own fortunes. From the standpoint of social identity theory and its extensions (Brewer, 1979; Tajfel, 1981; Turner et al., 1987), one's group memberships and social categories, rather than specific other individuals, are incorporated as part of the self so that other individuals who share those memberships and categories are treated specially.

Whether these are, in fact, two separate processes or two ways of conceptualizing the same phenomenon is, at present, unclear. Each perspective can be loosely translated into the other: Social identification may involve including those in one's group as part of the self (Aron et al., 1991), and close relationships may be characterized by categorizing oneself and another person as members of the same social group or relationship (cf. Turner et al., 1987). In any case, for our purposes, both analyses suggest that the degree to which people differentiate between themselves and other people influences social phenomena such as intimacy, closeness, discrimination, and intergroup competition.

The two perspectives also differ in the degree to which they view self–other differentiation and incorporation as generally desirable. Aron and Aron (1996, 2000) implied that including other people in the self is generally positive because it promotes relational closeness, satisfaction, interdependency, and relationship longevity. Similarly, self–other overlap may promote empathy and compassion (Cialdini et al., 1997; Wegner, 1980). Social identity theorists offer a more mixed picture in which social identification results in positive relationships with ingroup members but in negative, discriminatory, and sometimes hostile relationships with outgroups. Furthermore, in close relationships, including other people in the self to an excessive degree may heighten interpersonal dependency. People whose identities are too tied up with other people's may invest too much of themselves in the relationship, leading to dysfunctional reactions when relational problems arise or the relationship breaks up (Murphy, Meyer, & O'Leary, 1994). Many extreme cases of stalking and other forms of "obsessive relational intrusion" are perpetrated by individuals who have incorporated another person into their sense of self to an excessive and unrealistic degree (Cupach & Spitzberg, 1998).

EGOCENTRISM

All organisms' views of the world are inherently egocentric in the sense that it is much easier for them to see the world from their own perspectives than from others' viewpoints. Many factors contribute to egocentrism. Of course, mere physical perspective has an effect, as only one individual can experience the world from any particular vantage point. Beyond that, however, people's identities, experiences, personalities, values, and desires color their perception and interpretation of events. One of the earliest demonstrations of how ego involvement influences perceptions was provided by Hastorf and Cantril's (1954) classic study in which fans of

Princeton and Dartmouth provided very different accounts of a particularly acrimonious and controversial football game between the schools. Although fans of both schools watched the same film of the game, what they subjectively "saw" was influenced by their own identities, loyalties, and assumptions. Given that egocentrism is, in part, a consequence of people viewing events from different physical and psychological perspectives, it is perhaps not surprising that people are normally and automatically egocentric.

More surprising and interesting from the standpoint of research on the self is that people have great difficulty recognizing their own egocentrism and stepping outside of their own frame of reference even when they try to do so. In essence, people are not only egocentric but also display meta-egocentrism in which they egocentrically assume that they are not egocentric. Dozens of studies have shown that people consistently fail to appreciate the degree to which their personal experiences and subjective construals of events are egocentric even when they are warned to avoid egocentrism and encouraged to adopt others' views. People generally overestimate the accuracy of their perceptions of events, as well as the degree to which other people see things as they do (Griffin & Ross, 1991). Furthermore, although people readily perceive bias in other people's judgments, they do not seem to appreciate that their own judgments are similarly skewed. In one particularly interesting demonstration of this effect, Vallone, Ross, and Lepper (1985) showed pro-Israeli, pro-Arab, and neutral students television news coverage of the 1983 massacre of U.S. Marines in Beirut. Although the neutral students thought the news report was fairly evenhanded, both the pro-Israeli and pro-Arab groups perceived that the coverage was biased against their group.

Such meta-egocentric tendencies have important consequences for relationships. Many misunderstandings arise because people seem to function as naive realists who assume that their perceptions of the world are accurate. As a result, they tend to conclude that those who do not see things as they do are mistaken, misguided, or biased. Knowing that our views might be biased, we sometimes try to make adjustments in our views, but because we underestimate the magnitude of our egocentric bias, those adjustments are rarely sufficient to render our judgments impartial and objective (see Griffin & Ross, 1991).

Furthermore, when disagreements or conflicts arise, their resolution is impeded by each side's conviction that its perception of the situation is veridical. When people believe they have an inside track to reality, opportunities for negotiation and compromise are thwarted. Egotism has been identified as a primary obstacle to successful business and labor negotiations (Bazerman, Curham, Moore, & Valley, 2000), and it likely undermines compromise and reconciliation in close relationships as well (Nichols, 1995). Importantly, Thompson and Loewenstein (1992) found that the more egocentric the opposing parties, the harder it is for them to agree on a resolution. The perception by both sides of seemingly neutral responses as biased (cf. Vallone et al., 1985) suggests that objectively fair offers and proposals from one's opponents will be viewed as unfair. If people realized that their interpretation of events were as egocentrically biased as their opponents', compromise and reconciliation would be easier to achieve.

Given that people cannot step outside themselves to make simple decisions on the basis of limited information when explicitly instructed to do so in laboratory experiments (Griffin & Ross, 1991), we should not be surprised that they have difficulty avoiding egocentrism amid the complexities of the real world. Despite our best efforts, the self seems to be characterologically incapable of being automatically exocentric.

SELF-ESTEEM

All normal individuals beyond infancy show changes in how they feel about themselves as a function of events they experience. Furthermore, self-esteem—both stable trait self-esteem and momentary state self-esteem —relates to how people respond in interpersonal life (Baumeister, Tice, & Hutton, 1989; Hoyle, Kernis, Leary, & Baldwin, 1999). Compared to people who have high self-esteem, those with low self-esteem display a higher need for approval from other people, stronger desire for close relationships, greater fear of negative evaluation and rejection, greater dependency on other people, less optimistic view of relationships, higher sensitivity to relationship threats, and more negative emotional reactions to relational problems (for reviews, see Baumeister, 1993). However, despite the thousands of studies of aspects of self-esteem, there is no clear consensus about what self-esteem is, what it does, or why it is psychologically important.

Sociometer Theory

Sociometer theory suggests that the self-esteem system functions as a sociometer: a subjective, psychological gauge that monitors the degree to which the person is (or is likely to be) accepted or rejected by other people (Leary & Downs, 1995). In essence, self-esteem is an internal indicator of the degree to which one is valued as a relational partner or group member by other individuals. To the extent that people do things that others value and see themselves as generally acceptable to other people, self-esteem will be high. However, perceiving that one is not relationally valued or that one has engaged in behaviors that will lead others to devalue their relationships results in lower self-esteem (Leary, Tambor, Terdal, & Downs, 1995). According to sociometer theory, self-esteem is an inherent part of human life because it is the output of a psychological system that monitors one's interactions and relationships with other people.

In a review of the self-esteem literature, Leary and Baumeister (2000) described evidence that the self-esteem system does, in fact, function as a sociometer: Self-esteem is exquisitely sensitive to changes in social acceptance, most events that affect self-esteem have real or imagined implications for the person's relational value, public events have a much stronger effect on self-esteem than do private events, self-esteem is strongly associated with the perception of the degree to which one is valued by other people, and the behavior of people with low self-esteem appears designed to protect their acceptance by others. In addition, clinical interventions that raise self-esteem seem to do so by increasing the degree to which the individual perceives that he or she is valued by other people (Leary, 1999). Thus, self-esteem is important because it is the gauge of something that is necessary for human well-being and happiness, namely, relational value and belongingness. People need to know where they stand with other people, and the self-esteem system provides ongoing feedback about this.

State and trait self-esteem are aspects of the sociometer (Leary & Baumeister, 2000). State self-esteem provides relatively continuous information about the degree to which one is being relationally valued in immediate or upcoming contexts, whereas trait self-esteem provides a summary of one's potential for relational evaluation over time. Both are important because effective interpersonal regulation requires feedback about both one's current relational evaluation and one's potential evaluation in the future. How a person responds to a specific change in self-esteem at a particular time depends on his or her long-range prospects, much as an investor's response to a change in stock price depends on long-term projections.

Self-Esteem and Relationships

Research has shown that people with low versus high self-esteem (either state or trait) approach relationships differently. Conceptualizing self-esteem as a mechanism for monitoring relational evaluation helps to explain why.

People who have experienced a blow to self-esteem appear particularly motivated to attain others' approval and to avoid disapproval, and people who are chronically low in trait self-esteem score higher in need for approval and fear of negative evaluation than those whose trait self-esteem is higher (Crowne & Marlowe, 1964; Leary & Kowalski, 1993; Schneider, 1969). Furthermore, people whose state or trait self-esteem is low are more attracted to those who approve of them and more strongly dislike those who evaluate them negatively than do people whose self-esteem is high (Dittes, 1959; Hewitt & Goldman, 1974; Jacobs, Berscheid,

& Walster, 1971; Walster, 1965). Although many theorists have assumed that people who have experienced a drop in self-esteem are trying to raise it, sociometer theory suggests that their primary motive is to repair breaches in their interpersonal relationships and to increase their relational value rather than to repair their self-esteem per se (Leary, 1999; Leary & Baumeister, 2000). People's self-esteem may indeed rise when they obtain approval and acceptance but only because self-esteem is providing ongoing feedback about the state of their relationships.

Similarly, people with low trait self-esteem worry more about their relationships with other people than do people with high trait self-esteem. They are more concerned about how other people regard them and more afraid of being judged negatively (Watson & Friend, 1969). They are also more prone to feeling jealous when rivals threaten their relationships (and sometimes even when they do not), and their feelings are hurt more easily when they perceive that other people do not value their relationships as much as they would like (Salovey & Rodin, 1991; White, 1981). Low trait self-esteem is also associated with being highly sensitive to rejection and with extreme emotional reactions when one feels rejected (Downey & Feldman, 1996; Levy, Ayduk, & Downey, 2001). From the standpoint of sociometer theory, these effects may be explained by the fact that people who have low trait self-esteem generally perceive that other people do not value and accept them as much as they desire (Leary, Schreindorfer, & Haupt, 1995; Leary, Tambor, et al., 1995). Strictly speaking, these effects are mediated by perceived acceptance (or, more precisely, perceived relational evaluation) rather than by self-esteem. Self-esteem is simply the subjective, psychological indicator of relational value in the individual's social environment.

Self-esteem also moderates how people deal with events that may threaten their relationships. People with high self-esteem tend to react to potential threats in ways that foster connections with their partner, whereas those with low self-esteem distance themselves when the going gets rough (MacDonald & Holmes, 1999; Murray, Holmes, MacDonald, & Ellsworth, 1998). This pattern is somewhat ironic and difficult for sociometer theory to explain. Given that people with low self-esteem seem to desire approval and affection more than those with high self-esteem and are more dependent on their relationships (Crowne & Marlowe, 1964; Schneider, 1969), why would they be inclined to behave in ways that undermine their partner's affection when relational problems arise? One possibility is that they are trying to distance themselves from a partner whom they believe is likely to reject them.

One of the more intriguing findings related to self-esteem and relationships involves the seeming preference of people with low trait self-esteem for relationships with people who see them as they see themselves. Whereas people with high trait self-esteem are more committed to partners who perceive them very favorably, people with low trait self-esteem are more committed to partners who perceive them less favorably (Swann, De La Ronde, & Hixon, 1994; Swann, Hixon, & De La Ronde, 1992). The prevailing explanation for this effect comes from self-verification theory, which posits that people desire to maintain their existing views of themselves and thus want to associate with those whose perceptions of them are congruent with their own (Swann et al., 1992).

However, an equally plausible explanation may be derived from the sociometer theory assumption that self-esteem is a meter of relational evaluation. Imagine the situations of two people with relatively low self-esteem, both of whom are in romantic relationships with partners who love them. The first person's partner perceives him or her more positively than the person perceives himself or herself, whereas the second person's partner seems to perceive him or her accurately (i.e., consistently with the person's own, less-flattering self-views). We might guess that the second individual would feel more secure in the relationship than the first because he or she is loved by a partner who perceives him or her accurately. In contrast, the first individual is likely to feel less secure; despite the partner's current love and dedication, believing that the partner perceives him or her too positively opens the possibility of future difficulties once the partner learns the truth. Being loved in spite of one's shortcomings offers great comfort and security.

In brief, many relational phenomena that are moderated by self-esteem may be parsimoniously explained by sociometer theory. Self-esteem is a pervasive and familiar experience in interpersonal life because it is intimately involved in the fundamental human desire to form and maintain connections with other people.

EGOTISM

The tendency for people to evaluate themselves more positively than they evaluate other people, as well as to view themselves more positively than other people do, has been well-documented (Alicke, 1985; Blaine & Crocker, 1993; Hoyle et al., 1999; Kruger & Dunning, 1999; Taylor & Brown, 1988). Most people have an exaggerated estimate of their personal characteristics and tend to evaluate their and others' behavior in self-serving ways.

I wish to stress, however, that people are not the perpetual egotists they have sometimes been portrayed. Their responses are not always egotistically biased and, in fact, are sometimes biased in a "counterdefensive" direction that reflects negatively on their abilities, personalities, and motives. Many such instances are self-presentational efforts to be seen as magnanimous or nondefensive by other people (Leary & Forsyth, 1987; Miller

& Schlenker, 1985), but sometimes people really do recognize and admit the full extent of their personal failures and deficiencies. Furthermore, people's interpretations of events are sometimes biased in an explicitly anti-ego direction, as when people take failures, rejections, and other negative events more seriously or personally than warranted. Even so, the prevailing pattern tends to be toward egotism, leading Greenwald (1980) to compare the ego to a totalitarian political regime that distorts information and rewrites history to portray itself in a desirable light.

Theorists have debated the source of these self-serving perceptions and whether they are ultimately beneficial, but it is clear that they have implications for people's interpersonal relationships (Gilovich, Kruger, & Savitsky, 1999). In the following sections, we examine four consequences of egotism: (a) inequity, (b) attributional conflict, (c) symbolic ego-defense, and (d) relational illusions.

Inequity

Research shows that perceiving that one's ratio of inputs to outputs in a relationship is less than another party's creates dissatisfaction in peer, romantic, family, and occupational relationships (Walster, Walster, & Berscheid, 1978). What is often not acknowledged is that inequity often stems not from a true disparity in the relative contributions of the people involved but rather from each individual's egotistical perceptions that his or her contributions are more frequent or important than the other person's (Ross & Sicoly, 1979).

In group and work settings, for example, rewards, power, status, and other resources are allocated on the basis of group members' competence, contributions, and performance (Suchner & Jackson, 1976), but each member's natural egotistic proclivity virtually assures that many of them will feel that they are not being recognized adequately for their contributions. Because many members will expect a disproportionate share of the rewards, feelings of inequity will be widespread, resulting in dissatisfaction, conflict, reduced effort, and high turnover (Geurts, Buunk, & Schaufeli, 1994; Geurts, Schaufeli, & Rutte, 1994). Egotism also leads employees to rate their job performance higher than their supervisors do (Farh, Dobbins, & Cheng, 1991), which causes workers to feel that they are being unfairly evaluated and compensated. Our natural propensity to overestimate our own ability, performance, and effort sets us up for disappointment and frustration in many areas of social and occupational life.

Attributional Conflict

In hundreds of studies, researchers have examined the tendency for people to make attributions that portray them in a desirable light. Research shows, for example, that people tend to take more responsibility for their successes than their failures, derogate the source and accuracy of unflattering feedback about them, and claim more credit for successful joint endeavors than they assign to other people who were involved (Blaine & Crocker, 1993; Leary & Forsyth, 1987).

Many relational problems arise when two or more individuals each interpret an event in a self-serving manner. As Horai (1977) observed, "conflict rooted in disparate attributions concerning the cause of events appears to be prevalent in many situations" (p. 97). In group settings, for example, each member of a successful group tends to believe that he or she was particularly responsible for the group's success, and each member of a failing group tends to feel less responsible for the group's failure. These kinds of self-serving biases have been documented in many real-life contexts, including athletic contests, academic projects, group discussions, problem-solving groups, and marriages (e.g., Brawley, 1984; Forsyth & Schlenker, 1977; Ross & Sicoly, 1979; Schlenker & Miller, 1977; Wolosin, Sherman, & Till, 1973).

Conflict, discord, and resentment arise when members of such groups learn of one another's egotistical perceptions. Members who claim high responsibility for the group's success or downplay their responsibility for group failure are uniformly disliked (Forsyth, Berger, & Mitchell, 1981; Forsyth & Mitchell, 1979), and group cohesion declines when members perceive that others are interpreting their personal responsibility in a self-serving manner (Shaw & Breed, 1970). To make matters worse, people appear to overestimate the degree to which other people's perceptions are egotistically biased while underestimating their own egotism (Kruger & Gilovich, 1999). When most members construe events in an egotistical manner, not only does everyone feel a sense of inequity (as discussed earlier), but they may also argue about the discrepancies in their perceptions. Ironically, then, successful groups may be torn apart from the inside because their members disagree regarding the assignment of responsibility. Fortunately, group members often keep their egotistical attributions to themselves, knowing that the other members do not share their views (Miller & Schlenker, 1985).

Similarly, in close relationships, each person may overestimate the proportion of the responsibilities that he or she handles (Bradbury & Fincham, 1992; Ross & Sicoly, 1979; VanYperen & Buunk, 1991), leading again to conflict once each partner's egotistical perspective is known by the other. In addition, partners tend to make more benevolent attributions for their own than for their partner's negative behaviors, particularly if they are dissatisfied with the relationship (Fincham, Beach, & Baucom, 1987). These kinds of self-serving attributions may exacerbate relational conflicts because each person feels not only that he or she is being unfairly criticized but also that the partner is being egotistical (Fincham & Bradbury, 1993).

Symbolic Ego-Defense

In another manifestation of egotism, people protect particular images of themselves in their own minds. Most research has focused on the intrapsychic antecedents and consequences of ego-defense, but efforts to maintain certain images of oneself have important interpersonal implications as well.

Tesser (1988; Tesser & Campbell, 1983) has suggested that because people's self-evaluations are affected by the successes and failures of individuals with whom they have close relationships, people manage their relationships in ways that maintain a positive self-evaluation. So, for example, although people are more likely to help friends than strangers with tasks that are not relevant to their own egos, they actually help strangers more than friends when a friend's success might reflect badly on them (Tesser & Smith, 1980). They also distance themselves from friends who outperform them on ego-relevant tasks (Pleban & Tesser, 1981) and may even choose friends who do not excel on dimensions that are personally self-relevant (Tesser, Campbell, & Smith, 1984). This tendency for people to react negatively to friends who outperform them has obvious consequences for interpersonal relationships, creating tension, distance, avoidance, and hurt feelings.

At the same time, these patterns may enhance the individuals' relational value among their peers. Excelling in unique areas makes one a more valuable social interactant, group member, or relational partner than either excelling in areas in which close others also excel or being outperformed by close others. From this perspective, the domains that people view as most self-relevant may be those on which they heavily stake their acceptance by other people. Thus, when close others perform highly in these domains, people's social standing is threatened and, as sociometer theory predicts, their self-esteem declines (Leary & Baumeister, 2000).

In extreme cases, people may take strong actions to ward off threats to their ego, often with about the same vigor as if they were defending themselves against physical attack. On the basis of an extensive review of the literature, Baumeister, Smart, and Boden (1996) concluded that a great deal of violence can be traced to symbolic threats to people's self-images. Although their conclusion that aggression is linked to high rather than low self-esteem has been challenged (Larivière & Simourd, 2000), there seems little doubt that people sometimes react violently when their egos are threatened.

In addition, people tend to find other people's egotism annoying, exasperating, and unpleasant, as reflected in the disparaging labels we attach to egotistical people: *arrogant, conceited, stuck-up, narcissistic, pompous,* and worse. People derogate and dislike those who appear to think too highly of themselves (Schlenker & Leary, 1982). Leary, Bednarski, Hammon, and

Duncan (1997) discussed several reasons egotism evokes negative reactions from others: egotism often threatens the value and self-esteem of other people because it implies that they are inferior; egotism is sometimes viewed as personal misrepresentation, if not downright lying; egotistical people often feel entitled to a disproportionate share of deference, status, and resources; ego-defensive reactions, such as anger and aggression, are often aversive to other people; and people seem to believe that people should not enjoy the fruits of successes that they have not legitimately earned. Together, these factors lead people to react negatively to displays of egotism, thereby affecting the course of interactions and relationships.

Relational Illusions

One particularly interesting manifestation of egotism involves the tendency for people to see not only themselves but also their partners and relationships in an unrealistically positive light. In general, people tend to rate their partners more positively than is warranted and think that the relational difficulties that plague other people's relationships are less likely to happen to their own (Helgeson, 1994; Murray & Holmes, 1997; Murray, Holmes, & Griffin, 1996).

Although these kinds of positive illusions are well-documented, the mechanisms behind them are not clear. Most discussions of relationship illusions have suggested that they serve to maintain a sense of felt security, commitment, and relationship stability in the face of the inherent ups and downs of close relationships (Murray, 1999; Murray & Holmes, 2000). In support of this notion, positive illusions are linked to relationship satisfaction and stability (Murray & Holmes, 1997; Murray et al., 1996).

However, simply because illusions have positive relational consequences does not necessarily mean that they are motivated by a desire for felt security or commitment. In fact, it might be argued that a sense of relational security is higher if one perceives one's partner as fallibly human (and, thus, with a smaller range of relational options) than if one idealizes the partner. Furthermore, the quest for felt security may actually undermine satisfaction in the long run because it blinds people to relational difficulties when they are still small enough to be solved. If these beliefs are, in fact, illusions, it is difficult to see any long-term benefit of misperceiving the nature of one's relationship or partner. It is perfectly feasible to be in love with and committed to someone whom one does not overidealize and to face relationships with a realistic judgment of their difficulty and fragility, thereby reducing the likelihood of being blindsided by problems in the future. People who hold positive illusions of their partners and relationships may be happier and more committed at the moment (because they are slower to see problems on the horizon), but the jury is still out regarding what happens when the weight of evidence sends one's positive relational illusions crashing to the ground.

An alternative view is that positive relationship illusions arise from the more general egotistic tendency to construe the world in self-serving ways. Given the importance of significant others to people's self-concepts, believing that one is in a close relationship with an undesirable partner undermines one's own self-image. Thus, we may overestimate the positivity of our partners and relationships for the same reason that we overestimate our own qualities.

Overly positive views of one's partner may also reflect a self-presentational tactic designed to convince other people of one's own positive qualities. To the extent that people's choices of romantic or marital partners reflect on them personally, it is generally in their best interests that other people perceive their partners positively (Leary & Miller, 2000). Research indicates that people work to boost the public images of people with whom they are associated, even when the association is tenuous or superficial (Finch & Cialdini, 1989). Viewed in this way, so-called positive illusions may serve as much to manage other people's impressions of oneself as to allay one's personal concerns about the partner.

In brief, the tendency for people to idealize their romantic partners may stem as much from their egotistical inclinations to perceive themselves positively or to convey positive impressions of themselves to others as from their desire to feel secure in the relationship. This is not to deny that positive illusions may have positive effects on relationships or that they do not arise from the desire for security but rather to suggest that more research is needed on the processes that underlie such illusions.

SELF-REFLECTION AND SELF-RUMINATION

Unlike animals without the capacity for self-reflection, human beings invest a great deal of cognitive activity thinking about themselves. Although much theory and research has examined the antecedents and consequences of self-attention (e.g., Carver, Lawrence, & Scheier, 1996; Carver & Scheier, 1981; Duval & Wicklund, 1972), work in this area has tended to focus on internal cognitive and affective processes (e.g., self-regulation, self-knowledge, and self-conscious emotions), and interpersonal relationships have taken a back seat.

More than 30 years of research has shown that self-focused attention increases the likelihood that people will behave consistently with their personal standards and values (Duval & Wicklund, 1972). To the extent that people tend to hold prosocial rather than antisocial values, self-awareness thus should lead to more positive responses toward other people. Furthermore, the possession of a self allows human beings to think consciously about how they should best respond to other people's problems and misfortunes, as well as how to deal with particularly difficult social exchanges. In these ways, the self facilitates interpersonal interaction and benefits relationships.

However, research suggests that, although some self-relevant thought is undoubtedly useful in making informed decisions, planning for the future, and dealing with other people, much of it involves unnecessary rumination. People often think about themselves when doing so serves no useful purpose and may even be counterproductive. Furthermore, self-focused thinking can have negative consequences for people's interactions and relationships.

Self-preoccupation may take many forms. Often, it involves thinking about goals and problems in a search for solutions. Martin and Tesser (1989, 1996) suggested that rumination typically arises when goals are disrupted and tends to persist until the goal is achieved or the person finds some way to disengage from it. People may also reflect about their personal characteristics, try to understand or change themselves, or worry about real and imagined future events. People may also direct their attention to covert rehearsals of what they are going to say or do later. Self-preoccupation also occurs when people try to control their own thoughts and feelings, as when a person tries not to think about a traumatic event or feel a particular emotion (Wegner & Erber, 1993). Finally, some preoccupation takes the form of unfocused reminiscing and daydreaming that arise from boredom or lack of stimulation but that are not focused on solving particular problems or planning for the future. Animals that lack a self do not appear to get caught up in the reflection and rumination that characterizes much of human thought.

The relationship between self-reflection and interpersonal behavior is complex because different types of self-relevant thought relate to behavior in different ways. The most general effect of self-thought is to use attention and cognitive resources that are then not available for attending to the social environment. To the extent that people have limited attention capacity, self-preoccupation may interfere with the processing of other information, including information about ongoing social encounters.

First, because effective listening requires attention, people must suspend most of their self-chatter and rumination to be empathic listeners (Nichols, 1995). By implication, then, self-absorption may interfere with responses that require empathy, such as social support, advice-giving, or altruism (Davis, 1994). In addition, people who are self-absorbed during interactions have difficulty devoting sufficient attention to what other people say and do, thereby interfering with memory. Research on the "next-in-line effect" shows that ruminating about what one is going to say when it is one's turn to speak to a group interferes with memory for what other people say (Bond & Omar, 1990; Brenner, 1973). Similarly, feeling conspicuous undermines people's memories for what happens during social encounters (Kimble & Zehr, 1982), presumably because self-thoughts use cognitive resources needed to remember details about the encounter.

Furthermore, because attention capacity is also needed to enact deliberate behavioral choices, being overly preoccupied with oneself may result in a disruption of behavior. Research has shown that excessive rumination interferes with problem-solving and the execution of instrumental behaviors (Nolen-Hoeksema, 1993). In extreme cases, people may be so lost in their thoughts that they are unresponsive to the environment and essentially behaviorally paralyzed.

In addition to whatever effects self-attention has on information processing, inattentiveness may also convey an air of indifference to other people, which can lead to hurt feelings, anger, and breaches in relationships (Leary, Springer, Negel, Ansell, & Evans, 1998; Nichols, 1995). A common complaint among married couples, for example, is that one's partner does not pay adequate attention to what one says (Vangelisti, 1992). People also tend to become bored by those who are excessively self-preoccupied (Leary, Rogers, Canfield, & Coe, 1986), and boring individuals are typically not regarded as desired interactants or relational partners.

On the basis of the studies just cited, we might assume that people who think a great deal about themselves—those whose selves are particularly active—would have particular difficulty focusing on other people. The conclusion is not quite that straightforward, however, because the effects of self-attention on one's capacity to relate to other people depend not only on how much the person is self-focused but also on the content of their self-thoughts. People who think a great deal about themselves may be classified along two dimensions. *Reflection* refers to the tendency to engage in an "intellectual" form of self-awareness aimed toward exploring and understanding oneself, whereas *rumination* refers to the tendency to engage in a "neurotic" form of self-awareness that involves unnecessarily dwelling on past or future events or self-evaluations (Trapnell & Campbell, 1999). Joireman, Parrott, and Hammersla (in press) found that rumination was associated with a lower ability to take other people's perspectives but that reflection was associated with greater perspective-taking.

Most previous research on self-preoccupation has focused on the relationship between cognitive interference and performance either on intellectual, perceptual, or physical tasks or on emotional problems such as anxiety, depression, and shyness. Given that self-absorption has many implications for relationships, more attention should be devoted to the interpersonal consequences of thinking about ourselves.

CONCLUSION

As we have seen, the human self appears to be characterized by natural tendencies that lead people to do the following: (a) differentiate between themselves and others while incorporating some people into their sense of self; (b) egocentrically fail to recognize the egocentricity of their own perceptions; (c) experience changes in self-esteem; (d) respond in egotistical, self-serving ways; and (e) attend to, reflect on, and ruminate about themselves. Aside from their cognitive, motivational, and emotional effects on the individual, each of these features has implications for our relationships with other people. Human behavior and social life would be much different than they are if people did not differentiate themselves from others as they do, appreciated the depth of their own egocentricity, did not experience changes in self-esteem, were not egotistical, and could switch their self-attention on and off at will. These inherent aspects of the self channel people's perceptions, evaluations, emotions, and reactions in particular ways.

Some readers may object that the analysis offered in this chapter places the determinants of relationship events too firmly in the heads (and selves) of individuals rather than in what transpires between them. However, whatever happens when two or more people interact is necessarily constrained by their psychological apparatus, including the cognitive–affective structure that psychologists call the self. To the extent that human behavior is mediated partly by our ability to direct conscious attention toward ourselves and to think about ourselves in complex, symbolic ways, how we respond to one another is necessarily influenced by the properties of the self. The better we understand how the self operates and how its features relate to interpersonal behavior, the more likely we will be to find ways of directing its processes toward improving our relationships with other people.

REFERENCES

Alicke, M. (1985). Global self-evaluation as determined by the desirability and controllability of trait adjectives. *Journal of Personality and Social Psychology, 49,* 1621–1630.

Aron, A., & Aron, E. (1996). Self and self-expansion in relationships. In G. J. O. Fletcher & J. Fitness (Eds.), *Knowledge structures in close relationships: A social psychological perspective* (pp. 325–344). Mahwah, NJ: Erlbaum.

Aron, A., & Aron, E. (2000). Self-expansion motivation and including other in the self. In W. Ickes & S. Duck (Eds.), *The social psychology of personal relationships* (pp. 109–128). New York: Wiley.

Aron, A., Aron, E. N., & Smollan, D. (1992). Inclusion of other in the self scale and the structure of interpersonal closeness. *Journal of Personality and Social Psychology, 63,* 596–612.

Aron, A., Aron, E. N., Tudor, M., & Nelson, G. (1991). Close relationships as including other in the self. *Journal of Personality and Social Psychology, 60,* 241–253.

Aron, A., & Fraley, B. (1999). Relationship closeness as including other in the self: Cognitive underpinnings and measures. *Social Cognition, 17,* 140–160.

Baumeister, R. F. (Ed.). (1993). *Self-esteem: The puzzle of low self-regard.* New York: Plenum.

Baumeister, R. F., Smart, L., & Boden, J. M. (1996). Relation of threatened egotism to violence and aggression: The dark side of high self-esteem. *Psychological Review, 103,* 5–33.

Baumeister, R. F., Tice, D. M., & Hutton, D. G. (1989). Self-presentational motivations and personality differences in self-esteem. *Journal of Personality, 57,* 547–579.

Bazerman, M. H., Curham, J. R., Moore, D. A., & Valley, K. L. (2000). Negotiation. In S. T. Fiske, D. L. Schacter, & C. Zahn-Waxler (Eds.), *Annual review of psychology* (Vol. 51, pp. 279–314). Palo Alto, CA: Annual Reviews.

Blaine, B., & Crocker, J. (1993). Self-esteem and self-serving biases in reactions to positive and negative events: An integrative review. In R. F. Baumeister (Ed.), *Self-esteem: The puzzle of low self-regard* (pp. 55–85). New York: Plenum.

Bond, C. F., Jr., & Omar, A. S. (1990). Social anxiety, state dependence, and the next-in-line effect. *Journal of Experimental Social Psychology, 26,* 185–198.

Bradbury, T. N., & Fincham, F. D. (1992). Attributions and behavior in marital interaction. *Journal of Personality and Social Psychology, 63,* 613–628.

Brawley, L. R. (1984). Unintentional egocentric biases in attribution. *Journal of Sport Psychology, 6,* 264–278.

Brenner, M. (1973). The next-in-line effect. *Journal of Verbal Learning and Verbal Behavior, 12,* 320–323.

Brewer, M. B. (1979). In-group bias in the minimal intergroup situation: A cognitive–motivational analysis. *Psychological Bulletin, 86,* 307–334.

Carver, C. S., Lawrence, J. W., & Scheier, M. F. (1996). A control-process perspective on the origins of affect. In L. L. Martin & A. Tesser (Eds.), *Striving and feeling: Interactions among goals, affect, and self-regulation* (pp. 53–78). Hillsdale, NJ: Erlbaum.

Carver, C. S., & Scheier, M. F. (1981). *Attention and self-regulation: A control theory approach to human behavior.* New York: Springer-Verlag.

Cialdini, R. B., Brown, S. L., Lewis, B. P., Luce, C., & Neuberg, S. L. (1997). Reinterpreting the empathy–altruism relationship: When one into one equals oneness. *Journal of Personality and Social Psychology, 73,* 481–494.

Cooley, C. H. (1902). *Human nature and the social order.* New York: Scribner.

Crowne, D. P., & Marlowe, D. (1964). *The approval motive.* New York: Wiley.

Cupach, W. R., & Spitzberg, B. H. (1998). Obsessive relational intrusion and stalking. In B. H. Spitzberg & W. R. Cupach (Eds.), *The dark side of close relationships* (pp. 233–263). Mahwah, NJ: Erlbaum.

Davis, M. H. (1994). *Empathy: A social psychological approach.* Madison, WI: Brown & Benchmark.

Dittes, J. E. (1959). Attractiveness of group as a function of self-esteem and acceptance by group. *Journal of Abnormal and Social Psychology, 59,* 77–82.

Downey, G., & Feldman, S. I. (1996). Implications of rejection sensitivity for intimate relationships. *Journal of Personality and Social Psychology, 70,* 1327–1343.

Duval, S., & Wicklund, R. A. (1972). *A theory of objective self-awareness.* New York: Academic Press.

Farh, J., Dobbins, G. H., & Cheng, B. (1991). Cultural relativity in action: A comparison of self-rating made by Chinese and U.S. workers. *Personnel Psychology, 44,* 129–147.

Finch, J. F., & Cialdini, R. B. (1989). Another indirect tactic of (self-) image management: Boosting. *Personality and Social Psychology Bulletin, 15,* 222–232.

Fincham, F. D., Beach, S. R., & Baucom, D. H. (1987). Attribution processes in distressed and nondistressed couples: 4. Self-partner attribution differences. *Journal of Personality and Social Psychology, 52,* 739–748.

Fincham, F. D., & Bradbury, T. N. (1993). Marital satisfaction, depression, and attributions: A longitudinal analysis. *Journal of Personality and Social Psychology, 64,* 442–452.

Forsyth, D. R., Berger, R. E., & Mitchell, T. (1981). The effects of self-serving vs. other-serving claims of responsibility on attraction and attributions in groups. *Social Psychology Quarterly, 44,* 59–64.

Forsyth, D. R., & Mitchell, T. (1979). Reactions to others' egocentric claims of responsibility. *Journal of Psychology, 103,* 281–285.

Forsyth, D. R., & Schlenker, B. R. (1977). Attributing the causes of group performance: Effects of performance quality, task importance, and future testing. *Journal of Personality, 45,* 220–236.

Gallup, G. G., Jr., & Suarez, S. D. (1986). Self-awareness and the emergence of mind in humans and other primates. In J. Suls & A. G. Greenwald (Eds.), *Psychological perspectives on the self* (Vol. 3, pp. 3–26). Hillsdale, NJ: Erlbaum.

Geurts, S. A., Buunk, B. P., & Schaufeli, W. B. (1994). Social comparisons and absenteeism: A structural modeling approach. *Journal of Applied Social Psychology, 24,* 1871–1890.

Gilovich, T., Kruger, J., & Savitsky, K. (1999). Everyday egocentrism and everyday personal problems. In R. M. Kowalski & M. R. Leary (Eds.), *The social psychology of emotional and behavioral problems: Interfaces and clinical psychology* (pp. 69–95). Washington, DC: American Psychological Association.

Greenwald, A. G. (1980). The totalitarian ego: Fabrication and revision of personal history. *American Psychologist, 35,* 603–613.

Griffin, D. W., & Ross, L. (1991). Subjective construal, social inference, and human misunderstanding. In M. Zanna (Ed.), *Advances in experimental social psychology* (Vol. 24, pp. 319–359). San Diego, CA: Academic Press.

Hastorf, A., & Cantril, H. (1954). They saw a game: A case study. *Journal of Abnormal and Social Psychology, 49,* 129–134.

Helgeson, V. S. (1994). The effects of self-beliefs and relationship beliefs on adjustment to a relationship stressor. *Personal Relationships, 1,* 241–258.

Hewitt, J., & Goldman, M. (1974). Self-esteem, need for approval, and reactions to personal evaluations. *Journal of Experimental Social Psychology, 10,* 201–210.

Hogg, M. A., & Abrams, D. (1988). *Social identification.* London: Routledge & Kegan Paul.

Horai, J. (1977). Attributional conflict. *Journal of Social Issues, 33,* 88–100.

Hoyle, R. H., Kernis, M. H., Leary, M. R., & Baldwin, M. W. (1999). *Selfhood: Identity, esteem, regulation.* Boulder, CO: Westview Press.

Jacobs, L., Berscheid, E., & Walster, E. (1971). Self-esteem and attraction. *Journal of Personality and Social Psychology, 17,* 84–91.

James, W. (1890). *Principles of psychology.* New York: Dover.

Jarymowicz, M. (1998). Self–we–others schemata and social identifications. In S. Worchel, J. F. Morales, D. Páez, & J. Deschamps (Eds.), *Social identity: International perspectives* (pp. 44–52). London: Sage.

Jaynes, J. (1976). *The origin of consciousness in the breakdown of the bicameral mind.* Boston: Houghton-Mifflin.

Joireman, J. A., Parrott, L., & Hammersla, J. (in press). *Empathy and the self-absorption paradox: Support for distinguishing between self-reflection and self-rumination.* Self and Identity.

Kimble, C. E., & Zehr, H. D. (1982). Self-consciousness, information load, self-presentation, and memory in a social situation. *Journal of Social Psychology, 118,* 39–46.

Kruger, J., & Dunning, D. (1999). Unskilled and unaware of it: Difficulties in recognizing one's own incompetence lead to inflated self-assessments. *Journal of Personality and Social Psychology, 77,* 1121–1134.

Kruger, J., & Gilovich, T. (1999). "Naive cynicism" in everyday theories of responsibility assessment: On biased assumption of bias. *Journal of Personality and Social Psychology, 76,* 743–753.

Larivière, M. A. S., & Simourd, D. J. (2000, August). *Self-esteem and antisocial behavior: A meta-analytic review.* Paper presented at the annual meeting of the American Psychological Association, Washington, DC.

Leary, M. R. (1999). The social and psychological importance of self-esteem. In R. M. Kowalski & M. R. Leary (Eds.), *The social psychology of emotional and behavioral problems: Interfaces of social and clinical psychology* (pp. 197–221). Washington, DC: American Psychological Association.

Leary, M. R., & Baumeister, R. F. (2000). The nature and function of self-esteem: Sociometer theory. In M. Zanna (Ed.), *Advances in experimental social psychology* (Vol. 32, pp. 1–62). San Diego, CA: Academic Press.

Leary, M. R., Bednarski, R., Hammon, D., & Duncan, T. (1997). Blowhards, snobs, and narcissists: Interpersonal reactions to excessive egotism. In R. M. Kowalski (Ed.), *Aversive interpersonal behaviors* (pp. 111–131). New York: Plenum.

Leary, M. R., & Downs, D. L. (1995). Interpersonal functions of the self-esteem motive: The self-esteem system as a sociometer. In M. Kernis (Ed.), *Efficacy, agency, and self-esteem* (pp. 123–144). New York: Plenum.

Leary, M. R., & Forsyth, D. R. (1987). Attributions of responsibility for collective endeavors. In C. Hendrick (Ed.), *Review of personality and social psychology: Vol. 8. Group processes* (pp. 167–188). Newbury Park, CA: Sage.

Leary, M. R., & Kowalski, R. M. (1993). The Interaction Anxiousness scale: Construct and criterion-related validity. *Journal of Personality Assessment, 61,* 34–47.

Leary, M. R., & Miller, R. S. (2000). Self-presentational perspectives on personal relationships. In W. Ickes & S. Duck (Eds.), *The social psychology of personal relationships* (pp. 129–155). West Sussex, England: Wiley.

Leary, M. R., Rogers, P. A., Canfield, R. W., & Coe, C. (1986). Boredom in interpersonal encounters: Antecedents and social implications. *Journal of Personality and Social Psychology, 51,* 968–975.

Leary, M. R., Schreindorfer, L. S., & Haupt, A. L. (1995). The role of self-esteem in emotional and behavioral problems: Why is low self-esteem dysfunctional? *Journal of Social and Clinical Psychology, 14,* 297–314.

Leary, M. R., Springer, C., Negel, L., Ansell, E., & Evans, K. (1998). The causes, phenomenology, and consequences of hurt feelings. *Journal of Personality and Social Psychology, 74,* 1225–1237.

Leary, M. R., Tambor, E. S., Terdal, S. K., & Downs, D. L. (1995). Self-esteem as an interpersonal monitor: The sociometer hypothesis. *Journal of Personality and Social Psychology, 68,* 518–530.

Levy, S. R., Ayduk, O., & Downey, G. (2001). The role of rejection-sensitivity in people's relationships with significant others and valued social groups. In M. R. Leary (Ed.), *Interpersonal rejection* (pp. 251–289). New York: Oxford University Press.

Lewis, M., & Brooks-Gunn, J. (1979). *Social cognition and the acquisition of self.* New York: Plenum.

MacDonald, G., & Holmes, J. G. (1999, April). *Self-esteem and relationship conflict.* Paper presented at the conference of the Midwestern Psychological Association, Chicago.

Martin, L. L., & Tesser, A. (1989). Toward a motivational and structural theory of ruminative thought. In J. S. Uleman & J. A. Bargh (Eds.), *Unintended thought* (pp. 306–326). New York: Guilford.

Martin, L. L., & Tesser, A. (1996). Ruminative thoughts. In R. S. Wyer Jr. (Ed.), *Advances in social cognition* (Vol. 9, pp. 1–48). Hillsdale, NJ: Erlbaum.

Maslow, A. H. (1967). A theory of metamotivation: The biological rooting of the value-life. *Journal of Humanistic Psychology, 7,* 93–127.

Mead, G. H. (1934). *Mind, self, and society.* Chicago: University of Chicago Press.

Miller, R. S., & Schlenker, B. R. (1985). Egotism in group members: Public and private attributions of responsibility for group performances. *Social Psychology Quarterly, 48,* 85–89.

Moya, M. (1998). Social identity and interpersonal relationships. In S. Worchel, J. F. Morales, D. Páez, & J. Deschamps (Eds.), *Social identity: International perspectives* (pp. 154–165). London: Sage.

Murphy, C. M., Meyer, S., & O'Leary, K. P. (1994). Dependency characteristics of partner assaultive men. *Journal of Abnormal Psychology, 103,* 729–735.

Murray, S. L. (1999). The quest for conviction: Motivated cognition in romantic relationships. *Psychological Inquiry, 10,* 23–34.

Murray, S. L., & Holmes, J. G. (1997). A leap of faith? Illusions in romantic relationships. *Personality and Social Psychology Bulletin, 23,* 586–604.

Murray, S. L., & Holmes, J. G. (2000). Seeing the self through a partner's eyes: Why self-doubts turn into relationship insecurities. In A. Tesser, R. B. Felson, & J. Suls (Eds.), *Psychological perspectives on self and identity* (pp. 173–197). Washington, DC: American Psychological Association.

Murray, S. L., Holmes, J. G., & Griffin, D. W. (1996). The benefits of positive illusions: Idealization and the construction of satisfaction in close relationships. *Journal of Personality and Social Psychology, 70,* 79–98.

Murray, S. L., Holmes, J. G., MacDonald, G., & Ellsworth, P. (1998). Through the looking glass darkly? When self-doubts turn into relationship insecurities. *Journal of Personality and Social Psychology, 75,* 1459–1480.

Nichols, M. P. (1995). *The lost art of listening.* New York: Guilford.

Nolen-Hoeksema, S. (1993). Sex differences in control of depression. In D. M. Wegner & J. W. Pennebaker (Eds.), *Handbook of mental control* (pp. 306–324). Englewood Cliffs, NJ: Prentice-Hall.

Oakes, P. J., Haslam, S. A., & Turner, J. C. (1994). *Stereotyping and social reality.* Oxford, England: Blackwell.

Pleban, R., & Tesser, A. (1981). The effects of relevance and quality of another's performance on interpersonal closeness. *Social Psychology Quarterly, 44,* 278–285.

Ross, M., & Sicoly, F. (1979). Egocentric biases in availability and attribution. *Journal of Personality and Social Psychology, 37,* 322–336.

Salovey, P., & Rodin, J. (1991). Provoking jealousy and envy: Domain relevance and self-esteem threat. *Journal of Social and Clinical Psychology, 10,* 395–413.

Schlenker, B. R., & Leary, M. R. (1982). Audiences' reactions to self-enhancing, self-denigrating, accurate, and modest self-presentations. *Journal of Experimental Social Psychology, 18,* 89–104.

Schlenker, B. R., & Miller, R. S. (1977). Egocentrism in groups: Self-serving biases or logical information processing? *Journal of Personality and Social Psychology, 35,* 755–764.

Schneider, D. J. (1969). Tactical self-presentation after success and failure. *Journal of Personality and Social Psychology, 13,* 262–268.

Shaw, M. E., & Breed, G. R. (1970). Effects of attribution of responsibility for negative events on behavior in small groups. *Sociometry, 33,* 382–393.

Suchner, R. W., & Jackson, D. (1976). Responsibility and status: A causal or only a spurious relationship? *Sociometry, 39,* 243–256.

Swann, W. B., Jr., De La Ronde, C., & Hixon, J. G. (1994). Authenticity and positive strivings in marriage and courtship. *Journal of Personality and Social Psychology, 66,* 857–869.

Swann, W. B., Jr., Hixon, J. G., & De La Ronde, C. (1992). Embracing the bitter "truth": Negative self-concepts and marital commitment. *Psychological Science, 3,* 118–121.

Tajfel, H. (1981). *Human groups and social categories: Studies in social psychology.* Cambridge: England: Cambridge University Press.

Taylor, S. E., & Brown, J. D. (1988). Illusion and well-being: A social psychological perspective on mental health. *Psychological Bulletin, 103,* 193–210.

Tesser, A. (1984). Self-evaluation maintenance processes: Implications for relationships and for development. In J. C. Masters & K. Yarkin-Levin (Eds.), *Boundary areas in psychology: Social and developmental psychology* (pp. 271–299). New York: Academic Press.

Tesser, A. (1988). Toward a self-evaluation maintenance model of social behavior. In L. Berkowitz (Ed.), *Advances in experimental social psychology* (Vol. 21, pp. 181–227). San Diego, CA: Academic Press.

Tesser, A., & Campbell, J. (1983). Self-definition and self-evaluation maintenance. In J. Suls & A. G. Greenwald (Eds.), *Social psychological perspectives on the self* (Vol. 2). Hillsdale, NJ: Erlbaum.

Tesser, A., Campbell, J., & Smith, M. (1984). Friendship choice and performance: Self-evaluation maintenance in children. *Journal of Personality and Social Psychology, 46,* 561–574.

Tesser, A., & Smith, J. (1980). Some effects of friendship and task relevance on helping: You don't always help the one you like. *Journal of Experimental Social Psychology, 16,* 582–590.

Thompson, L., & Loewenstein, G. (1992). Egocentric interpretations of fairness and interpersonal conflict. *Organizational Behavior and Human Decision Processes, 51,* 179–197.

Trapnell, P. D., & Campbell, J. D. (1999). Private self-consciousness and the five-factor model of personality: Distinguishing rumination from reflection. *Journal of Personality and Social Psychology, 76,* 284–304.

Turner, J. C., Hogg, M. A., Oakes, P. J., Reicher, S. D., & Wetherell, M. S. (1987). *Rediscovering the social group: A self-categorization theory.* Oxford, England: Basil Blackwell.

Vallone, R. P., Ross, L., & Lepper, M. R. (1985). The hostile media phenomenon: Biased perception and perceptions of media bias in coverage of the Beirut massacre. *Journal of Personality and Social Psychology, 49,* 577–585.

Vangelisti, A. L. (1992). Communication problems in committed relationships:

An attributional analysis. In J. H. Harvey, T. L. Orbach, & A. L. Weber (Eds.), *Attribution, accounts, and close relationships* (pp. 144–164). New York: Springer-Verlag.

VanYperen, N. W., & Buunk, B. P. (1991). Sex role attitudes, social comparison, and satisfaction with relationships. *Social Psychology Quarterly, 54,* 169–180.

Walster, E. (1965). The effect of self-esteem on romantic liking. *Journal of Experimental Social Psychology, 1,* 184–197.

Walster, E., Walster, G. W., & Berscheid, E. (1978). *Equity: Theory and research.* Boston: Allyn & Bacon.

Watson, D., & Friend, R. (1969). Measurement of social–evaluative anxiety. *Journal of Consulting and Clinical Psychology, 33,* 448–457.

Wegner, D. M. (1980). The self in prosocial action. In D. M. Wegner & R. R. Vallacher (Eds.), *The self in social psychology* (pp. 131–157). New York: Oxford University Press.

Wegner, D. M., & Erber, R. (1993). Social foundations of mental control. In D. M. Wegner & J. W. Pennebaker (Eds.), *Handbook of mental control* (pp. 36–56). Englewood Cliffs, NJ: Prentice-Hall.

White, G. (1981). Some correlates of romantic jealousy. *Journal of Personality, 49,* 129–147.

Wolosin, R. J., Sherman, S. J., & Till, A. (1973). Effects of cooperation and competition on responsibility attribution after success and failure. *Journal of Experimental Social Psychology, 9,* 220–235.

6

DISTINCTIVENESS AND THE DEFINITION OF COLLECTIVE SELF: A TRIPARTITE MODEL

RUSSELL SPEARS, JOLANDA JETTEN, AND DAAN SCHEEPERS

Distinctiveness lies at the heart of self-definition in many senses (Brewer, 1991; Frable, 1993; Snyder & Fromkin, 1980; Tajfel & Turner, 1986; Vignoles, Chryssochoou, & Breakwell, 2000). Simply to define self implies distinctiveness from others, and this notion is the basis of the Cartesian notion of selfhood that grounds much Western philosophy: the independent, unique, preformed "subject" (Geertz, 1979). If embodiment gives the individual self a head (and body) start in the distinctiveness stakes, however, groups often have to make themselves distinctive. This chapter is concerned with the collective self and the problems of creating or maintaining a distinctive group identity in a social context. Our approach rests on the central assumption, derived from social identity theory (SIT), that we have and aspire to collective identities (that are distinct from the personal self) that distinguish us from other groups. Moreover,

We thank Marilynn Brewer, Geoffrey Leonardelli, Michael Schmitt, Vivian Vignoles, and particularly the editors, Diederik Stapel and Abraham Tesser, for their insightful comments on an earlier draft of this chapter.

although SIT talks of a motivation to achieve "positive group distinctiveness," we argue this distinctiveness motive is not reducible to enhancement concerns. However, this is only the start. There are many puzzles about group distinctiveness that have not always inspired faith in the precision of the available theory. We propose an integrated model of distinctiveness processes in an attempt to resolve some of the contradictions surrounding these issues.

A few decades of intergroup research and many more centuries of history show that group identity is very important to people and, in many contexts and at many times, no less important than individual identity (Spears, 2001). This is reflected in intergroup differentiation and discrimination, which often make little sense without the concept of collective identity (Tajfel & Turner, 1986). What is the role of group distinctiveness in explaining such behavior? Consider the following examples of intergroup discrimination that populate the textbooks: bigotry by Ku Klux Klan members directed at Black people, rivalry between neighboring college sports teams, and discrimination in "minimal groups" (groups in which people are categorized in the laboratory according to a trivial criterion, where members have no vested interests or even knowledge of fellow group members). In the first example, a feature of the discrimination is that it reflects differences, at least as these are all too readily perceived by the racists. By contrast, the groups in the second example are typically characterized by their similarity. And what do we make of discrimination in minimal groups in which there is little basis for either group difference or similarity? One thing that these examples share is that distinctiveness principles (among others) have been used to explain them. In short, both the presence of group distinctiveness and its absence have been used to account for differentiation and discrimination between groups (see Jetten, Spears, & Manstead, 1999).

The skeptical observer might then ponder whether distinctiveness processes really have much to tell about group differentiation that is not contradictory, circular, or post hoc. We claim that they do and that available theories such as SIT, self-categorization theory (SCT), and interdependence theories all present answers at least to parts of this puzzle.[1] What is needed is a framework that integrates the different explanatory principles of relevance, provides a theoretical vocabulary designed to recognize and distinguish different distinctiveness processes, and specifies the underlying motivational and cognitive principles and appropriate domains of application. This is the aim of this chapter.

---

[1]Although Brewer's (1991) Optimal Distinctiveness Theory might seem relevant here, this theory addresses a different form of distinctiveness (based on relative group size rather than on difference in group content). We address these differences in the discussion.

THEORETICAL FRAMEWORK: A TRIPARTITE INTEGRATION OF DISTINCTIVENESS EFFECTS (TIDE)

With the above aims in mind, we propose that there are actually three forms of distinctiveness process—what we call creative, reactive, and reflective distinctiveness—that together explain the patterns of intergroup differentiation found in the group distinctiveness literature. The model therefore aims to distinguish types of distinctiveness-based differentiation[2] and to specify conditions under which the explanatory principles implicated in these three forms will apply. The framework contains two classes of elements (inputs and functions or principles); the combination of inputs from the social context ("social reality") provides information about group distinctiveness ("input distinctiveness") that activates certain psychological principles or functions to produce the three characteristic forms of distinctiveness process (see Table 6.1).

We delineate three relevant forms of input distinctiveness provided by the social context. First, information concerning group distinctiveness may be essentially absent or indeterminate, a state often associated with group formation or the early stages of group life. However, it can also apply to existing groups involved in social comparisons with new outgroups, or comparison on new dimensions, where there is uncertainty about relative group distinctiveness. Second, the context can provide information suggesting similarity with a relevant comparison group. Third, the context can provide information suggesting difference from a relevant outgroup. Although we distinguish between these last two cases, in reality they form a continuum representing degrees of (perceived) similarity or difference.

Reactions to these classes of inputs can be understood in terms of three basic principles or functions (which are independent from the classes of input). An *identity* function addresses the definition of the collective self and is concerned with ensuring that the group is (positively) distinct from other comparison groups (Tajfel & Turner, 1986). A second function, *instrumental*, is premised on a group identity already being defined, distinct, and in place. It is instrumental because it relates to goals that can be achieved using this identity and deriving from interests or aims associated with the group. A third factor, the *reality* principle, simply relates to perceptions of the group identity as being distinctive based on evidence of input distinctiveness. As we show, this corresponds closely to the notion of "fit" or "metacontrast" detailed within SCT. We refer to the identity and instrumental principles as "functions" because they implicate a motivation: a striving for an end state, namely an identity or a goal, respectively.

---

[2]Intergroup differentiation is the central outcome or dependent variable of interest here, of which (behavioral) discrimination is just one specific form (and the only form available in the minimal group paradigm).

TABLE 6.1
A Tripartite Integration of Distinctiveness Effects (TIDE)

Social reality/ Input distinctiveness	Principles/ Functions	Relevant theory	Distinctiveness process	Moderators	Effect
Unknown	Identity	SIT	Creative distinctiveness	(identification prototypicality, group type, etc.)	Intergroup differentiation/ingroup bias
Similar groups	Identity	SIT (SCT)	Reactive distinctiveness		
Different groups	Reality	SCT	Reflective distinctiveness (reality-based)		
	Instrumental	CT/Interdependence	Reflective distinctiveness (instrumental)		

The reality principle is less clearly motivated in this way, being more perceptual or descriptive of reality, although self theorists have proposed that the related goals of accuracy and verification can form the basis of motives associated with the self (e.g., Sedikides, 1993). We now indicate how these functions or principles combine with input distinctiveness to form the three forms of distinctiveness process.

Creative Distinctiveness

Creative distinctiveness refers to a process that occurs when input distinctiveness is unknown, leading to a quest to define a distinctive group identity (implicating the identity function). In other words, we predict that one condition under which group members will differentiate their group from another is when group identity is insufficiently defined, precisely as a means to gain a distinctive group identity. Although not explicitly defined within SIT, the search for meaning in group identity has been touched on by several social identity theorists. In his earlier writing, Tajfel (1969) spoke of the importance of gaining a meaning through social categorization (see also Tajfel, 1981), but this theme somewhat disappeared from view in SIT as research focused more on self-esteem and enhancement motives. The quest for group distinctiveness is also often erroneously reduced to a quest for self-esteem or self-enhancement, but this is a misreading of the theory (see, e.g., Spears, Jetten, & Doosje, 2001; Turner, 1999). Abrams and Hogg (1988), noting the problems with the self-esteem hypothesis, suggest it might be fruitful to more directly consider meaning as a motive. This work has developed into uncertainty reduction (e.g., Hogg & Abrams, 1993; Mullin & Hogg, 1998). In our view this is different, however, from the motivation to gain a meaningful or distinctive identity (see also the empirical section below), and we have found no evidence that uncertainty drives creative distinctiveness (see also Stapel & Tesser, 2000).

Reactive Distinctiveness

Reactive distinctiveness refers to the situation in which group identity is already defined but group distinctiveness is threatened by comparison with a similar outgroup. As with creative distinctiveness, outgroup similarity should motivate the ingroup to differentiate from the outgroup, reflecting the operation of an identity function. Reactive distinctiveness is fundamental to SIT (Tajfel, 1982; Tajfel & Turner, 1979, 1986) and clearly has a motivated character. At first sight, this process seems to be absent from SCT, and it has been suggested as one dimension on which these theories can be distinguished (e.g., Jetten, Spears, & Manstead, 1998). However, we argue below that this reading is somewhat oversimplified and that SCT can also be used to predict reactive distinctiveness as well as to ground reflective distinctiveness.

Reflective Distinctiveness

Reflective distinctiveness has two forms that address the operation of two principles, namely the reality principle and the instrumental function. Both, however, can feed on input distinctiveness when it points toward a clear intergroup difference.

First, group differences can be used as the perceptual basis for intergroup differentiation (the reality principle). In this case differentiation simply reflects the perception of real differences between and similarities within groups. This principle can be traced back to ideas on the accentuation of categorical differences in Tajfel's work (e.g., Tajfel, 1981; Tajfel & Wilkes, 1963; see also Eiser & Stroebe, 1972; McGarty, 1999). The process of accentuation is essentially perceptual or judgmental, although the evaluative dimension can form the basis of a correlated dimension, providing a basis for accentuating differences (Tajfel, 1957, 1981). The categorical differentiation model of Doise and others (Doise, 1978; Doise, Deschamps, & Meyers, 1978) follows a similar principle.

This accentuation principle has been further developed in SCT (Turner, 1985). According to this theory, the perception of group difference will depend on the ratio of intragroup similarities to intergroup similarities and will be enhanced to the extent that the former exceeds the latter. This is captured by the "metacontrast ratio"—a computation of the differences between members of ingroup and outgroup, divided by the differences among the ingroup. The higher this ratio, the greater the "comparative fit" and the greater basis for distinct, distinguishable social categories. High fit is likely to heighten the salience of this basis for social categorization (e.g., in comparison with other social categorizations that have weaker fit). In other words, the greater the difference between groups, the greater the category salience will be and the more likely differentiation will occur (Oakes, 1987).

Cohesion within groups and differences between them can also feed instrumental motives associated with group interests and can exacerbate intergroup discrimination when groups are competing for valued resources. This process has its roots in the work of Lewin (1948/1997), who saw interdependence as the basis of group formation. The realistic group conflict theory of Sherif (1967) locates ingroup bias in the negative interdependence between groups and therefore sees intergroup differences, in the sense of dissimilarity as well as incompatible interests, as a potential source of group discrimination (see also Rokeach, 1960, for a more ideological analysis of difference-based discrimination). Group differences refer here to disparities in valued resources (e.g., wealth, status, prestige).

More recent accounts of group behavior in this Lewinian tradition also explain ingroup bias in terms of the (assumed) bonds of interdependence within the group that in turn may form expectations of reciprocity (e.g., L. Gaertner & Insko, 2000; Lodewijkx, K. Stroebe, & Spears, 2001; Rabbie, Schot, & Visser, 1989). However, differences from the outgroup can be seen as a source of ingroup entitativity (the extent to which a group is perceived as a real entity), which in turn stimulates ingroup bias (L. Gaertner & Schopler, 1998). The intergroup and intragroup forms of interdependence have in common the instrumental function (serving self- or group interest) as the driving principle. Whereas intergroup differentiation best fulfils the identity function, group enhancement and ingroup favoritism may often be sufficient to address the instrumental function of promoting group goals and interests.

These three processes form the core elements of the tripartite model (see Table 6.1). The first thing to note is that this model is able to account for group differentiation (or ingroup bias) resulting from group similarity (reactive distinctiveness), group difference (reflective distinctiveness), and no difference (creative distinctiveness). The problem of course is predicting when each of these will occur and accounting for apparently contradictory findings in the literature. This is one of the central aims of this chapter. The relevance of each of the three forms is in part objectively given by the input distinctiveness present (or absent) in a given social context. The social context may also affect the activation of certain functions. For example, the instrumental function may be prominent in contexts that emphasize intergroup competition for resources or a group goal, and the stage of group life and the nature of the intergroup comparison might influence activation of identity concerns. The relevance of functions may also vary with aspects of the perceiver. Below we consider contextual and person variables that can act as moderating variables influencing the likelihood that one distinctiveness process will dominate. The model does not rule out that different distinctiveness processes can operate in parallel and may be additive, cancel each other out, or even interact. Empirical tests allow us to evaluate these possibilities.

The elements of the three distinctiveness processes are not new and draw heavily on existing theoretical principles. The main aim is to specify the conditions under which these processes occur and to integrate the theoretical principles into a broader model, better able to account for available findings and predict future ones. We can locate the main theoretical contenders hitherto within the tripartite scheme. SIT is relevant to the identity function and to creative and reactive distinctiveness (optimal distinctiveness theory [ODT] has a similar relation). Self-categorization theory is particularly applicable to the reality principle operating within reflective distinctiveness, although we argue below that it can also accommodate reactive distinctiveness. Finally, interdependence approaches are particularly relevant to the form of reflective distinctiveness implicating instrumental motives. We now consider the potential effect of moderators that can influence the operation and extent of these three processes. Many, but not all, of these predictions are addressed in the subsequent empirical evaluation of the model.

Moderators

We consider two person-based factors and one context-based factor as potential moderator variables in the following empirical review. In general, person-based factors (e.g., identification) are likely to amplify the distinctiveness processes, whereas context-based factors may determine which form of distinctiveness process is likely to be set in motion. However, this classification is somewhat artificial in that person-based distinctions will often be the product (the experience of, interaction with) past contexts (Spears, Doosje, & Ellemers, 1999). The differential effects of these moderators should therefore provide further insights in the operation of these processes and independent evidence of their characteristic form. We focus here on group identification, group prototypicality, and "group type," although there doubtless will be other relevant factors that affect the distinctiveness processes.

Group Identification

Group identification is a crucial factor in any analysis of group processes, especially where motivational processes are concerned (Ellemers, Spears, & Doosje, in press; Spears et al., 1999). Some minimal degree of identification with the group is necessary to feel the need to generate distinctiveness (Tajfel & Turner, 1986). It is therefore relevant to the identity functions underlying both creative and reactive distinctiveness. However, in the case of creative distinctiveness, identity is largely unformed, and so variations in identification will be less relevant (but see Doosje, Spears, & Ellemers, in press). Degree of group identification is especially relevant to reactive distinctiveness. We would expect high identifiers to be particularly threatened by the similarity of another outgroup, and greater differentiation among high identifiers should provide evidence that the differentiation is motivated.

Group identification is less likely to affect the form of reflective distinctiveness that simply reflects social reality, as this is a more perceptual process. However, it may well enhance differentiation based on the instrumental form of reflective distinctiveness. People who identify strongly with their group are likely to favor their group more if this helps them to achieve group goals (e.g., winning a competition, maintaining group solidarity).

Prototypicality

Prototypicality is very closely related to group identification, although it is conceptually distinct (Spears, Doosje, & Ellemers, 1997); we define it as the extent to which people define themselves in group terms or as being central to the group on group-defining attributes. On the whole we would expect it to have effects similar to those of group identification. In particular we would expect those people who define themselves as central to the group to feel more threatened by the distinctiveness threat (reactive distinctiveness), based on the identity function. Prototypical group members should also feel more implicated by the instrumental form of reflective distinctiveness. For example, they may feel inclined to assume a more central or even leadership role in working toward group goals. In these cases, we would expect greater differentiation from prototypical group members under conditions of similarity (when identity concerns are central), but also under conditions of group difference (when instrumental concerns are evident), paralleling the case for identification. Prototypical group members might also perceive greater group difference than those who are actually more peripheral in the direction of the outgroup as a result of the reality principle (for them the outgroup *is* further away).

Prototypicality raises an interesting question in the case of creative distinctiveness, namely where evidence of group difference is not yet established. Logically speaking there should be little basis by which to establish prototypicality under these conditions (as for identification). Perceptions of oneself as prototypical may therefore best be considered as a means by which people already define the group as meaningful and thus distinct. On this basis, however, those who see themselves as less prototypical may actually be more motivated to display group differentiation as a means to attain the group distinctiveness they currently lack.

Group "Type"

The third critical moderator we consider concerns the nature of the group and the implications this may have for the functions and principles. There has been a recurring distinction in group research between groups based on interpersonal bonds (the classic group dynamics or Lewinian notion of the group as an interdependent unit), and the group defined in terms of a shared identity or social category membership (the social identity or self-categorization notion of the group). This dates back to the distinction that Durkheim (1893/1993) introduced between organic and mechanical solidarity (groups based on interdependence or similarity, respectively). More recently this has been crystallized in a distinction between "common bond" versus "common identity" groups (Prentice, Miller, & Lightdale, 1994; see also Moreland, 1987; Turner, 1982; Wilder & Simon, 1998). We should clarify some of our reservations about distinguishing two fundamentally different "types" of group. According to self-categorization principles, a prerequisite for all groups is that they share a common identity at some level. However, for some groups this group identity will be defined more in terms of the common bonds that comprise it. This interpretation fits well with the findings of Prentice et al. (1994), who were unable to distinguish common identity and common bond groups in terms of attachment to the group or to its members, respectively, especially for common bond groups. We suspect that most groups can best be considered as having these two components, with interpersonal bonds being more or less important or "group defining." For example, psychology students can often be considered a common identity group defined by their study major. However, in many situations this group will be defined by its members in terms of a network of friends and acquaintances, be it in the classroom or the café.

The relative weight given to these two elements may form an important distinction in the present context. We propose that the identity function may be especially important to groups defined primarily in terms of their "common identity." Where group identity is not yet known, it is especially important for group members to discover or create the shared basis of identity (creative distinctiveness). Similarly, the threat to group distinctiveness from a similar outgroup may be particularly acute for groups that define themselves in terms of a common identity and when this common identity is shown to differ little from the outgroup (reactive distinctiveness).

Groups defined primarily by common bonds (internal structure, interdependence), on the other hand, may be particularly suited to the pursuit of group goals and interests implicating the instrumental function. This should activate the instrumental form of reflective distinctiveness. That is, where group goals or interests are at stake, common bond groups may use evidence of intergroup difference as a basis for ingroup bias to further group goals and interests. Common bonds emphasize mutual interests (common fate, interdependence) and the means of furthering these interests (by working together as an interdependent unit).

It follows from this that emphasizing either the common identity of the group or the common bonds among group members may tip the balance in favor of the identity function (creative and reactive distinctiveness) or the instrumental function (reflective distinctiveness), respectively. One important additional contextual moderator that we consider in this regard is the visibility of group members. If we can see other group members and interact with them, this is likely to reinforce interpersonal bonds and strengthen this component of group definition. If we cannot see, or do not even (yet) know the people who make up the group, as is the case in many minimal group situations, then a group definition based on common bonds is less likely and the common identity group definition may prevail. Without any personal knowledge of fellow group members, all that members have in common is their group identity. This is consistent with research suggesting that the anonymity of ingroups and outgroups can actually exacerbate intergroup differentiation by depersonalizing perception and focusing attention on group identity (Reicher, Spears, & Postmes, 1995; Spears, 1995; Spears & Lea, 1994). We propose that, other things being equal, anonymity will tend to favor a common identity group definition and therefore forms of distinctiveness based on the identity function (creative and reactive distinctiveness). Identifiability of group members, and interaction among them, will shift the balance toward a common bond group definition and distinctiveness based in the instrumental form of reflective distinctiveness, at least where there are group interests at stake.

Illustrative Empirical Evidence

The next step is to evaluate empirical evidence for this integrative model. We consider some illustrative evidence for these three forms from our own research rather than attempt an exhaustive review of the literature. We then consider research that addresses the distinction between these forms where they appear to conflict or make conflicting predictions. As well as distinguishing the forms of distinctiveness, we attempt to provide evidence that distinctiveness, rather than self-enhancement, is the motivation for differentiation.

Creative Distinctiveness: The Search for Meaning and Identity in Groups

To study creative distinctiveness, we turned to the minimal group paradigm—a context in which the self is implicated in group membership, but where there is little a priori basis to distinguish between the groups in terms of difference or self-interest (Tajfel, Flament, Billig, & Bundy, 1971). In the first study we attempted to manipulate the central construct of the presence or absence of a meaningful and distinct group identity (Spears, Jetten, Arend, Van Norren, & Postmes, 2001). Participants were categorized on the basis of preference for paintings (Tajfel et al., 1971). To manipulate the presence of group distinctiveness, in one condition we informed participants that their preference tended to be associated with either extroversion or introversion, with the reverse being true of members of the other category. In the other condition, no such extra information was given (the classic "minimal" condition). In this way we provided a more meaningful and distinct basis for categorization than the basic minimal condition.

To assess evidence of intergroup differentiation, we used the Tajfel reward matrices, in which respondents are asked to choose between a range of paired numbers that represent rewards (symbolic points or money) that would be allocated to a member of the ingroup and a member of the outgroup (not to the group or the self, to rule out self-interest). We also measured evaluations of the two groups on evaluative trait ratings. As predicted, we found greater ingroup bias on both evaluative ratings and reward matrices in the minimal or meaningless condition, and no significant bias when a meaningful identity was added.

In a later study we attempted to replicate this finding and rule out some alternative explanations. One possibility was that knowing that outgroup members were either extroverted or introverted may have individuated them; individuation of the outgroup has been known to attenuate outgroup discrimination (Wilder, 1978). This study ruled out the individuation interpretation, although the effects of meaning on ingroup bias were more complicated here (see Spears, Jetten, Arend, et al., 2001). However, we did obtain evidence that when groups were perceived as less meaningful, they displayed more ingroup bias on evaluative ratings, particularly for those participants who rated themselves as low on group prototypicality. This is consistent with the idea that those people who lack a clear identity are most motivated to differentiate, supporting the argument that differentiation provides a meaningful identity.

To summarize, these studies provide some initial evidence for a process of creative distinctiveness whereby group members who lack a distinctive or meaningful group identity try to create one through a process of intergroup differentiation on available indices. Note that neither of these studies provided any evidence that uncertainty reduction motives could account for the differentiation (meaning and group distinctiveness are more than the absence of uncertainty).

Reactive Distinctiveness: Protecting and Maintaining Group Distinctiveness

Once group identity has been formed, the identity function does not disappear. Distinctive group identity has to be protected and preserved, and this distinctiveness can be brought into question by social comparison with groups that are very similar on relevant dimensions to the ingroup. Unlike the case of creative distinctiveness, there is already considerable support in the literature for reactive distinctiveness (see e.g., Hornsey & Hogg, 2000; Jetten et al., 1999, for recent reviews). Two ways of investigating this is to confront groups with evidence of the similarity of outgroup norms or to provide information about the distance between and relative distribution of groups on a given dimension (Jetten et al., 1999).

Jetten, Spears, and Manstead (1996; Study 2) provided feedback about the nature of group norms concerning reward allocation behavior using the Tajfel matrices. This adapted the minimal group paradigm such that participants received feedback about the reward allocation strategies of other group members. This feedback revealed bias in favor of the ingroup or fairness, for either ingroup and outgroup, resulting in four combinations of ingroup and outgroup behavior, two of which were distinctive (ingroup discriminatory, outgroup fair; ingroup fair, outgroup discriminatory) and two of which were similar (both groups fair or both groups discriminatory). In this study we used an existing social categorization with a history of competitive social comparisons (students from the University of Amsterdam vs. Free University students). The similarity of group norms led to greater discrimination and differentiation on reward allocations and evaluative measures, especially for the condition in which both norms were discriminatory.

Studies that threaten group distinctiveness by displaying high levels of overlap between ingroup and outgroup distributions on a relevant comparison dimension also show evidence of enhanced intergroup differentiation (e.g., Jetten, Spears, & Manstead, 1997, in press; Pickett & Brewer, 2001). However, the evidence suggests that group identification and prototypicality moderate reactive distinctiveness (Jetten et al., 1997; Jetten et al., in press). These studies show that high identifiers (Jetten et al., in press) and prototypical group members (Jetten et al., 1997) are most likely to respond to a distinctiveness threat with differentiation on available measures.

These studies also provide indirect evidence for the motivated character of reactive distinctiveness. More direct evidence that reactive distinctiveness is a motivated process was presented in a study designed to assess the evidence for motivation more directly. In this experiment (Fransen, 2000), the researcher confronted University of Amsterdam students with the possibility of a merger of their university with another institution in Amsterdam. This information was designed as a form of distinctiveness threat. She also measured identification with the university beforehand, predicting that primarily those who identified strongly with their group would be affected by the distinctiveness threat and motivated to differentiate their group.

One feature of motivations that distinguishes them from cognitions is that they persist and grow until satisfied (Gollwitzer & Moskowitz, 1996; Kuhl, 1986). The critical manipulation used in the Fransen (2000) study to test for a motivational process was the thwarting of the opportunity to express some level of the reactive distinctiveness. Her prediction was that this motivation should intensify when blocked. For half the participants, the computer "crashed" during a crucial phase of the experiment in which the participants were to give their views on the planned merger. In fact, this crash was preprogrammed and designed to frustrate participants motivated to express opposition to the plans. Consistent with a motivational process, high identifiers who had been thwarted in giving their views devoted more time to distinguishing their university on both positive and negative attributes than did other participants, resulting in a two-way interaction. This finding provides evidence of the motivational basis of reactive distinctiveness. The fact that this occurred for negatively distinguishing features indicates that distinctiveness rather than self-enhancement motives are critical here (see Spears, Doosje, & Ellemers, 1999).

Reflective Distinctiveness: Differentiation Based on Differences Between Groups

What is the evidence for reflective distinctiveness based on the reality principle? Several studies provide evidence that input distinctiveness can underlie differentiation between groups (Doise, 1978; Hensley & Duval, 1976; Mummendey & Schreiber, 1984; Rokeach, 1960; see Jetten, Spears, & Manstead, 1999, for a review). We provide illustrative evidence for this from one study (Jetten, Spears, & Manstead, 1996; Study 1) identical in design to the earlier one in which norms of reward allocation behavior were manipulated (Jetten et al., 1996; Study 2). In this case, however, minimal rather than natural groups were used. Once again the feedback revealed evidence of distinctive groups (incongruent group norms) or indistinct groups (congruent norms).

The pattern of differentiation on the reward allocations for these minimal groups was quite different than that for the established groups using the same paradigm. Whereas the groups tended to maximize rewards to both ingroup and outgroup in the indistinct conditions, they tended to maximize less relative to a differentiation strategy in the distinctive norm conditions. We interpreted this as evidence that the distinctive groups exhibited reflective distinctiveness. This pattern was repeated on measures of group identification and group prototypicality: Group members in the distinct norm conditions scored higher on these measures. In other words, on several measures differentiation responses reflected group differences and were not triggered by similarity for these minimal groups.

This study (Jetten et al., 1996; Study 1) raises several questions, however. Whether these responses were the product of the reality principle or more instrumental concerns is not clear. Differences between the ingroup and the outgroup provided a perceptual basis for group differentiation in line with accentuation and self-categorization principles. They also provided the entitativity that may influence perceived interdependence and mutual reciprocation. These are not mutually exclusive possibilities, and group difference may have increased perceptions of interdependence within the group. In the following section, we provide further evidence for the operation of the reality principle and the instrumental function.

A second question the study (Jetten et al., 1996; Study 1) raises is why the difference between these fairly minimal groups, rather than intergroup similarity, should lead to greater differentiation, as might be predicted by reactive (or even creative) distinctiveness. The similarity of the design of this study to the earlier one using natural groups suggests that the group identity of the minimal groups was not sufficiently established (or group identification high enough) to evoke reactive distinctiveness. Why did creative distinctiveness not prevail for the indistinct groups? Remember that these groups were not entirely minimal; information about group behavior was provided by the normative feedback. As we saw in the section on creative distinctiveness, some meaning to group identity may well be enough to fulfill the identity function associated with creative distinctiveness. This may have tipped the balance in favor of reflective distinctiveness processes. However, the general issue of specifying "which distinctiveness process will dominate when" is a central task of TIDE. We now consider contexts where these processes are likely to conflict and compete.

DISTINCTIVENESS PROCESSES IN CONFLICT: WHICH, WHEN, AND WHY?

We now try to assess evidence of competition between the distinctiveness processes and the ability of the model to account for these in terms of moderating variables. Creative and reactive distinctiveness are unlikely to compete because these refer to different phases of group life, different forms of input distinctiveness, and both predict the same outcomes deriving from the same identity function (differentiation based on distinctiveness threat). The main conflicts between principles are likely to arise between reflective distinctiveness and these two other forms where the effects of input distinctiveness on differentiation are predicted to be opposite. We therefore consider the tension between reflective distinctiveness and creative and reactive distinctiveness, respectively.

Creative Versus Reflective Distinctiveness

A study using the same paradigm developed in the earlier section on creative distinctiveness makes clear the tension between creative and reflective distinctiveness processes (Arend, 1999; Spears, Jetten, et al., 2001). In this study, participants were informed (vs. not informed) that painter preference associated with group membership was related to personality. In this case, the presence of a meaningful ingroup identity (rather than its absence) led to enhanced differentiation, both on the reward matrices and evaluative measures. Moreover, this effect was mediated by measures of group entitativity. This pattern suggests that the relation between input distinctiveness and differentiation is more consistent with reflective distinctiveness than creative distinctiveness in this case.

This finding is consistent with other recent research by L. Gaertner and Schopler (1998), indicating that ingroup favoritism can reflect perceptions of group entitativity. L. Gaertner and Schopler (1998) manipulated entitativity differently to input distinctiveness, namely in terms of the degree of interaction and interdependence within the group. This study provides a good example of the instrumental function leading to ingroup bias. However, we would argue that entitativity and group distinctiveness are closely related (Spears et al., in press). Consistent with the operation of an instrumental function, these authors found more evidence of ingroup favoritism than of intergroup differentiation per se (that would serve an identity function).

The obvious questions then arise: How do we distinguish when the presence of group distinctiveness rather than the lack of distinctiveness will lead to differentiation, and specifically how do we explain the divergence of the Arend (1999) study from the earlier ones in the same paradigm? One approach outlined in our model is to consider moderators that might tip the balance in favor of one process. Considering the role of identification does not help, as this would be predicted to motivate both creative and reflective distinctiveness. The nature of the group may be more critical in this case. The group Gaertner and Schopler investigated was clearly an interacting task group that may evoke interdependence concerns and the instrumental function associated with reflective distinctiveness. The Arend (1999) study is less clear-cut, however, being similar in design and manipulation to the earlier studies of creative distinctiveness by Spears, Jetten, et al. (2001; Study 1 and 2). One critical factor was that the Arend (1999) study was conducted in the class, over two sessions, whereas the earlier studies were run in separate cubicles. As outlined in the theoretical section, the visibility of other group members (and copresence over sessions) may make salient a more common-bond representation of the group, emphasizing the interdependence concerns associated with the instrumental function. Anonymity, on the other hand, should emphasize a common identity representation of the group, which may in turn trigger creative distinctiveness aimed at defining the group identity (the identity function).

In a social influence study we tested the hypothesis that anonymity would enhance group effects for common identity groups but that visibility would enhance group effects for common-bond groups (Postmes & Spears, 1999; Spears & Postmes, 1998). This idea received clear support. Anonymity increased group effects (social influence, entitativity) for common identity groups but undermined them for common bond groups. In short, it is possible that anonymity in the first two studies in the meaning paradigm strengthened the construal of the group context in terms of a shared group identity. By contrast, the visible interaction between group members in the Arend (1999) study may have focused people on a different basis for group identity, one based more on interpersonal bonds. However, this analysis needs to be subjected to experimental scrutiny in a paradigm designed to assess group differentiation (Spears, Jetten, et al., 2001).

A more direct means of distinguishing between the identity and instrumental functions associated with creative and reflective distinctiveness, respectively, is desirable, however. We addressed this in two studies in which we attempted to manipulate the critical conditions favorable to these two functions (Scheepers, Spears, Doosje, & Manstead, 2000). In these studies we categorized participants into minimal groups on the basis of their painter preference.

In Study 1 all participants had the opportunity to differentiate their group by evaluating abstract artworks of varying color combinations made by ingroup and outgroups. As predicted, the minimal groups showed reliable levels of intergroup differentiation in favor of ingroup products, in keeping with creative distinctiveness. However, only those who had received feedback that their group would engage in a competition with another group showed enhanced levels of ingroup bias on subsequent group product ratings, reflecting an instrumental function (negative interdependence at the intergroup level). For those without such a goal, ingroup bias actually reduced. This finding is consistent with the operation of a motivational dimension to this process: Once the goal has been achieved (group distinctiveness), the striving disappears (Gollwitzer & Moskowitz, 1996; Kuhl, 1986).

In a second study we manipulated the opportunity to engage in intergroup differentiation between participants and group competition as independent factors in a 2 × 2 design. We found a crossover interaction on measures of differentiation. High levels of differentiation were obtained in the condition with no prior differentiation opportunity and no group goal (the "meaningless" cell), consistent with creative distinctiveness. Differentiation was also high in the condition in which both a prior differentiation opportunity and a competitive group goal were present, supporting the instrumental form of reflective distinctiveness. Note that the prior differentiation seems to be a prerequisite for subsequent differentiation when the goal is present. This is consistent with the argument that intergroup difference facilitates differentiation for the instrumental form of reflective distinctiveness: Having a clear group identity seems to be a prerequisite for group-based action.

To summarize, distinctiveness can sometimes form the goal of differentiation (creative) and sometimes the basis for it (reflective). In cases in which instrumental motives are present (e.g., furthering goals), a distinctive group identity will be functional for achieving group goals. Cases in which an ideological or some other value basis to group difference is present may also be associated with motivated differentiation (e.g., Rokeach, 1960), rather than merely reflecting perception of group differences (the reality principle). Although these group differences may reflect material conflicts of interests (invoking realistic conflict), the identity function is not absent here but forms the bedrock on which instrumental concerns are grounded (as in Study 2 of Scheepers et al., 2000, discussed earlier). Few would dispute that "differences" between Protestants and Catholics in Northern Ireland and between Palestinians and Jews in Israel are the sources of motivated differentiation based on conflicts of interests. At the same time, these religious differences are invested with such emotion and meaning that identity and instrumental concerns become closely bound up with each other and difficult to separate (Spears et al., in press).

Reactive Versus Reflective Distinctiveness

Just as we have the problem of deciding when creative or reflective distinctiveness will produce more differentiation, we have the same sort of dilemma between reflective and reactive distinctiveness. Here we propose two general types of solution to this issue. First, the range or degree of distinctiveness may determine which process will predominate, and this may be further moderated by degree of group identification. We have addressed this possibility more fully elsewhere (see Jetten, Spears, & Manstead, 1998, 1999, in press). The basic argument and finding is that increasing outgroup similarity enhances differentiation in line with the reactive distinctiveness principle for high identifiers (Jetten et al., in press). However, the relation between input distinctiveness will be more curvilinear for low identifiers (Jetten et al., in press) and on dimensions of less importance to the group (Jetten et al., 1998), because intergroup similarity will undermine the intergroup distinction, shifting self-categorization to a superordinate level for those less committed to the group or dimension. Reflective distinctiveness based on the reality principle should therefore predominate for low identifiers (Dywer, 2000; Jetten et al., in press).

A second resolution between the opposite pulls of reactive and (reality-based) reflective distinctiveness can be sought at the level of theoretical integration between social identity and self-categorization principles. We propose that SCT is not just a theory of reflective distinctiveness but, like SIT, is also able to account for reactive distinctiveness. It is important here to distinguish the overall level of metacontrast, which is indeed a function of intergroup difference (the reality principle basis of reflective distinctiveness), from the tendency to differentiate governed by the shifts of prototypicality within the group. A measure of the most prototypical position is determined by calculating the mean difference between any given position in the ingroup and the available outgroup positions, divided by the mean difference between this position and the ingroup positions (Turner, 1985). It transpires that the nearer two groups are (keeping the internal distribution of the ingroup constant), the more extreme the most prototypical position within the group, contrasted away from the outgroup, becomes.

To illustrate this, take the following three distributions on any underlying dimension (e.g., attitude positions) representing the relative positions of ingroup members (i) and outgroup members (o):

Example 1:	-4	-3	-2	-1	0	1	2	3	4
	o1	o2	o3				i1	i2	i3
Example 2:	-4	-3	-2	-1	0	1	2	3	4
		o1	o2	o3			i1	i2	i3
Example 3:	-4	-3	-2	-1	0	1	2	3	4
				o1	o2	o3/i1	i2	i3

If we calculate the prototypicality of the ingroup positions (see Table 6.2), we can see that the prototypicality of the most extreme ingroup member (i3) becomes more prototypical within the group the closer the outgroup gets. Setting the prototypicality of the most prototypical group member to 1 (and calibrating less-prototypical positions as a proportion of this metric) makes this clearer by giving a measure of the relative prototypicality of group members. The most prototypical position is the middle person (i2) when the outgroup is distant (Example 1), but when the outgroup is close (Example 3), the most extreme group member (i3) becomes just as prototypical as the middle group member (i2). Thus, despite the higher level of metacontrast in the distant condition (as reflected in the high absolute prototypicality scores), the tendency to differentiate between the groups by conforming to the prototypical position should increase the closer or more similar the groups become. We obtained empirical support for this analysis within a group polarization paradigm in which we manipulated intergroup distance (Spears & Schippers, 1999). Differentiation from the outgroup was strongest in the small-distance condition.

In sum, SCT appears able to combine elements of both reflective and

TABLE 6.2
Absolute and Relative Prototypicality (P_{abs}, P_{rel}) of the Three Ingroup Members as a Function of Outgroup Distance

| | Outgroup distance | | | | | |
| | Example 1 (distant) | | Example 2 (intermediate) | | Example 3 (close) | |
Ingroup member	P_{abs}	P_{rel}	P_{abs}	P_{rel}	P_{abs}	P_{rel}
i1	3.33	0.55	2.00	0.50	0.66	0.33
i2	6.00	1.00	4.00	1.00	2.00	1.00
i3	4.66	0.77	3.33	0.83	2.00	1.00

reactive distinctiveness. This analysis also helps to clarify the differences between these two forms of distinctiveness and differentiation. One form is based on real, gross, group differences (a perceptual process based on social reality), whereas the other is an impetus to preserve group distinctiveness when it is threatened (reactive distinctiveness). Both reflective and reactive distinctiveness processes may occur in parallel; reflective distinctiveness acknowledges the reality of group differences, whereas reactive distinctiveness protects the group from being assimilated into similar outgroups.

CONCLUSION

We have presented evidence for three types of distinctiveness processes that play a role in differentiation of the collective self or ingroup from other groups. This tripartite distinction is necessary, to explain the variability and the apparent contradictions in the relation between input distinctiveness and differentiation. As should be clear, the distinctiveness–differentiation relation is complex. However, it is possible to see some sort of pattern emerging, making it possible to integrate different forms of distinctiveness within a common framework.

In proposing a motivational basis to group distinctiveness grounded in SIT, our approach has affinities with the ODT of Brewer (1991; see also Pickett & Brewer, 2001). We do not see our integrative approach as contradictory or competing with ODT. However, it is appropriate to indicate differences and points of contact. First, optimal distinctiveness theory is primarily concerned with group preference, based on the relative size or frequency of the ingroup compared to other groups in the frame of reference. Brewer (1991) also posited a drive state underlying the need for group distinctiveness. Like SIT and the present integration, an identity function is central to optimal distinctiveness theory. Although we agree that group distinctiveness has motivational bases, we have not made strong assumptions about the degree to which these reflect universal drives or psychological needs. Motivations are obviously located within individuals rather than groups, but conceptualizing them as drives tends to undermine the element of codetermination of these motives by context and social factors. The motivations we discuss have a group basis in that they may stem from the concerns of collective identity and group priorities as much as from individual needs. Having said this, optimal distinctiveness theory makes many similar predictions regarding distinctiveness in terms of relative group size as we do for relative group similarity, and for closely related reasons (Pickett & Brewer, 2001).

In this chapter we have drawn heavily from social identity and self-categorization theories. However, we hope that we have added some insight to these theories and shown that there is less contradiction and more unity here than is sometimes supposed. Distinctiveness motives, although not neglected in the social identity tradition, have unfortunately received less attention than self-esteem or enhancement motives. We hope our research helps to restore the ascendancy of distinctiveness, which we regard as more central to this theoretical tradition and truer to its social character (before we can talk of a positive social identity, we need a distinctive social identity). One criticism sometimes leveled at SIT, perhaps more in the conference corridor or in anonymous reviews than in more visible forums, is that it can account for almost any finding. When we look back at the work of Tajfel, this impression may not be so surprising because we can find in his writing the roots of all three forms of distinctiveness discussed in this chapter. Whether this is good or bad is open to debate. However, in making explicit the different forms of the distinctiveness process, we hope that we have specified at least when and why group distinctiveness may result in its diverse effects.

REFERENCES

Abrams, D., & Hogg, M. A. (1988). Comments on the motivational status of self-esteem in social identity and intergroup discrimination. *European Journal of Social Psychology, 18*, 317–334.

Arend, S. (1999). *The effects of perceived group meaningfulness on ingroup bias*. Unpublished honors thesis, University of Queensland, Brisbane, Australia.

Brewer, M. B. (1991). The social self: On being the same and different at the same time. *Personality and Social Psychology Bulletin, 17*, 475–482.

Doise, W. (1978). *Groups and individuals: Explanations in social psychology*. Cambridge, England: Cambridge University Press.

Doise, W., Deschamps, J. C., & Meyers, G. (1978). The accentuation of intra-category similarities. In H. Tajfel (Ed.), *Differentiation between social groups* (pp. 159–168). London: Academic Press.

Doosje, B., Spears, R., & Ellemers, N. (in press). Social identity as both cause and effect: The development of group identification in response to anticipated and actual changes in the intergroup status hierarchy. *British Journal of Social Psychology*.

Durkheim, E. (1993). *The division of labour in society*. London: Macmillan. (Original work published 1893)

Dwyer, L. (2000). *Distinctiveness based differentiation: The role of group identification*. Unpublished honors dissertation, University of Queensland, Brisbane, Australia.

Eiser, J. R., & Stroebe, W. (1972). *Categorization and social judgment*. London: Academic Press.

Ellemers, N., Spears, R., & Doosje, B. (in press). Self and social identity. *Annual Review of Psychology*.

Frable, D. E. S. (1993). Being and feeling unique: Statistical deviance and psychological marginality. *Journal of Personality, 61*, 85–110.

Fransen, J. (2000). *Reactions to group distinctiveness threat: Cognitive or motivational?* Unpublished masters thesis, University of Amsterdam, the Netherlands.

Gaertner, L., & Insko, C. A. (2000). Intergroup discrimination in the minimal group paradigm: Categorization, reciprocation or fear? *Journal of Personality and Social Psychology, 79*, 77–94.

Gaertner, L., & Schopler, J. (1998). Perceived group entitativity and intergroup bias: An interconnection of self and others. *European Journal of Social Psychology, 28*, 963–980.

Geertz, C. (1979). From the native's point of view: On the nature of anthropological understanding. In P. Rabinow & W. M. Sullivan (Eds.), *Interpretive social science* (pp. 225–241). Berkeley: University of California Press.

Gollwitzer, P. M., & Moskowitz, G. B. (1996). Goal effects on action and cognition. In E. T. Higgins & A. W. Kruglanski (Eds.), *Social psychology: Handbook of basic principles* (pp. 361–399). New York: Guilford.

Hensley, V., & Duval, S. (1976). Some perceptual determinants of perceived similarity, liking and correctness. *Journal of Personality and Social Psychology, 34*, 159–168.

Hogg, M. A., & Abrams, D. (1993). Towards a single-process uncertainty-reduction model of social motivation in groups. In M. A. Hogg & D. Abrams (Eds.), *Group motivation: Social psychological perspectives* (pp. 173–190). New York: Harvester Wheatsheaf.

Hornsey, M. J., & Hogg, M. A. (2000). Assimilation and diversity: An integrative model of subgroup relations. *Personality and Social Psychology Review, 4*, 143–156.

Jetten, J., Spears, R., & Manstead, A. S. R. (1996). Intergroup norms and intergroup discrimination: Distinctive self-categorization and social identity effects. *Journal of Personality and Social Psychology, 71*, 1222–1233.

Jetten, J., Spears, R., & Manstead, A. S. R. (1997). Distinctiveness threat and prototypicality: Combined effects on intergroup discrimination and collective self-esteem. *European Journal of Social Psychology, 27*, 635–657.

Jetten, J., Spears, R., & Manstead, A. S. R. (1998). Intergroup similarity and group variability: The effects of group distinctiveness on the expression of ingroup bias. *Journal of Personality and Social Psychology, 74*, 1481–1492.

Jetten, J., Spears, R., & Manstead, A. S. R. (1999). Group distinctiveness and intergroup discrimination. In N. Ellemers, R. Spears, & B. Doosje (Eds.), *Social identity: Context, commitment, content* (pp. 107–126). Oxford, England: Blackwell.

Jetten, J., Spears, R., & Manstead, A. S. R. (in press). Similarity as a source of discrimination: The role of group identification. *European Journal of Social Psychology*.

Kuhl, J. (1986). Motivation and information processing: A new look at decision making, dynamic change and action control. In R. M. Sorrentino & E. T. Higgins (Eds.), *Handbook of motivation and cognition* (Vol. 1, pp. 404–434). New York: Guilford.

Lewin, K. (Ed.). (1997). *Resolving social conflicts: Selected papers on group dynamics.* Washington, DC: American Psychological Association. (Original work published 1948)

Lodewijkx, H., Stroebe, K., & Spears, R. (2001). *Do unto others as they do unto you: Bounded and unbounded reciprocation versus social identification as determinants of ingroup favoritism among minimal groups.* Unpublished manuscript, University of Utrecht, the Netherlands.

McGarty, C. (1999). *Categorization in social psychology.* London: Sage.

Moreland, R. L. (1987). The formation of small groups. *Review of Personality and Social Psychology, 8,* 80–110.

Mullin, B., & Hogg, M. A. (1998). Dimensions of subjective uncertainty in social identification and minimal group discrimination. *British Journal of Social Psychology, 37,* 345–365.

Mummendey, A., & Schreiber, H. J. (1984). "Different" just means "better": Some obvious and some hidden pathways to ingroup favoritism. *British Journal of Social Psychology, 23,* 363–368.

Oakes, P. J. (1987). The salience of social categories. In J. C. Turner, M. A. Hogg, P. J. Oakes, S. D. Reicher, & M. S. Wetherell (Eds.), *Rediscovering the social group: A self-categorization theory* (pp. 117–141). Oxford, England: Basil Blackwell.

Pickett, C. L., & Brewer, M. B. (2001). Assimilation and differentiation needs as motivational determinants of perceived ingroup and outgroup homogeneity. *Journal of Experimental Social Psychology, 37,* 341–348.

Postmes, T., & Spears, R. (1999). *Anonymity in computer-mediated communication: Different groups have different SIDE effects.* University of Amsterdam, the Netherlands. Manuscript submitted for publication.

Prentice, D., Miller, D., & Lightdale, J. (1994). Asymmetries in attachments to groups and to their members: Distinguishing between common identity and common-bond groups. *Personality and Social Psychology Bulletin, 20,* 484–493.

Rabbie, J. M., Schot, J. C., & Visser, L. (1989). Social identity theory: A conceptual and empirical critique from the perspective of a behavioural interaction model. *European Journal of Social Psychology, 19,* 171–202.

Reicher, S. D., Spears, R., & Postmes, T. (1995). A social identity model of deindividuation phenomena. *European Review of Social Psychology, 6,* 161–198.

Rokeach, M. (1960). *The open and closed mind.* New York: Basic Books.

Scheepers, D., Spears, R., Doosje, B., & Manstead, A. S. R. (2000). *Integrating identity and instrumental approaches to intergroup differentiation: Different contexts, different motives.* Manuscript submitted for publication.

Sedikides, C. (1993). Assessment, enhancement, and verification determinants of the self-evaluation process. *Journal of Personality and Social Psychology, 65,* 317–338.

Sherif, M. (1967). *Group conflict and co-operation: Their social psychology.* London: Routledge.

Snyder, C. R., & Fromkin, H. L. (1980). *Uniqueness: The human pursuit of difference.* New York: Plenum Press.

Spears, R. (1995). Isolating the collective self. In A. Oosterwegel & R. Wicklund (Eds.), *The self in European and North American culture: Development and processes* (NATO ASI series, Vol. 84, pp. 309–322). Amsterdam: Kluwer.

Spears, R. (2001). The interaction between the individual and the collective self: Self-categorization in context. In C. Sedikides & M. B. Brewer (Eds.), *Individual self, relational self, and collective self: Partners, opponents or strangers?* (pp. 171–198). Philadelphia, PA: Psychology Press.

Spears, R., Doosje, B., & Ellemers, N. (1997). Self-stereotyping in the face of threats to group status and distinctiveness: The role of group identification. *Personality and Social Psychology Bulletin, 23,* 538–553.

Spears, R., Doosje, B., & Ellemers, N. (1999). Commitment and the context of social perception. In N. Ellemers, R. Spears, & B. Doosje (Eds.), *Social identity: Context, commitment, content* (pp. 59–83). Oxford, England: Blackwell.

Spears, R., Jetten, J., Arend, S., Van Norren, M., & Postmes, T. (2001). *Meaning and differentiation in minimal groups: Creative and reflective distinctiveness.* Manuscript in preparation, University of Amsterdam/University of Queensland.

Spears, R., Jetten, J., & Doosje, B. (2001). The (il)legitimacy of ingroup bias: From social reality to social resistance. In J. Jost & B. Major (Eds.), *The psychology of legitimacy: Emerging perspectives on ideology, justice, and intergroup relations* (pp. 332–362). New York: Cambridge University Press.

Spears, R., & Lea, M. (1994). Panacea or panopticon? The hidden power in computer-mediated communication. *Communication Research, 21,* 427–459.

Spears, R., & Postmes, T. (1998, October). *Anonymity in computer-mediated communication: Different groups have different SIDE effects.* "Social Psychology on the Web" symposium conducted at the meeting of the Society for Experimental Social Psychology, Lexington, KY.

Spears, R., Scheepers, D., Jetten, J., Doosje, B., Ellemers, N., & Postmes, T. (in press). Group homogeneity, entitativity and social identity: Dealing with/in social structure. In V. Yzerbyt, C. M. Judd, & O. Corneille (Eds.), *The psychology of group perception: Contributions to the study of homogeneity, entitativity and essentialism.* Philadelphia: Psychology Press.

Spears, R., & Schippers, K. (1999). *When less distance makes more difference: The comparative and normative dimensions of decision polarization in an intergroup context.* Unpublished manuscript, University of Amsterdam, the Netherlands.

Stapel, D. A., & Tesser, A. (2000). *Self-activation increases social comparison.* Unpublished manuscript, Universities of Groningen, Amsterdam.

Tajfel, H. (1957). Value and the perceptual judgment of magnitude. *Psychological Review, 64,* 192–204.

Tajfel, H. (1969). Cognitive aspects of prejudice. *Journal of Social Issues, 25,* 79–97.

Tajfel, H. (1981). *Human groups and social categories.* Cambridge, England: Cambridge University Press.

Tajfel, H. (1982). Social psychology of intergroup relations. *Annual Review of Psychology, 33,* 1–39.

Tajfel, H., Flament, C., Billig, M. G., & Bundy, R. F. (1971). Social categorization and intergroup behaviour. *European Journal of Social Psychology, 1,* 149–177.

Tajfel, H., & Turner, J. C. (1979). An integrative theory of intergroup conflict. In W. G. Austin & S. Worchel (Eds.), *The social psychology of intergroup relations* (pp. 33–48). Monterey, CA: Brooks/Cole.

Tajfel, H., & Turner J. C. (1986). The social identity theory of intergroup behavior. In S. Worchel & W. G. Austin (Eds.), *Psychology of intergroup relations* (pp. 7–24). Chicago: Nelson Hall.

Tajfel, H., & Wilkes, A. L. (1963). Classification and quantitative judgment. *British Journal of Social Psychology, 54,* 101–114.

Turner, J. C. (1982). Towards a cognitive redefinition of the group. In H. Tajfel (Ed.), *Social identity and intergroup relations* (pp. 15–40). Cambridge, England: Cambridge University Press.

Turner, J. C. (1985). Social categorization and the self-concept: A social cognitive theory of group behaviour. In E. J. Lawler (Ed.), *Advances in group processes: Theory and research* (Vol. 2, pp. 77–122). Greenwich, CT: JAI.

Turner, J. C. (1999). Some current issues in research on social identity and self-categorization theories. In N. Ellemers, R. Spears, & B. Doosje (Eds.), *Social identity: Context, commitment, content* (pp. 6–34). Oxford, England: Blackwell.

Vignoles, V. L., Chryssochoou, X., & Breakwell, G. (2000). The distinctiveness principle: Identity, meaning and the bounds of cultural relativity. *Personality and Social Psychology Review, 4,* 337–354.

Wilder, D. A. (1978). Reduction of intergroup discrimination through individuation of the outgroup. *Journal of Personality and Social Psychology, 36,* 1361–1374.

Wilder, D. A., & Simon, A. F. (1998). Categorical and dynamic groups: Implications for social perception and intergroup behavior. In C. Sedikides, J. Schopler, & C. A. Insko (Eds.), *Intergroup cognition and intergroup behavior* (pp. 27–44). Mahwah, NJ: Erlbaum.

7

MODELING THE STRUCTURE OF SELF-KNOWLEDGE AND THE DYNAMICS OF SELF-REGULATION

JAY G. HULL

The ideas outlined in this chapter represent an attempt to build a general theory that can integrate a representation of the structure of the self-concept with psychological processes basic to self-regulation. Given a confusing array of "principles" and "mini-theories" regarding the self, the theory attempts to impose a semblance of conceptual order on a large and somewhat unwieldy theoretical and empirical literature. In addition to lending a certain coherence to this literature, such an approach holds the promise of connecting research on the self to broader issues in social psychology and connecting social psychological research to broader issues in psychology as a field.

This approach involves the development of a formal, mathematical model. Essential aspects of the model are described in this chapter, together with illustrations and arguments for its ability to integrate major findings in the empirical literature on self and a brief overview of some original

The research reported in this chapter was supported in part by a Social Sciences Grant from the Rockefeller Center at Dartmouth College.

research generated to test various aspects of the model. Using dynamic systems software, the principles that constitute the formal model have been implemented as a computer simulation of the self: a sort of Self-Sim, if you will, that is referred to in this chapter as the Interactive Self and Identity System, or ISIS. Although it is conceptually useful and occasionally important to maintain a distinction between the formal theory and the computer simulation based on its principles, these are treated interchangeably here for expository purposes.

Writing such a model is an intellectually bracing experience: It requires that the exact form of any theorized association between two variables be stated explicitly. Equally important, it requires that any theorized null association between two variables also be stated explicitly. Addition of any new variable to the system thus requires a stand on the exact form of that variable's direct, indirect, and nonassociations with all other variables in the system. Associations that seem psychologically plausible in terms of some variables can carry absurd implications in terms of their indirect consequences for other elements in the model. The flip side of such difficulties is that the addition of any new variable instantly yields predictions with respect to the association of that variable and all other variables in the system. If each variable has plausible empirical referents in the form of experimental manipulations or validated measures, one instantly has multiple, testable hypotheses. In many cases, these hypotheses are associated with an existing literature such that the ability of the model to generate predictions consistent with known results becomes an important test of its plausibility. In other cases, the hypotheses generated by the model have not been tested, and in this sense the model can stimulate programmatic research.

The model examined in this chapter has two components that are useful to distinguish: (a) a hierarchical model of the structure of self-knowledge and (b) a dynamic systems model of self-regulatory functions.

INTEGRATION OF STRUCTURE AND FUNCTION

A Structural Model of Self-Knowledge

A central component of this theory involves a structural model of self-knowledge. This structural model consists of a hierarchical representation of knowledge regarding specific behaviors nested beneath (a) knowledge of specific traits, (b) knowledge of relevant social roles, and (c) an evaluative (good–bad) sense of identity. As a hierarchical representation of self-knowledge, this aspect of the model is similar in certain respects to other hierarchical models of self-control (e.g., Carver & Scheier, 1981, 1998; Powers, 1973; Vallacher & Wegner, 1987). The model in this chapter is distinguished from other models by the specific behavior–trait–type–

identity hierarchy it proposes, and it is based on a more general, hierarchical model of the structure of personality traits proposed by Hull, Lehn, & Slone (2001). Whereas alternative models of personality traits (e.g., the five-factor model; see John, 1990) have been repeatedly shown to provide a poor account of trait intercorrelations when tested using structural equation modeling techniques (e.g., Church & Burke, 1994), the hierarchical model proposed by Hull, Lehn, et al. (2001) provided a good fit in both an initial and a replication sample, fit substantially better than a five-factor model, and provided a similar fit in male and female subsamples. The trait-based version of this hierarchical model is depicted in Figure 7.1.

It is important to recognize that the Hull, Lehn, et al. (2001) model is intended as a general model of the structure of personality in the same spirit as other measurement models (e.g., factor models, circumplex models). In addition to arguing for its statistical utility, however, Hull, Lehn, et al. (2001) also provided a rational account of the source of this structure. Specifically, they argued that human social interaction is structured in terms of specific types of relationships that form the basis of three major roles: (a) personal social-interaction roles (those that involve intimacy relations with others; e.g., friendship roles), (b) impersonal social-interaction roles (those that involve status relations with others; e.g., leadership roles), and (c) relatively non-social-interaction roles (those that do not require or necessarily imply specific relations with others; e.g., performance-based work roles). Individual traits are defined as differentially relevant to these relationships and role-types. The hierarchical trait–type–identity structure is thus proposed to have its basis in the essential dimensions of human interaction (see Hogan, 1983, for a related model and argument).

Hull, Lehn, et al. (2001) assumed that covariation of trait reports has its basis in covariation of behaviors, and as such their model serves as a general model of the structure of personality. However, the hierarchical trait–type–identity model can also be viewed as an implicit personality theory. As such, the structural parameters of the model serve as precise predictions about the strength with which individuals make judgments about which specific traits belong together. Using the model in this manner, Hull and Renn (2000) demonstrated that it was superior to a variety of alternative models in its ability to predict the speed with which individuals make trait co-occurrence judgments. Finally, and most important for the present arguments, the hierarchical trait–type–identity model can be viewed as characterizing the structure of self-representations and thus can serve as the basis of self-regulation.

A Dynamic Systems Model of Self-Regulation Processes

As a structural model of self-knowledge, the parameters and associative links depicted in Figure 7.1 can be viewed in terms of the relevance of particular traits to major social roles and the relevance of particular roles to the individual's sense of identity and self-worth. The structure does not change or act. A dynamic systems model proposed by Hull (2000) provided an account of the processes involved in rendering the structural model of self-representations "operational" as a self-regulative system. The variables and their assumed relationships as defined in this model are briefly described.

It is helpful to think of the dynamic model as a set of five interacting systems that serve to operationalize seven theoretical postulates: (a) a Perceptual System (Postulates I, II, and III), (b) an Inference System (Pos-

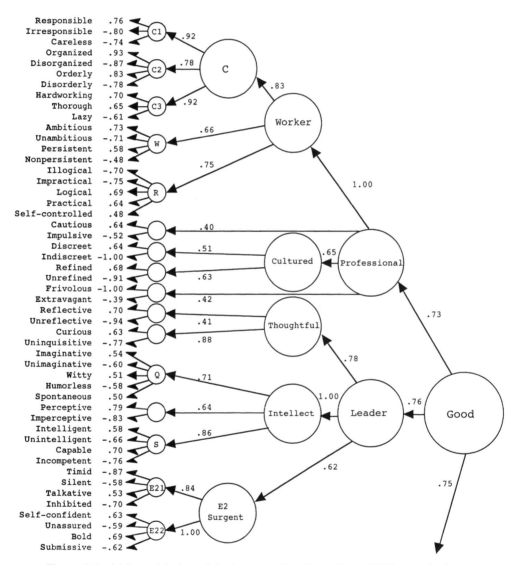

Figure 7.1. A hierarchical model of personality. *Note.* From "A Typological Model of the Structure of Personality," by J. G. Hull, D. A. Lehn, and L. B. Slone, 2001, manuscript submitted for publication. Reprinted with permission.

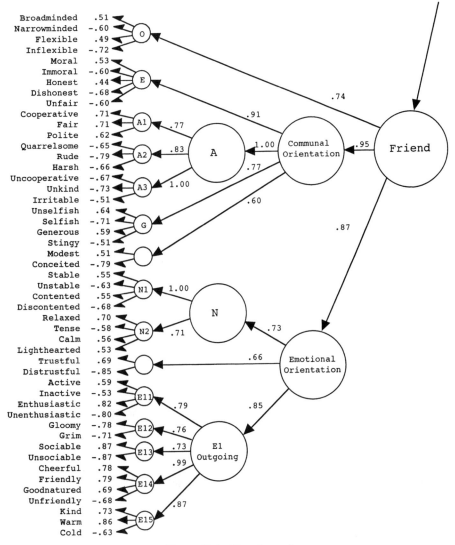

Figure 7.1. (Continued)

tulate IV), (c) a Motivational System (Postulate V), (d) an Affective System (Postulate VI), and (e) a Behavioral Regulation System (Postulate VII). These systems are depicted in Figure 7.2.[1] In ISIS, each postulate is operationalized using a set of definitions and equations. The basic rela-

[1]Not depicted in Figure 7.2, but defined in the set of equations that constitute the model, are four feedback loops that connect (a) Affect to Perception, (b) Behavioral Regulation to Motivation, (c) Behavioral Regulation to Inferences, and (d) Motivation to Inferences. Note that the system as defined is not intended to include all of the causes and effects of the variables that constitute the model. Indeed, some of these variables have no stated causes (in modeling language, they are "exogenous" variables). Rather, the equations that define the system should be interpreted as representing some of the causes and consequences of variables central to the process of self-regulation.

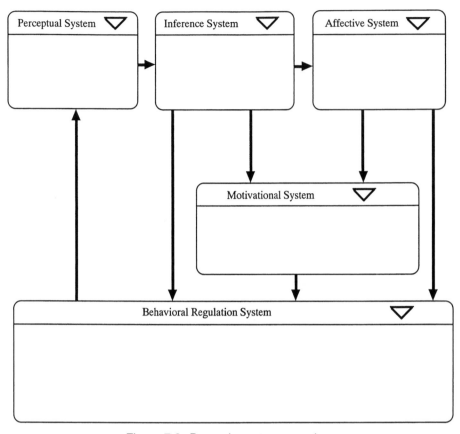

Figure 7.2. Dynamic system overview.

tionships between the system variables as defined by these equations appear in an appendix at the end of this chapter.[2] The trait–type–identity hierarchy depicted in Figure 7.1 is formalized within the dynamic systems model as a hierarchical structure that characterizes both inference and motivational systems defined in the appendix.

[2]The appendix is intended to illustrate the general form of the relations between variables in the model. Some details have been excluded to streamline the presentation (e.g., some variables have maximum caps to avoid infinite values). The actual equations and the dynamic systems program used to implement it with the computer application STELLA can be obtained directly from the author. In the language of STELLA, variables that accumulate and dissipate values over time are represented as "reservoirs" whose values ebb and flow as a function of other variables in the model. The current value of any reservoir in the appendix is defined to be a function of the contribution of "inflow" variables at a discrete point in time (t), "outflow" variables at the same moment in time, and the reservoir's specific accumulation at the point immediately preceding inflow and outflow adjustments (i.e., accumulation at time $t - 1$). Variables that do not accumulate or dissipate values as a function of time simply represent constants or mathematical functions of other variables at a specific moment in time. Interested readers should see Nowak and Vallacher (1998) and Nowak, Vallacher, Tesser, and Borkowski (2000) for other examples of the application of dynamics systems modeling to social psychological processes.

Postulate I: Discrepancy Definition

Overt behavior is postulated to be a function of (a) relatively automatic dispositional tendencies of an individual to respond to a particular situation with a particular response adjusted by (b) more controlled, self-regulatory processes. Automatic behaviors are evoked as a learned disposition to act in a particular manner in the presence of a specific cue that is encoded as self-relevant (see Chartrand & Bargh, chapter 1, this volume). Controlled self-regulatory processes follow from a discrepancy between the resultant perceived behavior and a perceived behavioral standard (Equations 1 and 2).

Postulate II: Discrepancy Perception

Discrepancies affect self-regulation only to the extent that they are perceived as such. Discrepancy perception is postulated to be a function of (a) the size of the discrepancy, (b) attention devoted to it, and (c) the degree to which it is encoded as self-relevant. In addition, perception is biased by the individual's current affective state: Negative affect is postulated to increase and positive affect to decrease the perceived size of the discrepancy (Equation 3). Self-referent encoding is a direct function of self-awareness.

Postulate III: Discrepancy Memory

Perceived discrepancies are maintained in active memory through rehearsal and decay from active memory through forgetting and dismissal as unimportant to the self. The rate at which discrepancy memory decays is a function of affect; the degree to which discrepancies are dismissed as unimportant is a function of the accessibility of stored self-affirming memories (Equations 4–6).

Postulate IV: Inference System

Trait–Type–Identity Hierarchy. Discrepancies that are maintained in memory form the basis of inferences about the self. Trait inferences are drawn to the extent that the behavior in question corresponds to particular trait characteristics. More general inferences are drawn depending on the relevance of the trait to higher order self-constructs (defined in fractional units). Specifically, perceived discrepancies may reflect on the successful enactment of a role to the extent that the particular trait is relevant to the role. Role discrepancies reflect on the general construct of the person as a worthy individual to the extent that enactment of the role is relevant to an evaluative (good–bad) identity (Equations 7–9).

Match-to-Self Subsystem. Inferences about the self are referenced to self-standards. Inferences that are relatively close to such standards (within a latitude of acceptance) are considered a "match"; inferences that are relatively distant from such standards (outside a latitude of acceptance) are considered a "mismatch." Such matches and mismatches exist with respect to each level of the hierarchy described above (traits, role types, and identities; Equations 10a–12b).

Expectancy Violations and Correspondence. Because they constitute a violation of expectancies, mismatches result in a drop in the perceived correspondence of the behavior to the trait in question (Equation 13).

Postulate V: Motivation

Motivation exists with respect to each level of the trait–type–identity hierarchy that serves to structure inferences. The amount of motivation at a particular level is a function of (a) the degree of mismatch at the level in question, (b) the amount of motivation at the immediately superordinate level, (c) the strength of association of sub- and superordinate levels, and (d) negative affect in the form of specific negative emotions. Thus, higher level motivation has a direct influence on lower level motivation as a function of the degree of association between levels (e.g., the relevance of an identity to a particular role; the relevance of a role to a particular trait). Furthermore, negative emotions magnify the degree of motivation that exists at each level (Equations 14–16).

Postulate VI: Affective System

Matches and mismatches have direct implications for positive and negative affect. Mismatches are associated with increased negative affect and matches with increased positive affect as a consequence of concomitant arousal conceived in terms of activation in particular centers in the brain. Changes from baseline positive and negative affect decay over time (Equations 17–23). Attributional labels applied to diffuse positive and negative affective states yield specific positive and negative emotions, respectively (Equations 24 and 25).[3]

---

[3]Of direct relevance to the affective system, it is conceptually important to note that within the model, perceived discrepancies function as cues for reward and punishment. If the perceived discrepancy is referenced to a potential reward, the system is described as regulating with respect to a "positive standard." If it is referenced to a potential punishment, the system is described as regulating with respect to a "negative standard." With respect to the match–mismatch system, matches to positive standards yield anticipated reward, matches to negative standards yield anticipated no-punishment, mismatches to positive standards yield anticipated no-reward, and mismatches to negative standards yield anticipated punishment. These positive and negative standards can be linked to either action or inaction such that regulation can be in the service of increasing or inhibiting behavior. By conceptualizing the specific emotions associated with positive and negative affect as dependent on the activated standard (positive vs. negative) and the state of the system (match vs. mismatch), the result is a fourfold structure of affect (see Higgins, 1997, and Mowrer, 1960, for related arguments; see Russell, 1980, and Feldman Barrett & Russell, 1998, for a related structure of affect): reward-based positive affects, no-reward-based negative affects, no-punishment-based positive affects, and punishment-based negative affects. Within the model, attributions are required to move from these general, diffuse affects to specific emotions (e.g., joy, dejection, tranquility, and anxiety, respectively).

Postulate VII: Behavioral Regulation

Approach–Avoidance. Trait-level motivation yields approach to the extent that the system regards itself as capable of undertaking actions that will reduce the operative discrepancies (i.e., as efficacious). Trait-level motivation yields avoidance to the extent that the system regards itself as incapable of undertaking actions that will reduce operative discrepancies (i.e., as inefficacious; Equation 26).

Judgments of Self-Efficacy. As noted, whether the system engages in approach or avoidance is a function of perceived self-efficacy (see Bandura, 1977, for related arguments). Self-efficacy is itself a function of (a) the size of the match or mismatch, (b) the current affective state, and (c) the accessibility of self-affirming memories. Larger mismatches, greater negative affect, and less-accessible self-affirming memories increase the perception of self-inefficacy and the behavioral choice to avoid. Matches, positive affect, and more-accessible self-affirming memories increase the perception of self-efficacy and the behavioral choice to approach. Finally, changes in self-efficacy have consequences for the perceived relevance of the discrepancy: Perceptions of efficacy result in increased relevance and perceptions of inefficacy result in decreased relevance (Equations 27–29).

Behavioral Self-Regulation. Approach takes the form of (a) increased attention to relevant feedback and (b) enactment of behaviors intended to reduce the perceived discrepancy. Avoidance can take the form of disengagement through decreased attention to feedback (mental or behavioral disengagement) or denial of a mismatch through adjustment of the latitude of acceptance (Equations 30–32).

Effective approach behaviors feed back to reduce the size of the behavioral discrepancy from a behavioral standard (see Postulate I). In addition, they add to the store of self-affirmational memories and boost the automatic dispositional tendencies of the individual to respond to similar situations with similar responses. The latter response is regarded as a learned increment in a baseline response that is subject to extinction (Equations 33–34).

Illustration and Issues

Obviously, the foregoing definition of the dynamics systems model as theoretical postulates is necessarily abstract. As an illustration of these processes, imagine the effects of a supervisor's stare on an employee who is supposed to be working hard, typing a report. Processing the supervisor's stare in terms of its self-relevance is proposed automatically to increase work on the report. In addition to evoking automatic, learned patterns of behavior, the model also assumes that situational cues define behavioral standards against which one's own action can be judged. An essential element in the operation of the model is the discrepancy between one's perceived behavior and this perceived behavioral standard. Thus, in addition to evoking the automatic dispositional tendency to act (e.g., type faster), the cue (stare) can also be processed as implying that one's current behavior is discrepant from the cued behavior. This cued behavior thus serves as a standard against which to judge one's current action. Thus, whereas situational cues may automatically activate a particular level of industrious behavior (e.g., typing faster), perceptions of one's behavior in response to this cue together with perceptions of situationally cued behavioral standards can also yield perceived behavioral discrepancies (e.g., I am not typing fast enough). This will be true to the extent that the individual attends to the behavior-standard discrepancy and processes it as self-relevant. Furthermore, this perception will be biased by the individual's pre-existing affective state. These perceptions activate knowledge in memory that persists and decays over time and forms the basis of (a) trait inferences ("I am not industrious") as a function of the correspondence of the behavior (typing speed) to the trait (industriousness), (b) role inferences ("I am not a good worker") as a function of the relevance of the trait (industriousness) to the role type (Worker), and (c) identity inferences ("I am a bad person") as a function of the relevance of the role type to the general evaluative identity (Good–Bad Person).

Note that to this point, the model is processing behavioral discrepancies. To the extent that the individual is not acting consistently with the behavioral standards implies that the individual is "not industrious" (as in correspondent inference theory; Jones & Davis, 1965). Whether this inference is consistent with the individual's view of self is another matter. The latter concerns the individual's self-knowledge, and it is at this point in the model that trait, type, and identity inferences are compared to trait, type, and identity self-representations, respectively. Comparison of self-inferences to self-representations constitutes one form of a matching-to-standard (or test–operate–test–exit, TOTE; Miller, Galanter, & Pribram, 1960) sequence that I refer to as "matching-to-self."

Note that it is not the case that self is involved whenever matching-to-standard processes are engaged.[4] If the behavioral discrepancy does not exist, is not attended to, or is not encoded as self-relevant, the individual will not make trait–type–identity inferences and ultimately will not engage a matching-to-standard process with respect to a self-knowledge structure. Although the individual may regulate behavior, and this regulation may be based on behavioral discrepancies and TOTE-like sequences, regulation

---

[4]This is in contrast to models in which self-awareness determines whether individuals engage TOTE sequences (Carver & Scheier, 1981, p. 144). According to Miller, Galanter, and Pribram (1960, p. 64), organisms that do not engage TOTE sequences and execute plans are asleep or dead, not non-self-aware. Within the current model, as in our previous models, self-awareness is associated with processing information (in this case, the behavioral discrepancy) in terms of its self-relevance (see Hull & Levy, 1979; Hull, Van Treuren, Ashford, Propsom, & Andrus, 1988).

will not occur with respect to self-representations (and does not constitute self-regulation in its current use).

This matching-to-self process occurs at the trait, type, and identity level. Mismatches at a particular level are associated with motivation at that level. Furthermore, motivation at a superordinate level is transmitted to subordinate levels as a function of relevance. Thus, an industrious mismatch that is sufficient to trigger a Worker mismatch yields industriousness motivation as well as Worker motivation. The Worker motivation boosts industriousness motivation as a function of the relevance of the trait industriousness to the Worker role type. However, Worker motivation boosts motivation to any subordinate trait as a function of the relevance of those traits to the Worker role type. In this way, an industriousness mismatch sufficient to trigger a Worker mismatch yields motivation to become more organized and responsible and not simply more industrious. Furthermore, identity-level mismatches yield motivation to enact alternative role types as a function of their relevance to the individual's general evaluative sense of identity. In this way, industriousness mismatches may actually trigger the system to become more sociable as a consequence of motivating the role of Friend if the individual's sense of identity is sufficiently challenged (mismatched).

All of the relationships within the model are defined using mathematical equations akin to those that appear in the appendix. For the most part, these are linear equations; some are conditionals (e.g., matching or mismatching to self is governed by latitudes of acceptance); some are positively or negatively accelerating curves. Each operationalizes psychological variables with clear empirical referents (e.g., attention, positive affect, negative affect, and self-referent encoding). In this sense, the effects of "manipulations" of these variables on other variables within the system constitute empirically testable hypotheses. One question, then, becomes, How well does the behavior of the system capture the dynamics of self-regulation?

DYNAMIC PROPERTIES OF THE SYSTEM

Self-Regulation With Respect to a Behavioral Standard

A key variable that affects the behavior of the system is the situationally cued behavioral standard. Varying the extremity or salience of situational cues results in automatic behavior to the extent that the system processes the cues as self-relevant and has some baseline disposition (learned behavioral association) to act accordingly (see Postulate I). In the present system, such behavior does not involve discrepancy perception, affect, or self-regulation. On the other hand, if the automatically invoked baseline level of behavior is discrepant from the perceived behavioral standard, a series of reactions occur, some of which appear in Figure 7.3.

Figure 7.3 is a direct product of an ISIS simulation. The x axis represents time, and the y axis represents units for the respective dependent variables. In this simulation, two units of time were allowed to pass before a behavioral standard was primed by a situational cue. Given that this standard was discrepant from the system's automatic behavioral response, it (a) perceives a behavioral discrepancy, (b) infers a trait, (c) experiences negative affect, and (d) increases its behavioral response. As can be seen, all of these reactions are phased in time. Although not depicted, the system also experiences decreased positive affect, increased trait-relevant motivation, and increases in its automatic tendency to behave accordingly in the future. If the system is effective in reducing the size of the perceived discrepancy, negative affect declines, positive affect rebounds, memory of the discrepancy decays, and positive self-memories are stored (but then slowly decay over time). A host of additional processes follow similar curves through time: Judged correspondence of the behavior to the trait and judged relevance of the trait to the larger role identities initially decline and then rebound; focal attention on the discrepancy increases as the sys-

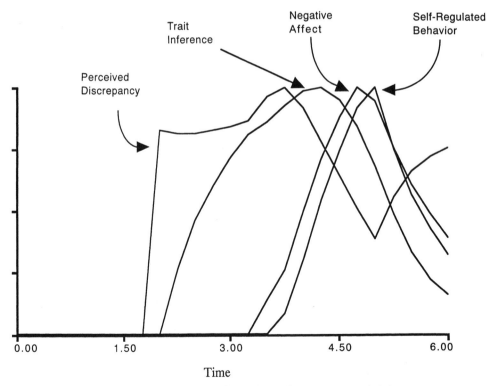

Figure 7.3. Normal self-regulation: Perceived discrepancy, trait inference, affect, and behavior.

tem is approach motivated; and the latitude of what the system is willing to tolerate as a match widens briefly and then narrows with self-regulatory success. Again, all of these changes occur in response to manipulation of a single variable: the extremity of the cued behavioral standard.

It is important to recognize that, characterized as such, the system not only responds but also adapts: Dispositions (which affect automatic behavior) develop as a function of encounters with behavioral standards. Thus, over time, as a consequence of perceiving discrepancies between the behavior signaled by a salient cue and its own actions, the system evolves from automatic baseline responses of zero toward responses that reflect the situational standards of conduct. Conceptually, insofar as these standards reflect the essential form of social relationships and interactions (i.e., major social roles), the dispositionally based behaviors (i.e., personality) are structured accordingly.

Self-Regulatory Collapse

In addition to responding to the perception of a behavioral discrepancy with the systematic evocation of a series of psychological responses, the system also varies in the intensity of its response depending on the size of the perceived discrepancy. As depicted in Figure 7.4, greater discrepancies (25 vs. 15) result in greater motivation and more intense responses. However, this is true only up to a point defined by the perceived self-

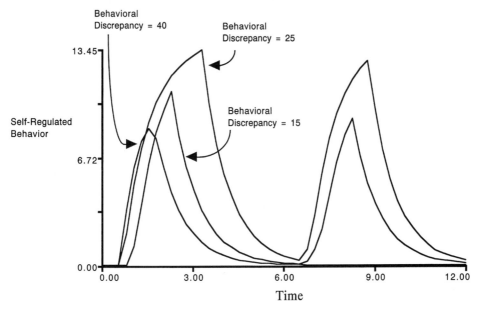

Figure 7.4. Self-regulation and regulatory collapse as a function of discrepancies of varying size.

efficacy of the system. When the system perceives that a discrepancy is so large that it exceeds its capacity to effectively respond, it switches from behavioral engagement to disengagement and avoidance. The result is self-regulatory collapse: Rather than working to reduce the discrepancy, after an initial token effort, work-related acts diminish to zero (see Figure 7.4; behavioral discrepancy = 40). In addition, negative affect asymptotes at maximum, perceived discrepancies decay more slowly from memory (i.e., the system ruminates), and the judged relevance of the specific role type for the system's identity achieves a minimum. Interestingly, with discrepancies of sufficient size, the judged relevance of all role types to the system's identity are reduced, resulting in a system that can plausibly be described as perceiving its "life" (the totality of its role identities) as less "meaningful" (relevant). Such self-regulatory collapse has relevance to the psychological state of depression (see Hull, 2000, for an extended discussion).

System Model as Formal Theory

Obviously, the extremity of a behavioral standard is only one variable in a much larger system. On the one hand, manipulating it provides an elaborate if straightforward illustration of the dynamics of the system and its plausibility as an account of self-regulation. On the other hand, the system itself constitutes a formal mathematical theory of the manner in which various psychological processes associated with processing resultant discrepancies are related to each other and interact. The observed functional relations among these variables constitute the predictions of the theory.

It is interesting in this regard that social psychological theorizing has remained relatively impervious to formal mathematical approaches. Virtually all physical theories are mathematically expressed (as are many psychological theories of nonsocial behavior). Perhaps the perception has been that social psychology cannot yet specify the measurement and manipulation of its variables in a manner amenable to equations. Rather, theories are stated in the form "if x is increased, y will increase" or "for x to increase when y increases, condition z must hold." But that is a mathematical expression. Furthermore, it is the type of expression that characterizes the current model. Thus, the specific units of measurement in the model are to some extent arbitrary: The predictions of the model regarding the effects of "manipulations" of independent variables on dependent variable "measures" exist as functional relationships rather than specific scaled values in conceptually meaningful units.

To illustrate this point, consider the model as a theory of self-awareness. Let us define self-awareness in terms of self-referent encoding (Hull & Levy, 1979). As a consequence of encoding situational cues as self-relevant, self-awareness is associated with the automatic invocation of the dispositional baseline behavior. As a consequence of encoding behavioral discrepancies as self-relevant, self-awareness is associated with the process of deriving inferences about the self on the basis of a behavioral discrepancy and self-regulation.

Such an analysis is consistent with our long-standing account of self-awareness as having its effects by increasing self-referent encoding of cues due to heightened accessibility of self-knowledge (Hull & Levy, 1979; Hull, Van Treuren, Ashford, Propsom, & Andrus, 1988). All of the effects of self-awareness are proposed to follow as a consequence of this effect. Note that this is qualitatively distinct from identifying self-awareness with self-focused attention (e.g., Duval & Wicklund, 1972), self-evaluation (see Wicklund, 1975), greater awareness of internal states (e.g., Gibbons, 1990), or a matching-to-standard TOTE process (e.g., Carver, 1979; Carver & Scheier, 1981). This is not to deny that self-awareness is sometimes associated with matching-to-self processes or self-evaluation, but rather to state that whether it is associated with such a process in any particular situation depends on the nature of the information encoded as self-relevant (in this case, discrepancy information) rather than existing as a defining feature of self-awareness per se (see Hull & Levy, 1979, pp. 757–758).

The present dynamic systems model provides an illustration of this point. Using ISIS, if a moderate standard is set regarding behavioral "industriousness" that is sufficiently discrepant from the baseline dispositional response, self-regulation occurs as detailed earlier. Consider this as the response of a "control" model. If the system's level of self-awareness is increased (i.e., the mathematical value of the system variable Self-Referent Encoding is increased), then compared to the control model, the "heightened self-awareness" version of ISIS shows (a) a larger perceived behavioral discrepancy, (b) increased negative affect, (c) increased motivated industriousness, (d) increased behavioral approach, and (e) heightened subsequent attention to feedback. All of these differential responses occur as a consequence of a manipulation of one variable in the system: its level of self-awareness as self-referent encoding. Indeed, the heightened self-awareness model differs from the control model in other ways as well: (f) the relevance of industriousness to its sense of self becomes lower, (g) its judgment regarding the correspondence of the behavior to the trait of industriousness becomes lower, and (h) its self-efficacy becomes lower. With a standard set at a very high level, the self-aware model is more likely to (i) try to compensate on other dimensions of self or even (j) give up (i.e., experience self-regulatory collapse), subsequently (k) engage in mental disengagement and avoidance, and (l) become more flexible in what it is willing to consider as an acceptable performance. Several of these predicted effects have empirical support (e.g., a, b, d, e, g, k); others do not appear to have been tested (e.g., f, h, i, j, l). Furthermore, virtually all of these effects include time as a dimension of the dependent variable. Thus, it is not only the case that the self-aware version of ISIS experiences a higher level of negative affect as a consequence of the perception that it is not acting in concert with a behavioral standard of performance; it is also the case that it begins experiencing negative affect sooner than the less self-aware system. Similarly, it is not simply the case that a self-aware system facing a very large discrepancy is more likely to give up but rather that it exerts an initial effort more quickly and then gives up sooner and with respect to a discrepancy that is smaller in objective magnitude than the control system. Again, none of these hypotheses appears to have been empirically tested.

The general point, then, is that the model is not simply a computer simulation but rather the mathematical instantiation of a theory of the interrelation of every variable in the system (e.g., positive affect, negative affect, trait inferences, self-efficacy, role identity structure). All predictions regarding the direct and indirect effects of all variables are explicit in the functional equations. This does not mean that the theorized system renders predictions in units that directly correspond to the intensity of specific manipulations or the scale of specific measures. Rather, it means that the effects of increases or decreases in the system variables have clear directional (or null) consequences for all of the remaining variables in the system.

An Integrated Approach to Psychological Theories of the Self

Quite apart from the relevance of the model to empirical literatures regarding specific variables, the model also adopts characteristic patterns of responding that involve the simultaneous invocation of multiple variables. These patterns of responses have parallels in various theories of self. Thus, for example, the theory of Self-Evaluation Maintenance (Tesser, 1988; Tesser & Campbell, 1983) is not a theory about the consequences of a manipulation of a single variable but rather is a characterization of the distinct patterns of response associated with qualitative shifts in psychological processing (social comparison vs. reflection; see Tesser, 2000).

The most obvious pattern discontinuity addressed by the present system involves the break from non-self-regulation to self-regulation as discussed earlier. More than simply characterizing associations between specific variables, then, a self-regulation theory seeks to capture the multifaceted pattern associated with this break. As such, a theory couched in terms of linked equations is extremely economical: In addition to the formally specified direct and indirect associations among the variables, patterns of joint responses to individual manipulations are explicit in the way the system functions or behaves.

In addition to the automatic or self-regulated pattern shift, a second relevant discontinuity involves the break between self-regulation and regulatory collapse. Once again, as the system shifts from regulation to collapse, its responses change qualitatively and not simply quantitatively. Now larger discrepancies do not result in greater motivation and effort; rather, they lead to the opposite: greater avoidance and disattention. Once again, this pattern shift is characteristic of certain theories of self-regulation, most notably the Wortman and Brehm (1975) model of reactance (as self-regulation) and learned helplessness (as regulatory collapse). It is interesting to note that just as in the present model, Wortman and Brehm (1975) identified the key variable governing this break as perceived controllability (here treated as perceived self-efficacy).

A third example of discontinuity involves the break between matches versus mismatches at different levels of the trait–type–identity hierarchy. With linearly increasing discrepancies, such breaks adopt a stair-step function: What initially is a problem with industriousness jumps to being a problem with work, which jumps to an issue of whether one is a good, worthy person. As the problem becomes defined at higher levels, the system engages in qualitatively different actions. Whereas before its efforts were narrowly constrained to boosting work performance, now it may engage in friendly behavior as a means of boosting its sense of identity. In the self literature, this shift in what the system attempts to accomplish with its actions is consistent with the notion of compensatory self-enhancement (Baumeister & Jones, 1978; Greenberg & Pyszczynski, 1985). If the model succeeds in enacting such alternative, valued role identities (and stores positive memories of self), it becomes less motivated to respond to the original discrepancy and less likely to experience regulatory collapse or helplessness, a pattern consistent with self-affirmation theory (Steele, 1988; as applied to helplessness, see Liu & Steele, 1986). Furthermore, the more relevant the model's alternative role identities are to its sense of identity, the more successful it can be in adopting this strategy, a pattern consistent with the finding that individuals with multifaceted self-concepts are better able to cope with life stress and avoid becoming depressed (Linville, 1987; Oatley & Bolton, 1985). Simulations using ISIS have been conducted that illustrate that the model produces each of these patterns of effects (see Hull, 2000).

Beyond accounting for specific consequences of particular variables, then, the theorized model yields patterns of effects among multiple variables in a manner consistent with existing, isolated theories of self-regulation. Viewed somewhat differently, those theories describe specific patterns of interplay among a common set of variables that constitute the core elements of the presently theorized model. As such, the model has heuristic value in demonstrating the ability of a single framework to integrate multiple unique models of specific aspects of self-regulatory dynamics. Beyond this, however, by taking into account a larger set of variables than any single theory, the model has the ability to identify dependent variables that may not have been considered or subjected to empirical tests in more circumscribed accounts.

Dimensions of Standards and Self-Representations

As described to this point, the system is relatively general with respect to the form of self-representations operationalized by the model. Nonetheless, the form of the self-representations in large part determines the specific nature of the behavioral response. Thus, the same psychological processes engaged with respect to different self-representations will yield qualitatively distinct patterns of behavior. A key question thus becomes: What are the essential forms of self-representations?

Elsewhere I have distinguished four dimensions along which representations relevant to self-regulation can vary (Hull, 2000): (a) private–public, (b) actual–desired, (c) past–present–future, and (d) self–other. These are conceptualized as dimensions insofar as any particular image that forms the basis of self-regulation can be characterized according to all four categories (e.g., regulation with respect to a present–private–desired–self image). In each case, the specific form of self-representation used in self-regulation is theorized to be a direct function of its relative level of activation in memory where activation is itself a function of situational factors (e.g., priming, salience) and dispositional factors (i.e., chronic differences in relative accessibility based on experience; see Higgins, 1987, for related arguments). The general processes associated with self-regulation are proposed to be relatively constant across a wide variety of distinct phenomena. Nothing is changed within the theorized model to account for phenomena in these apparently distinct literatures other than the particular form of self-image that is specified as the focus of self-regulation and the conceptualization of the specific inferences and acts that result (see Tetlock & Manstead, 1985). By defining the operative self-image to be a function of cognitive activation–accessibility, the application of the model to each of these literatures can be tested using relevant situational manipulations and individual differences.

Private–Public

One major dimension of self-representations concerns private versus public self-images (see Carver & Scheier, 1981; Snyder, 1974; and see Hull et al., 1988, for an earlier discussion of the present argument). The large self-awareness and self-consciousness literature (see Carver & Scheier, 1998) clearly illustrates the importance of the distinction between regulation with respect to a personally held image of self (private) and an image of how one appears to others (public). Beyond this literature, the private dimension is directly relevant to much of the foregoing discussion on self-regulation and is specifically relevant to the system's attempt to counteract feedback that does not match its sense of itself (paralleling work on the effects of self-schema; see, e.g., Markus, 1977) and to change its perception of itself when it cannot discount or correct such feedback (paralleling a self-concept driven account of cognitive dissonance; see Aronson, 1969; Festinger, 1957). In contrast, the public dimension is characteristic of self-regulated impression management and is specifically relevant to the system's attempt to act consistently with self-representations that will affect audience perceptions (paralleling an account of self-presentation offered by Tetlock & Manstead, 1985).

Actual–Desired

A second dimension of self-representations involves what is perceived to be an accurate characterization of self versus a desired or undesired form of self. Distinctions between actual and desired self-images have a long history within social psychology (e.g., Duval & Wicklund, 1972; Higgins, 1987, 1989b; James, 1890; Ogilvie, 1987; Wylie, 1968). Note, however, that the present distinction concerns whether a self-inference based on current behavior is referenced to an image of what the self is actually like or to an image of what the self is desired to be like. Such an analysis has interesting conceptual implications. For example, individual differences in "motivation to self-verify" versus "motivation to self-enhance" are accounted for in terms of differences in levels of chronic activation of actual versus desired self-images. Viewed from such a perspective, debates concerning which self-motivations are more psychologically "basic" (e.g., Sedikides & Strube, 1997) devolve into issues regarding situational variables and individual differences that affect relative accessibility–activation.

Past–Present–Future

A third dimension along which forms of self-representations vary is time. Much of social psychological research on the self is implicitly or explicitly concerned with the present insofar as self-regulation is characterized as following from a conflict (or mismatch) between a self-inference based on current behavior and an image of the current self. This conflict may exist with reference to a current image of the actual self (e.g., as in self-verification theory; Swann, 1983) or a current image of an ideal self (e.g., as in self-discrepancy theory; Higgins, 1987, 1989b). At the same time, self-regulation can occur with respect to a projected or future self. Such self-images may concern the immediate future, the long-term future, or various stages of self along the way. The importance of time as a dimension of self-images is illustrated by work on possible and feared selves (see Carver, Lawrence, & Scheier, 1999; Markus & Nurius, 1986), the effects of imagined scenarios on coping (see Aspinwall & Taylor, 1997), and the dynamics of regret over past actions and inactions (see Gilovich & Medvec, 1995).

Once again, in addition to broadening the applicability of the model, inclusion of time as a dimension has interesting conceptual implications. Consider, for example, the effects of rate of progress toward a goal on emotional reactions (e.g., Carver & Scheier, 1990; Hsee, Abelson, & Salovey, 1991). The current model lacks a "rate of progress" variable. However, it is plausible that rate of progress functions to increase the activation of an image of future behavior that matches or mismatches a future self-image. Emotion in the present model follows directly from such match or mismatch processes (in this case with respect to projected actions and representations of the future self). As such, the emotional effects of rate of progress toward a goal are mediated by the level of activation of future self-images and the perception of a future match (see Read, Jones, & Miller, 1990, for an elaboration of the relation between goals and traits).

Self–Other

A final dimension along which self-images are distinguished concerns the involvement of others. Up to this point, self-regulation has been conceived in terms of a self-image that is relatively devoid of the other. Other is implicitly included in the social character of the enacted roles (e.g., Friendship roles) and as a source of behavioral standards (e.g., the supervisor in the earlier example), but such roles do not require others (e.g., there are solitary work roles), and the individual can serve as his or her own source of cued behavioral standards.

Others are held to be more explicitly involved in the image that forms the basis of self-regulation in at least five ways. First, one may regulate with respect to particular self-images because they are provided by a specific other (as in reflected appraisals, see Felson, 1993; or as in self-fulfilling prophecies, see Madon, Jussim, & Eccles, 1997; Rosenthal, 1994). Second, the action of the other can serve as a behavioral standard with reference to one's own self-regulation (as in imitation and social comparison; see Wood, 1989). Third, one can adopt the image one holds of other as one's own desired self-image (as in identification). Fourth, one can adopt a perceived discrepancy experienced by the other (other-discrepancy) as a self-discrepancy as a function of the strength of self–other links (as in reflection, see Cialdini, Borden, Thorne, Walker, Freeman, & Sloan, 1976). Finally, one can adopt an image of the relationship with an other as the focus of self-regulation (e.g., Baldwin, 1992; Baldwin, Carrell, & Lopez, 1990).

To illustrate some of these distinctions with respect to a specific example, perceiving an other as doing well or poorly has different behavioral implications depending on the particular image that is sufficiently active to form the basis of self-regulation. If the action of the other serves as a cued behavioral standard, then (a) perceived behavioral discrepancies motivate attempts to improve performance through self-regulation; (b) with increases in the size of the discrepancy, negative affect increases and the perceived relevance of the dimension declines; and (c) if the discrepancy is sufficiently large, the individual becomes motivated to avoid (decrease closeness to) the other. Each reaction is consistent with social comparison processes that are central to the theory of self-evaluation maintenance (SEM) proposed by Tesser and Campbell (1983; Tesser, 1988). On the other hand, if the action of the other is itself referenced to a cued behavioral standard and this other-discrepancy is adopted as one's own, then as the other does well or poorly relative to the standard, self experiences positive or negative affective responses; the stronger the self–other link, the greater the emotional response. This reaction is consistent with reflection processes in the Tesser and Campbell (1983) model.

According to Tesser and Campbell, whether one engages in social comparison or reflection processes is a function of the relevance of a particular action to one's own sense of self. According to the present analysis, these processes follow from the relative accessibility of behavioral standards, self-images, other-images, and self–other links. Although highly personally relevant dimensions will tend to be associated with greater accessibility of relevant self-images and as a consequence social comparison, heightened accessibility of other-images together with increased salience of self–other links will increase the likelihood of reflection processes even when personal relevance is high. In certain key respects, such an analysis is consistent with a more recent account of SEM processes offered by Beach, Tesser, Fincham, Jones, Johnson, and Whitaker (1998).

Summary

The current model captures patterns of responses that characterize shifts between distinct psychological states in a manner that relates directly to key aspects of existing theories of self-regulation. Couching these distinctions as dimensions of images that form the basis of self-regulation makes apparent the multifaceted nature of the present model and the breadth of the literatures it seeks to embrace. Some of these accounts are consistent with reasoning advanced by existing models; other accounts are relatively novel.

ORIGINAL RESEARCH

In terms of research, I feel that the model is useful in four primary respects: (a) as an account of the consequences of manipulations of individual dynamic process variables, (b) as an account of qualitative shifts in psychological processes as revealed in discontinuous patterns of responses, (c) as an account of the structure of the self-concept and the functional consequences of differences in structural variables, and (d) as a general framework for developing a self-regulatory account of specific social behaviors. I describe research from my own lab as illustrations of the first two uses of the model.

Dynamic Processes of Self-Regulation: Generating New Predictions With Respect to Old Variables

One distinct aspect of the model is that self-awareness is not defined in terms of a conscious, reflective process but rather is associated with the encoding of information according to its self-relevance. If the information being encoded is not relevant to a behavioral discrepancy, then no process of comparison-to-self is evoked. On the other hand, even under these circumstances, self-awareness stimuli may have direct, automatic consequences involving the invocation of dispositional baseline levels of responses by virtue of encoding the situational cue as self-relevant. Although relatively unique to this model, we made similar claims regarding the nature of self-awareness more than 20 years ago:

> Specifically, we propose that self-awareness corresponds to the encoding of information in terms of its relevance for the self and as such directly entails a greater responsivity to the self-relevant aspects of the environment.... feature encoding corresponds to the automatic activation of specific cognitive structures in response to a particular input configuration and as such operates through a set of associative connections in long-term memory. On the other hand, controlled processing corresponds to a capacity-limited comparison or search process.... Since feature encoding defines the form of information available to the individual, it need not be associated with different kinds of controlled processes to lead to different behavioral effects. Thus, encoding may be associated with automatic responses that do not require controlled processing, or, by its inherently constructive nature, encoding may determine the outcomes of those controlled processes that do occur. (Hull & Levy, 1979, p. 757)

These claims are similar in key respects to Bargh's proposal that situational cues can act to evoke behavior automatically (see Chartrand & Bargh, chapter 1, this volume). For example, Bargh, Chen, and Burrows (1996) found that individuals who were implicitly primed with characteristics of the elderly stereotype subsequently walked down a hallway more slowly than did those primed with neutral content stimuli. Using the Bargh et al. (1996) elderly prime, Hull, Slone, Meteyer, and Matthews (2001) found that this effect held only among individuals high in dispositional private self-consciousness. A subsequent study replicated this prime by self-consciousness interaction. This pattern of results is particularly interesting because of the apparent irrelevance of the elderly stereotype to participants' sense of self (i.e., all of the participants were young adults). According to traditional accounts of stereotypes, primes only bias processing of information about targets for whom the prime is applicable (e.g., Banaji, Hardin, & Rothman, 1993; Higgins, 1989a). How, then, to account for the elderly stereotype prime biasing the behavior of individuals who do not conceive of themselves as elderly? Furthermore, why would individuals high in private self-consciousness show a greater influence of such primes? If self-consciousness involves a process of matching the prime to a personal standard (e.g., Carver, 1979; Carver & Scheier, 1981), then at the very least it should not influence behavior when the prime is clearly irrelevant to self. Indeed, one could easily argue that such individuals should be less influenced by such primes than should low private self-conscious individuals. The current analysis resolves these contradictions by proposing that the prime has its effects because it is processed as self-relevant (i.e., applicable) despite its "objective" status as irrelevant, and this induces action via a non-matching-to-self process whereby a prime-to-behavior link is automatically evoked.

A subsequent study in our lab demonstrated related effects using primes masked to non-consciousness. Specifically, the prime "success" or "failure" preceded each of 100 lexical decision trials but was presented for only 17 ms and was both backward and forward masked. Once again, private self-consciousness interacted with the priming manipulation to influence behavior. High private self-conscious participants were faster at the lexical decision task following the success prime and slower following the failure prime. Low self-conscious participants fell between these extremes and showed a slightly reversed pattern. This behavioral pattern was not present during the practice phase of the task (when a neutral prime was shown to all participants), and the pattern became more exaggerated over the 100 experimental trials. These effects occurred despite the fact that no participants reported any knowledge of the primes. Again, we see such results as consistent with a model of self-awareness as a self-referent encoding process that can occur at an automatic level. Similarly, the reasoning advanced by Chartrand and Bargh (chapter 1, this volume) is consistent with the argument that any individual element in the model can be directly and automatically activated with consequences for elements in all subsequent equations. Thus, automatically activated motivation can yield overt behavior without requiring controlled self-evaluation. At the same time, such automatic behavior can itself feed back to create a discrepancy and subsequent non-automatic behavior as a consequence of controlled self-regulation (e.g., controlled behavioral inhibition of an automatic behavior that is inconsistent with self-standards).

Qualitative Shifts in Processing: Assimilation and Contrast in the Self-Concept

The model distinguishes, then, between (a) the automatic behavioral consequences of a situational cue and (b) the self-regulatory consequences of processing a discrepancy between the behavioral standard implied by such a cue and one's own behavior. Self-awareness as a self-referent encoding process can have effects on both. According to the model, then, the self-aware individual's initial and automatic tendency will be to act consistently with the situational cue. In a recent set of studies, we (Hull, Slone, & Koepsel, 2000) have proposed that in such cases, accessible self-knowledge follows directly from characteristics implied by the cued behavior. Based on such self-knowledge, self-descriptions will appear to have been assimilated to the primed construct. In addition, the model engages in a parallel process of coding the cue and current action as a behavioral discrepancy. This behavioral discrepancy yields a trait inference that either falls within or outside a latitude of acceptance with respect to an existing self-representation. When the implied characteristics fall outside this latitude, the model engages in self-regulation. In this case, self-descriptions are proposed to follow from the behavioral-discrepancy self-regulatory system, specifically the discrepancy-derived trait inference. As such, self-descriptions will appear to have been contrasted against the primed construct (because the trait implied by the discrepancy is that one does not have a sufficient amount of the trait implied by the cued behavior). As noted earlier (see earlier quote from Hull & Levy, 1979), the comparison processes that give rise to such a reaction are capacity limited such that increasing an individual's cognitive load should interfere with such contrast effects.

In an initial study designed to examine such self-concept shifts, participants anticipated that they would be interviewed for a job by a graduate student (activating the complex of traits associated with the Worker role). All participants were then seated before a two-way mirror and left to imagine how they would respond to a series of questions to be asked by the interviewer. At the end of 5 minutes, the experimenter returned and told the participant that the interviewer was delayed and that they should answer a series of computer-presented questions regarding their self-perceptions on multiple personality traits. All participants had completed similar questions in a booklet distributed 4–6 weeks earlier. Consistent with the notion that anticipation of a job interview would lead to an anticipatory self-concept shift with respect to the Worker role, relative to their premeasures participants shifted their self-descriptions on multiple traits that define this role in the Hull et al. model of personality (e.g., they rated themselves as more orderly and thorough and less disorganized and irresponsible). Indeed, they showed few changes on any traits not associated with this role. One way to characterize these results is that participants assimilated their self-representations to the situationally appropriate role definition.

In addition to the procedures described earlier, in this initial study all participants were told to present themselves either as sociable or unsociable during the interview. Although this manipulation had relatively minor effects on participants' self-descriptions compared to the general shift seen on Worker-related traits, we thought that this might have been a consequence of the irrelevance of sociability to the Worker role. In addition, we hypothesized that anticipated presentation on a nonrelevant trait might actually have acted as a cognitive load (see Gilbert, Krull, & Pelham, 1988; Experiment 2) and functioned to facilitate assimilation to the primed role.

In a second study, half of the participants were told that they would be interviewed for a job (to activate the Worker role) and half that they would interact with another participant in a get-acquainted interaction (to activate the Friend role). Crossed with this manipulation, participants were told that in the upcoming interview or interaction they were to present themselves as either hardworking (a trait from the Worker role) or sociable (a trait from the Friend role). Participants for whom the self-presentational trait and anticipated role were inconsistent were expected to replicate the findings from Study 1 and show self-concept assimilation to the primed role (as a consequence of load). Participants for whom the traits were consistent with the role were not expected to show consequences of a presentational load and hence were predicted to be more likely to show self-concept contrast effects. Finally, whereas in the initial study all participants were self-aware (seated in front of a mirror), in this second study the mirror was removed and individual differences in private self-consciousness were assessed.

The results of Study 2 provided a conceptual replication of Study 1: Relative to low private self-conscious individuals, high self-conscious individuals showed anticipatory shifts in their trait self-descriptions consistent with the Worker role when anticipating a job interview and consistent with the Friend role when anticipating a get-acquainted social interaction. Again, this suggests greater assimilation of the self-concept to the situationally appropriate role definition among private self-conscious individuals (recall that a mirror was present for all participants in Study 1). However, statistically significant interactions revealed that this was the case only when participants were told to present themselves with respect to a trait that fell outside the role (present self as sociable when anticipating job interview—as in Study 1; present self as hardworking when anticipating social interaction). When told to present themselves with respect to a trait that was a key component of the role (hardworking when anticipating job interview; sociable when anticipating get-acquainted interaction), high private self-conscious individuals showed less assimilation than did low self-conscious individuals and in some cases showed contrast effects (e.g., describing themselves as less hardworking when anticipating a job interview than on their premeasure trait rating).

Our account of these findings is as follows: Anticipatory identity shifts in the form of assimilation occur automatically as a judgment consistent with the implications of the behavioral cue (anticipated role). Because this requires processing the role cues as self-relevant, the extent to which it occurs is moderated by private self-consciousness or self-awareness. Anticipatory contrast effects involve a judgment with reference to a perceived discrepancy between the cue and anticipated behavior. If inferences based on the discrepancy are sufficiently extreme so as to fall outside the individual's latitude of acceptance regarding the inferred traits ("I am going to present myself as hardworking"; "I am not *that* hardworking"), a mismatch occurs that yields a contrast effect. Once again, such an effect is a function of private self-consciousness. Finally, explicit instructions to present oneself with respect to a trait that is not part of the role definition is cognitively taxing (see Gilbert et al., 1988), and this load disrupts the discrepancy-driven process responsible for the observed contrast effects.

In a final study, we investigated the potentially opposite implications that this analysis suggests for self-descriptions versus overt behavior: Thus, (a) prior to action discrepancy-based inferences suggest reduced self-descriptions on the trait dimension being regulated, but (b) the process of self-regulation should function to increase subsequent trait-relevant behaviors. In support of this hypothesized pattern, in a study in which participants anticipated occupying a position of leadership in a brainstorming task, high private self-conscious participants rated themselves less "capable" than did low self-conscious participants (a contrast to the role requirements of Leader) but subsequently acted more leader-like according to an objective judge. Conversely, when they anticipated occupying a position of Follower in the same task, high private self-conscious participants rated themselves more capable than did low self-conscious participants (again, in contrast to their role as Follower) but subsequently acted less leader-like according to an objective judge.[5] These opposite self-descriptive versus behavioral patterns are consistent with the preceding account of discrepancy-based inferences and self-regulation.

CONCLUSION

As I hope is apparent from the foregoing discussion, the proposed dynamic system, when combined with a structural model of self-knowledge,

---

[5]Although the self-consciousness by role manipulation interaction achieved conventional levels of significance on measures of judged leaderlike behavior, it approached significance on the self-ratings of capable ($p = .08$).

holds promise for integrating a variety of models of self-regulation. Beyond its heuristic value as an integrative framework, however, it constitutes a meaningful and unique theory of specific relations among fundamental psychological processes and variables. As illustrated by our research on trait structures, this theory is useful in explaining the basic organization of personality. As illustrated by our research on trait judgments, it is useful as an "implicit personality theory" of how individuals organize trait knowledge. As illustrated by our research on self-consciousness, automaticity, and assimilation and contrast in the self-concept, the theory is useful in generating unique predictions regarding variables central to self-regulation.

We are currently pursuing additional ways in which the theory can be used to advance our understanding of the causes and dynamics of social behavior. For example, we have considerable empirical support for the value of the model as a systematic roadmap for identifying sources of individual differences in attachment styles and grounding these differences in more basic psychological processes of general relevance to self-regulation. In addition, in research on the consequences of stressful life events for the experience of depression, we have demonstrated the empirical utility of the distinction in the model between the number of major roles individuals perceive as highly relevant to their sense of identity and their degree of interconnectedness (Koepsel & Hull, 2000).

Ultimately, the value of the model depends on its empirical utility in pushing research in new directions. To some extent, this depends on the value of the model in associating areas of research and experimental paradigms that have proceeded relatively independently; to some extent, it depends on the utility of hypotheses derived directly from the model itself. Certainly, I have no illusions as to the limitations of the present approach or the likelihood of mis-specifications in the proposed model. However, one reasonable approach to advancing social psychological theory and research is to identify the nature of such mis-specifications empirically and propose specific alternative models that correct them while retaining the breadth and explanatory power of the current model.

REFERENCES

Aronson, E. (1969). The theory of cognitive dissonance: A current perspective. In L. Berkowitz (Ed.), *Advances in experimental social psychology* (Vol. 4, pp. 1–34). New York: Academic Press.

Aspinwall, L. G., & Taylor, S. E. (1997). A stitch in time: Self-regulation and proactive coping. *Psychological Bulletin, 121*, 417–436.

Baldwin, M. W. (1992). Relational schemas and the processing of social information. *Psychological Bulletin, 112*, 461–484.

Baldwin, M. W., Carrell, S. E., & Lopez, D. F. (1990). Priming relationship schemas: My advisor and the Pope are watching me from the back of my mind. *Journal of Experimental Social Psychology, 26,* 435–454.

Banaji, M. R., Hardin, C., & Rothman, A. J. (1993). Implicit stereotyping in person judgment. *Journal of Personality and Social Psychology, 65,* 272–281.

Bandura, A. (1977). Self-efficacy: Toward a unifying theory of behavior change. *Psychological Review, 84,* 191–215.

Bargh, J. A., Chen, M., & Burrows, L. (1996). Automaticity of social behavior: Direct effects of trait construct and stereotype activation on action. *Journal of Personality and Social Psychology, 71,* 230–244.

Baumeister, R. F., & Jones, E. E. (1978). When self-presentation is constrained by the target's knowledge: Consistency and compensation. *Journal of Personality and Social Psychology, 36,* 608–618.

Beach, S. R. H., Tesser, A., Fincham, F. D., Jones, D. J., Johnson, D., & Whitaker, D. J. (1998). Pleasure and pain in doing well, together: An investigation of performance-related affect in close relationships. *Journal of Personality and Social Psychology, 74,* 923–938.

Carver, C. S. (1979). A cybernetic model of self-attention processes. *Journal of Personality and Social Psychology, 37,* 1251–1281.

Carver, C. S., Lawrence, J. W., & Scheier, M. F. (1999). Self-discrepancies and affect: Incorporating the role of feared selves. *Personality and Social Psychology Bulletin, 25,* 783–792.

Carver, C. S., & Scheier, M. F. (1981). *Attention and self-regulation: A control-theory approach to human behavior.* New York: Springer-Verlag.

Carver, C. S., & Scheier, M. F. (1990). Origins and functions of positive and negative affect: A control-process view. *Psychological Review, 97,* 19–35.

Carver, C. S., & Scheier, M. F. (1998). *On the self-regulation of behavior.* Cambridge, England: Cambridge University Press.

Church, A. T., & Burke, P. J. (1994). Exploratory and confirmatory tests of the big five and Tellegen's three- and four-dimensional models. *Journal of Personality and Social Psychology, 66,* 93–114.

Cialdini, R. B., Borden, R. J., Thorne, A., Walker, M. R., Freeman, S., & Sloan, L. R. (1976). Basking in reflected glory: Three (football) studies. *Journal of Personality and Social Psychology, 34,* 366–375.

Duval, S., & Wicklund, R. A. (1972). *A theory of objective self-awareness.* New York: Academic Press.

Feldman Barrett, L., & Russell, J. A. (1998). Independence and bipolarity in the structure of current affect. *Journal of Personality and Social Psychology, 74,* 967–984.

Felson, R. B. (1993). The (somewhat) social self: How others affect self-appraisals. In J. Suls (Ed.), *Psychological perspectives on the self* (Vol. 4, pp. 1–26). Hillsdale, NJ: Erlbaum.

Festinger, L. (1957). *A theory of cognitive dissonance.* Evanston, IL: Row Peterson.

Gibbons, F. X. (1990). Self-attention and behavior: A review and theoretical update. In M. P. Zanna (Ed.), *Advances in experimental social psychology* (Vol. 23, pp. 249–303). San Diego, CA: Academic Press.

Gilbert, D. T., Krull, D. S., & Pelham, B. W. (1988). Of thoughts unspoken: Social inference and the self-regulation of behavior. *Journal of Personality and Social Psychology, 55,* 685–694.

Gilovich, T., & Medvec, V. H. (1995). The experience of regret: What, when, and why. *Psychological Review, 102,* 379–395.

Greenberg, J., & Pyszczynski, T. (1985). Compensatory self-inflation: A response to threat to self-regard of public failure. *Journal of Personality and Social Psychology, 49,* 273–280.

Higgins, E. T. (1987). Self-discrepancy: A theory relating self and affect. *Psychological Review, 94,* 319–340.

Higgins, E. T. (1989a). Knowledge accessibility and activation. In J. S. Uleman & J. A. Bargh (Eds.), *Unintended thought* (pp. 75–123). New York: Guilford.

Higgins, E. T. (1989b). Self-discrepancy theory: What patterns of self-beliefs cause people to suffer? In L. Berkowitz (Ed.), *Advances in experimental social psychology* (Vol. 22, pp. 93–136). New York: Academic Press.

Higgins, E. T. (1997). Beyond pleasure and pain. *American Psychologist, 52,* 1280–1300.

Hogan, R. (1983). Socioanalytic theory of personality. In M. M. Page (Ed.), *Nebraska Symposium on Motivation: Personality—Current theory and research* (pp. 55–89). Lincoln: University of Nebraska Press.

Hsee, C. K., Abelson, R. P., & Salovey, P. (1991). The relative weighting of position and velocity in satisfaction. *Psychological Science, 2,* 263–266.

Hull, J. G. (2000). *A dynamic theory of personality and self.* Manuscript submitted for publication.

Hull, J. G., Lehn, D. A., & Slone, L. B. (2001). *A role-type model of the structure of personality.* Manuscript submitted for publication.

Hull, J. G., & Levy, A. S. (1979). The organizational functions of the self: An alternative to the Duval and Wicklund model of self-awareness. *Journal of Personality and Social Psychology, 37,* 756–768.

Hull, J. G., & Renn, R. J. (2000). *Implicit personality theory: Testing alternative models of the architecture of trait cognitions.* Manuscript submitted for publication.

Hull, J. G., Slone, L. B., & Koepsel, K. D. (2000). *Anticipatory identity shifts: Assimilation and contrast in the self-concept.* Unpublished manuscript.

Hull, J. G., Slone, L. B., Meteyer, K. B., & Matthews, A. R. (2001). *The nonconsciousness of self-consciousness.* Manuscript submitted for publication.

Hull, J. G., Van Treuren, R. R., Ashford, S. J., Propsom, P., & Andrus, B. W. (1988). Self-consciousness and the processing of self-relevant information. *Journal of Personality and Social Psychology, 54,* 452–465.

James, W. (1890). *The principles of psychology.* New York: Holt, Rinehart, & Winston.

John, O. P. (1990). The "big five" factor taxonomy: Dimensions of personality in the natural language and in questionnaires. In L. A. Pervin (Ed.), *Handbook of personality theory and research* (pp. 66–100). New York: Guilford.

Jones, E. E., & Davis, K. E. (1965). From acts to dispositions: The attribution process in person perception. In L. Berkowitz (Ed.), *Advances in experimental social psychology* (Vol. 2, pp. 220–266). New York: Academic Press.

Koepsel, K., & Hull, J. G. (2000). *The independent effects of self-complexity components: Number of self-aspects and redundancy*. Unpublished manuscript.

Linville, P. W. (1987). Self-complexity as a cognitive buffer against stress-related illness and depression. *Journal of Personality and Social Psychology, 52,* 663–676.

Liu, T. J., & Steele, C. M. (1986). Attributional analysis as self-affirmation. *Journal of Personality and Social Psychology, 51,* 531–540.

Madon, S., Jussim, L., & Eccles, J. (1997). In search of the powerful self-fulfilling prophecy. *Journal of Personality and Social Psychology, 72,* 791–809.

Markus, H. R. (1977). Self-schemata and processing information about the self. *Journal of Personality and Social Psychology, 35,* 63–78.

Markus, H., & Nurius, P. (1986). Possible selves. *American Psychologist, 41,* 954–969.

Miller, G. A., Galanter, E., & Pribram, K. H. (1960). *Plans and the structure of behavior.* New York: Holt, Rinehart, & Winston.

Mowrer, O. H. (1960). *Learning theory and behavior.* New York: Wiley.

Nowak, A., & Vallacher, R. R. (1998). *Dynamical social psychology.* New York: Guilford.

Nowak, A., Vallacher, R. R., Tesser, A., & Borkowski, W. (2000). Society of self: The emergence of collective properties in self-structure. *Psychological Review, 107,* 39–61.

Oatley, K., & Bolton, W. (1985). A social–cognitive theory of depression in reaction to life events. *Psychological Review, 92,* 372–388.

Ogilvie, D. M. (1987). The undesired self: A neglected variable in personality research. *Journal of Personality and Social Psychology, 52,* 379–385.

Powers, W. T. (1973). *Behavior: The control of perception.* Chicago: Aldine.

Read, S. J., Jones, D. K., & Miller, L. C. (1990). Traits as goal-based categories: The importance of goals in the coherence of dispositional categories. *Journal of Personality and Social Psychology, 58,* 1048–1061.

Rosenthal, R. (1994). Interpersonal expectancy effects: A 30-year perspective. *Current Directions in Psychological Science, 3,* 176–179.

Russell, J. A. (1980). A circumplex model of affect. *Journal of Personality and Social Psychology, 39,* 1161–1178.

Sedikides, C., & Strube, M. J. (1997). Self-evaluation: To thine own self be good, to thine own self be sure, to thine own self be true, to thine own self be better. In M. P. Zanna (Ed.), *Advances in experimental social psychology* (Vol. 29, pp. 209–269). San Diego, CA: Academic Press.

Snyder, M. (1974). Self-monitoring of expressive behavior. *Journal of Personality and Social Psychology, 30,* 526–537.

Steele, C. M. (1988). The psychology of self-affirmation: Sustaining the integrity of the self. In L. Berkowitz (Ed.), *Advances in experimental social psychology* (Vol. 21, pp. 261–302). New York: Academic Press.

Swann, W. B. (1983). Self-verification: Bringing social reality into harmony with the self. In J. Suls & A. G. Greenwald (Eds.), *Psychological perspectives on the self* (Vol. 2, pp. 33–66). New York: Erlbaum.

Tesser, A. (1988). Toward a self-evaluation maintenance model of social behavior. In L. Berkowitz (Ed.), *Advances in experimental social psychology* (Vol. 21, pp. 181–227). New York: Academic Press.

Tesser, A. (2000). On the confluence of self-esteem maintenance mechanisms. *Personality and Social Psychology Review, 4,* 290–299.

Tesser, A., & Campbell, J. (1983). Self-definition and self-evaluation maintenance. In J. Suls & A. G. Greenwald (Eds.), *Psychological perspectives on the self* (Vol. 2, pp. 1–32). Hillsdale, NJ: Erlbaum.

Tetlock, P. E., & Manstead, A. S. (1985). Impression management versus intrapsychic explanations in social psychology: A useful dichotomy? *Psychological Review, 98,* 59–77.

Vallacher, R. R., & Wegner, D. M. (1987). What do people think they're doing? Action identification and human behavior. *Psychological Review, 94,* 3–15.

Wicklund, R. A. (1975). Objective self-awareness. In L. Berkowitz (Ed.), *Advances in experimental social psychology* (Vol. 8, pp. 233–275). New York: Academic Press.

Wood, J. V. (1989). Theory and research concerning social comparison of personal attributes. *Psychological Bulletin, 106,* 231–248.

Wortman, C. B., & Brehm, J. W. (1975). Responses to uncontrollable outcomes: An integration of reactance theory and the learned helplessness model. In L. Berkowitz (Ed.), *Advances in experimental social psychology* (Vol. 8, pp. 278–336). New York: Academic Press.

Wylie, R. C. (1968). The present state of self theory. In E. F. Borgatta & W. W. Lambert (Eds.), *Handbook of personality theory and research* (pp. 728–787). Chicago: Rand McNally.

APPENDIX: INTERACTIVE SELF AND IDENTITY
SYSTEM EQUATIONS

Perceptual System

Perceptual Subsystem I: Behavioral Discrepancies

Overt Behavior = Auto Behavior + Self-Regulated Behavior [1]

Behavior Discrepancy = Behavior Standard − Overt Behavior [2]

Perceptual Subsystem II: Perception of Discrepancies

Behavior Discrepancy Perception = Behavior Discrepancy * Attention * Self-Referent Encoding * ((Negative Affect + Constant)/(Positive Affect + Constant)) [3]

Perceptual Subsystem III: Storage of Discrepancies in Memory

Behavior Discrepancy Memory Reservoir

    Inflows: Behavior Discrepancy Perception (see Equation 3)

    Outflows: Forgetting (see Equations 4 and 5)

                  Attributional bias (see Equation 6)

Forgetting = Behavior Discrepancy Memory * Salience Decay [4]

Salience Decay = f(Mood) [5]

Attributional Bias = Affirmational Memories [6]

Inference System

Inference Subsystem I: Trait–Type–Identity Inference Hierarchy

Trait Inference = Behavioral Discrepancy Memory * Correspondence of Behavior to Trait [7]

Type Inference = Trait Inference * Relevance of Trait to Type [8]

Identity Inference = Type Inference * Relevance of Type to Identity [9]

Inference Subsystem II: Match-to-Self System

Trait Match:

    IF ($0 \leq$ Trait Inference $\leq$ Latitude Boundary)

    THEN (Trait Match = |Trait Inference − Latitude Boundary|)

    ELSE (Trait Match = 0) [10a]

Type Match:

    IF ($0 \leq$ Type Inference $\leq$ Latitude Boundary)

    THEN (Type Match = |Type Inference − Latitude Boundary|)

    ELSE (Type Match = 0) [11a]

Identity Match:

    IF ($0 \leq$ Identity Inference $\leq$ Latitude Boundary)

    THEN (Identity Match = |Identity Inference − Latitude Boundary|)

    ELSE (Identity Match = 0) [12a]

Trait Mismatch:

    IF (Trait Inference > Latitude Boundary)

    THEN (Trait Mismatch = Trait Inference)

    ELSE (Trait Mismatch = 0) [10b]

Type Mismatch:

IF (Type Inference > Latitude Boundary)
THEN (Type Mismatch = Type Inference)
ELSE (Type Mismatch = 0)   [11b]
Identity Mismatch:
IF (Identity Inference > Latitude Boundary)
THEN (Identity Mismatch = Identity Inference)
ELSE (Identity Mismatch = 0)   [12b]
Inference Subsystem III: Correspondence and Expectancy Violations
Correspondence = f(Expectancy Violation)   [13]

Motivational System

Identity Motivation = S(Identity Mismatches) * Negative Emotion *
    Identity Relevance   [14]
Type Motivation = (Identity Motivation * Relevance Type to Identity)
    + (Type Mismatch * Negative Emotion * Relevance Type to
    Identity)   [15]
Trait Motivation = (Type Motivation * Relevance Trait to Type) +
    (Trait Mismatch * Negative Emotion * Relevance Trait to Type) [16]

Affective System

Positive Affect Reservoir:
    Inflows: PA Arousal (see Equations 17 and 18)
    Outflows: PA Decay (see Equation 19)
PA Arousal = Match-based Arousal + PA Resting Level   [17]
    Where: Match-based Arousal = S(S Matches)   [18]
PA Decay = Positive Affect Reservoir * PA Decay Fraction   [19]
Negative Affect Reservoir:
    Inflows: NA Arousal (see Equations 20 and 21)
    Outflows: NA Decay (see Equation 22)
NA Arousal = Mismatch-based Arousal + NA Resting Level   [20]
    Where: Mismatch-based Arousal = S(S Mismatches)   [21]
NA Decay = Negative Affect Reservoir * NA Decay Fraction   [22]
    Mood = Positive Affect − Negative Affect   [23]
Negative Emotion = Negative Affect * NA attribution   [24]
Positive Emotion = Positive Affect * PA attribution   [25]

Behavioral Regulation System

Behavioral Subsystem I: Approach/Avoidance
Approach vs. Avoidance = f(Trait Motivation * Self-Efficacy)   [26]
Behavioral Subsystem II: Judgments of Self-Efficacy
Self-Efficacy = f(Trait Match − Trait Mismatch)
    + Mood + Affirmational Memories)   [27]
Affirmational Memory Reservoir
    Inflows: Perception of Self-Affirming Acts (see Equation 26)
    Outflows: Memory Decay

Perception of Self-Affirming Acts = constant * (Self-Regulated
  Behavior)   [28]
Relevance = f(Self-Efficacy)   [29]
Behavioral Subsystem III: Behavioral Self-Regulation
Self-Regulated Behavior = constant * Approach   [30]
Attention = f(Approach − Avoidance)   [31]
Latitude Adjustment = f(Avoidance or Approach)   [32]
Behavioral Disposition = f(constant * Self-Regulated Behavior)   [33]
Auto Behavior = f(Situational Cue * Self-Referent Encoding | Behavior
  Disposition)   [34]

AUTHOR INDEX

Numbers in italics refer to listings in the reference sections.

Bornstein, R. F., 63, *116*
Bourne, E. J., 77, 95
Bowlby, J., 47, *64*
Bradbury, T. N., 132, *139*, *140*
Bratslavsky, E., 34, *36*
Brawley, L. R., 132, *139*
Breakwell, G., 147, *171*
Breed, G. R., 132, *144*
Brehm, J. W., 51, 52, 59, *64*, 66, 68, 73,
    76, 81, *91*, 189, *203*
Brekke, N., 14, *41*
Brenner, M., 136, *139*
Breuer, J., 60, *64*
Brewer, M. B., 25, *37*, 124, *139*, 147,
    148n, 159, 166, *167*, 169, *170*
Brooks-Gunn, J., 121, 122, *142*
Brown, J. D., 49, 55, *64*, 73, 95, 130,
    144
Brown, R. J., 25, *37*
Brown, S. L., 122, *139*
Bryant, J., 46, *64*
Bundy, R. F., 157, *171*
Burggraf, S. A., 105, *114*, *116*
Burish, T. G., 52, *64*
Burke, P. J., 175, *200*
Burling, J., 66
Burrows, L., 14, *36*, 194, *200*
Butner, J., 81, *91*
Buunk, B. B., 131, 132, *140*, *145*

Cacioppo, J. T., 22, *37*, 45, 46, 51n, 52,
    56, 57, 61, *64*, *65*, 67
Campbell, J., 133, 137,*144*, 188, 193,
    203
Canfield, R. W., 137, *142*
Cantor, J. R., 46, *64*
Cantor, N., 3, *11*, 14, *37*
Cantril, H., 125, *141*
Carlsmith, J. M., 51, *65*
Carlston, D. E., *39*
Carrell, S. E., 192, *199*
Carver, C. S., 14, 28, *37*, 135, *139*, 174,
    182n, 187, 190, 191, 192, 195,
    200
Chaiken, S., 34, *36*
Chambers, J., 73, *92*
Chanowitz, B., 34, *39*
Chartrand, T. L., 14, 16, 17, 19, 22, 23,
    27, 28, 29, 30, 31, 32, 33, 34,
    35, *36*, *37*, 179
Chen, M., 14, 34, *36*, *37*, 194, *200*

Chen, S., 27, 27–28, *37*
Cheng, B., 131, *140*
Cheng, C. M., 30, *37*
Christie, M. J., 45, 69
Chryssochoou, X., 147, *171*
Church, A. T., 175, *200*
Cialdini, R. B., 81, 89, *91*, 122, 125,
    135, *139*, *140*, 192, *200*
Clark, F., *113*
Clark, M. S., 27, *37*, *64*
Clayton, P., *113*
Clore, G. L., 28, 40, 44, *64*
Coe, C., 137, *142*
Collins, B. E., 72, 73, *92*
Condry, J., 73, *92*
Condry, J. C., 73, *92*
Cooley, C. H., 119, *139*
Cooper, J., 46, 51, 56, 59, *65*, 68, 69, 72,
    73, 88, 90, *92*, *93*, *94*
Cordess, C., *115*
Cordova, D. I., 74, 75, 79, 83, *92*
Corneille, O., *170*
Cornell, D. P., 30, *41*, 44, 50, 68, 69
Costello, C. G., *116*
Cox, M., *115*
Crites, S. L., Jr., 22, *37*, 45, *64*
Crocker, J., 130, 132, *139*
Crowne, D. P., 128, 129, *139*
Croyle, R. T., 51, *65*
Cullen, F. T., *113*
Cummings, E. M., *114*
Cupach, W. R., 125, *139*
Curham, J. R., 126, *139*

Damhuis, I., 100, *114*
Damon, W., 98, *114*
Darwin, C., 45, *65*
Davis, K. E., 182, *202*
Davis, M. H., 136, *140*
Dawson, M. E., 45, *65*
Dearing, R., 101, 103, 104, 106, *117*
deCharms, R., 71, 73, *92*
Deci, E. L., 14, 17, *37*, 73, 73–74, 74,
    76, 77, *92*, *94*, 96
DeFour, D., 60, *65*
De La Ronde, C., 130, *144*
Dember, W. N., 73, 83, *92*
Deschamps, J., *141*, *143*
Deschamps, J. C., 152, *167*
Detweiler, J. B., 74, *92*
Devine, P. G., 44, 57, 60, *65*

Trope, Y., 84, *93*
Trötschel, R., 18, *36*
Tudor, M., 123, *138*
Turner, J. C., 124, 125, *143*, *144*, 147,
     148, 149, 151, 152, 154, 155,
     164, *169*, *171* Turner, R. H., 67
Tversky, A., 84, *93*, *95*

Uleman, J. S., *142*, *201*

Vallacher, R. R., *145*, 174, 178n, *202*,
     203
Valley, K. L., 126, *139*
Vallone, R. P., 126, 127, *144*
Vance, K. M., 60, *65*
Vangelisti, A. L., 137, *145*
van Knippenberg, A., 14, 37–38, *38*
Van Norren, M., 157, *170*
Van Treuren, R. R., 182n, 187, *201*
VanYperen, N. W., 132, *145*
Vargas, P., 31, *41*
Venables, P. H., 45, *69*
Verma, G. K., *95*
Vignoles, V. L., 147, *171*
Villareal, M. J., 79, *95*
Visser, L., 153, *169*
von Hippel, W., 31, *41*

Wagner, P. E., 99, 101, 103, 105, 106,
     116, *117*
Walder, L. O., *115*
Walker, M. R., 192, *200*
Wallbott, H. G., 100, *117*
Walster, E., 128–129, 131, *141*, *145*
Walster, G. W., 131, *145*
Warm, J. S., 73, 83, *92*
Waschull, S. B., 60, *66*
Wasel, W., 25, *40*
Watson, D., 129, *145*
Weary, G., 28, *41*, 50, 54, *69*
Weber, A. L., *145*
Weber, E. U., 87, *96*

Wegner, D. M., 14, *41*, 122, 125, 136,
     143, *145*, 174, *203*
Weinberg, R. S., 28, *41*
Weiner, B., 99, *117*
Weinert, F. E., *39*
Weisenberg, M., 73, *96*
Wetherell, M. S., 124, *144*, *169*
Wheatley, T., 14, *41*
Whitaker, D. J., 193, *200*
White, G., 129, *145*
Whitehead, A. N., 91, *96*
Wicker, F. W., 99, 100, 103, *117*
Wicklund, R. A., 28, *39*, 135, *140*, 187,
     191, *200*, *203*
Wiegand, A. W., 59, *68*
Wilder, D. A., 155, 158, *171*
Wilkes, A. L., 152, *171*
Williams, A. O., *113*
Wilson, T. D., 14, *40*, *41*, 44, 67, 73, *92*
Wolfe, C. T., 24, *41*
Wolosin, R. J., 132, *145*
Wood, J. V., 25, *41*, 192, *203*
Worchel, S., *141*, *143*
Wortman, C. B., 189, *203*
Wosinka, W., 81, *91*
Wyer, R. S., Jr., 16, *36*, *39*, *41*, 142
Wylie, R. C., 191, *203*

Yarkin-Levin, K., *144*
Yates, B. T., *96*
Yzerbyt, V., *170*

Zahn-Waxler, C., 102, 104, *114*, *117*,
     139
Zajonc, R. B., 44, *67*
Zamble, E., 107, *117*
Zanna, M. P., 46, 51, 56, 64, 66, 67, *68*,
     69, *141*, *201*, *202*
Zehr, H. D., 137, *141*
Zemore, R., 44, 58, 58n, 59, *69*
Zillmann, D., 46, 54, 64, *69*
Zimbardo, P. G., 73, *96*
Zinger, I., *113*
Zuckerman, M., 50, 69, 74, 79, 90, *96*
Zurawski, R. M., 52, *68*

SUBJECT INDEX

Jails, and moral emotions, 109
Justice, restorative, 108–109
Just-world beliefs, and self-esteem tasks, 53

Lateralization, of activation, 22
Left-hemisphere activation, and self-serving attribution, 55n
Lewin, Kurt, 72
Longitudinal Family Study, of moral emotions, 104

Matching-to-standard process, 182
Match-to-self Subsystem, in ISIS model, 179–180, 182
Memorization goal, 4, 16–17
Memory, and automatic goals, 22
Metacontrast ratio, 152
Mimicking, automatic, 34
Misattribution of arousal paradigms, 46
and self-serving attribution, 54
Misattribution research, and influence of arousal on dissonance reduction, 56
Moderator variables, for distinctiveness processes, 154–157
Mood
   and automatic goal pursuit, 28–29
   and self-enhancement mechanisms, 30–31
Moral behavior, and shame vs. guilt, 104
Moral emotions, 6–7, 97, 98
   Longitudinal Family Study of, 104
   See also Guilt; Shame
Mortality salience-induced worldview defense, 56, 62
Motivation
   vs. cognition, 159
   and drives, 166
   emphasis on, 3
   increasing interest in, 10
   intrinsic and extrinsic, 17–18 (see also Intrinsic motivation)
   in ISIS model, 180
   nonconscious processes in, 14 (see also at Automatic)
   See also Goals
Motivational states
   as increasing over time, 19

and priming, 19–21
Motivational system, in ISIS model, 176, 205

Negative feedback
   derogation of, 132
   as threats to self-esteem, 49–50, 52
Neurophysiological evidence, for activation of goal states, 21–22
Nonconscious goals, and stimulus-response link, 32–33
Nonconscious mental processes, 14. See also at Automatic
Nonconscious motives, intrinsic and extrinsic, 18
NS-SCRs (nonspecific skin conductance responses), 45

Obsessive relational intrusion, 125
Optimal Distinctiveness Theory (ODT), 148n, 153, 166
Other, incorporation of in self, 8, 121–123, 124–125
Other-oriented empathy. See Empathy

Parafoveal vigilance task, 29
Parenting, and shame vs. guilt, 109–111
Past-present-future dimension of self-representations, 191–192
Perceptions, ego involvement as influence on, 125–126
Perceptual priming effects, 19
Perceptual System, in ISIS model, 176, 204
Persistence
   and automatic goals, 4, 20–21
   and motivational states, 19
Physiological arousal, and self-esteem, 5, 44, 46, 61–63
   and arousal as influence on self-esteem defense, 54–57
   directions for research on, 60–61
   and generalized view of self-esteem threat and maintenance, 49–50
   and reduction of arousal, 57–60
   threats to, 50–53
Physiological indices of arousal, 44–47

Self-evaluation maintenance model, 49
and arousal, 55
Self-evaluation maintenance (SEM) patterns, 51n
Self-image threat, and stereotyping, 24
Self-knowledge, structural model of (Hull ISIS model), 10, 174–175, 176–177
Self-other differentiation and incorporation, 8, 121–125
Self-other dimension of self-representation, 192–193
Self-preoccupation, 136–137
Self-reflection, 8, 120, 121, 135–137
Self-regulation, 3–4, 13
auto-motive model of, 4, 14–16
behavioral, 181
conscious choice as, 13–14
dynamic processes of, 194–195
dynamic systems model of, 175–181
Hull model of, 10 (*see also* Interactive Self and Identity System)
and motivational states of goal pursuit, 19
nonconscious, 34, 35
with respect to behavioral standard, 183–185
Self-regulatory collapse, 185–186, 188–189
Self-representations, dimensions of, 190–193
Self-rumination, 136–137
Self-serving attributions
from left-hemisphere activation, 55n
as self-esteem defense, 54–55
Self-serving bias, 49–50
Self theory of Rogers, 13
Self-verification, 130
and self-enhancement, 61
Sexual harassment, and power-sex association, 26
Shame, 98
vs. guilt, 6–7, 99–100, 112–113
and anger or aggression, 103
and child-rearing, 109–111
and criminal justice system, 106–109
and deterrence of transgression or socially undesirable behavior, 104–105
and hiding vs. amending, 100
and other-oriented empathy, 100–102

and psychological symptoms, 105–106
and teaching, 111–112
as self-conscious emotion, 97
Situations
as automatically associated with goals, 23–28, 32
See also Environment
Social comparison or reflection processes, 193
Social identification, 123–124, 125
Social identities, 123–124, 125
Social identity theory (SIT), 8, 166–167
and collective identity, 147–148
and discrimination, 124
and identity function, 153
Social power, and relationship orientation, 27
Social psychological theorizing, and formal mathematical approaches, 186
Sociometer model and theory, 8, 127–128, 130
Stalking, 125
Standards, rules, and goals (SRGs), 97–98
STELLA computer application, 178n
Stereotypic Explanatory Bias (SEB) scale, 31
Stereotyping
automatic activation of goals leading to, 24–26
and automatic goal pursuit, 30–31
and primes, 194–195
Stimulus-response link, and nonconscious goals, 32–33
Subsequent goal-relevant performance, and automatic goal pursuit, 31–32
Suppression, physiological consequences of, 59
Symbolic ego-defense, 133–134
Symptoms, psychological, and shame vs. guilt, 105–106

Tajfel reward matrices, 157–158
Teaching, and shame vs. guilt, 111–112
Terror management theory, 5, 57
and affect, 62
and anxiety, 5, 47, 48–49
and threat of mortality, 62

ABOUT THE EDITORS

Abraham Tesser completed his PhD in social psychology at Purdue University in 1967. Currently, Dr. Tesser is a research professor emeritus in psychology at the University of Georgia. He has been a visiting fellow at Yale University, Princeton University, the Center for Advanced Study in the Behavioral Sciences, and Ohio State University. Dr. Tesser has served as director of the University of Georgia's Interdisciplinary Institute for Behavioral Research, as an associate editor of *Personality and Social Psychology Bulletin,* and as editor of the Attitude and Social Cognition Section of the *Journal of Personality and Social Psychology.* He has served on and chaired the National Institute of Mental Health's Social, Personality, and Group Processes Review Committee and is a past president of the Society for Personality and Social Psychology, Division 8 of the American Psychological Association. The recipient of many awards for his research, Dr. Tesser has published numerous articles, chapters, and books on self-esteem, attitudes, thought and ruminative processes, interpersonal communication, and attraction.

Diederik A. Stapel is the Van der Leeuw Professor in Cognitive Social Psychology at the University of Groningen in The Netherlands. He holds master's degrees in psychology and communication science and earned his PhD in psychology (1997) from the University of Amsterdam. Dr. Stapel was a visiting fellow at the Universities of Exeter (UK), Chicago, Michigan, and Georgia. Although Dr. Stapel has a wide variety of research interests, including self-perception and social comparison, person perception and social judgment, prejudice and stereotyping, and consumer psychology, most recently he has focused especially on automatic context effects on person and self-judgment. Currently, he is beginning a series of projects that focus on the affect–cognition interface in the earliest (automatic)

225

stages of affective processing. A core theme in this research concerns the automaticity of self-maintenance and self-defense mechanisms.

Joanne V. Wood completed her PhD in clinical psychology at the University of California–Los Angeles in 1984. She was a faculty member at the State University of New York at Stony Brook for five years and in 1989 moved to the University of Waterloo, where she serves on the faculty of the Psychology Department. Dr. Wood has served as an associate editor of *Personality and Social Psychology Bulletin*; on the editorial boards for *Journal of Personality and Social Psychology*, *Journal of Experimental Social Psychology*, *Personality and Social Psychology Bulletin*, and *Self and Identity*; and as an ad hoc reviewer for many other journals. She is a Fellow of the Society for Personality and Social Psychology, Division 8 of the American Psychological Association. Her publications concern social comparison, affect regulation, coping with illness, and mechanisms underlying the maintenance of self-esteem.